DUNDEE

University Library

Date of Return - Subject to Recall

Women and Ideology in the
Soviet Union

Women and Ideology in the Soviet Union

Mary Buckley
Lecturer in Politics, University of Edinburgh

Harvester Wheatsheaf

New York   London   Toronto   Sydney   Tokyo

First published 1989 by
Harvester Wheatsheaf,
66 Wood Lane End, Hemel Hempstead,
Hertfordshire, HP2 4RG
A division of
Simon & Schuster International Group

Printed and bound in Great Britain by
Billing and Sons Ltd, Worcester

British Library Cataloguing in Publication Data

Buckley, Mary, *1951–*
    Women and ideology in the Soviet Union.
    1. Soviet Union, Society. Role of women
    I. Title
    305.4′2′0947

    ISBN 0–7450–0279–X
    ISBN 0–7450–0669–8 pbk

1 2 3 4 5   93 92 91 90 89

To my Mother
and for the Memory of my Father

Contents

List of tables

Acknowledgements

Many of the sources upon which this book is based were found in the USSR. I am indebted to the British Council and the Soviet Ministry for Higher and Special Education for enabling me to make three extended visits to the USSR between 1979 and 1987 and to the Society for Cultural Relations with the USSR for making possible a fourth in 1984.

My hosts in the USSR were the Department of International Law at Kiev University, the Department of the History of the USSR of the Soviet Period at Moscow University, the Department of History at Azerbaidzhan University and the Department of Russian Language for Foreigners at Moscow University. I am grateful to them all for guidance, encouragement and support. I also wish to record thanks to the Lenin and INION libraries in Moscow, including the dissertation room of the Lenin library, Kiev University library and the libraries of the Academy of Sciences in Kiev and Baku. Above all, however, I am grateful to Soviet social scientists and members of the women's councils for allowing me to interview them and to Soviet citizens of various walks of life for showing me clearer than any book has done what different aspects of life in the USSR are like.

This book finally began to take shape when I was a Senior Associate Member of St Antony's College in the Hilary term of 1988, on leave from the University of Edinburgh. I am grateful to Archie Brown for his sponsorship and to the College for providing a pleasant and stimulating environment. A Research Grant from the Leverhulme Trust and supplementary financial support from the Travel and Research Committee of Edinburgh University and the Initiative Fund of the Faculty of Social Sciences at Edinburgh made my time in Oxford possible.

Some of the chapters which follow draw on material published elsewhere: 'Soviet interpretations of the woman question' in Barbara Holland (ed.) (1985) *Soviet Sisterhood* (London, Fourth Estate; Bloomington, Indiana, Indiana University Press), pp. 24–53; 'Soviet ideology and female roles' in Stephen White and Alex Pravda (eds) (1988) *Ideology and Soviet Politics* (London, Macmillan), pp. 159–79; and 'The woman question in the contemporary Soviet Union' in Sonia Kruks, Rayna Rapp and Marilyn B. Young, (eds) (1989) *Promissory Notes: Women in the Transition to Socialism* (New York, Monthly Review Press), pp. 251–81. Unlike the first two of these articles, this manuscript uses the Library of Congress transliteration system, with the exception of names whose more customary English form are now widely adopted. Thus 'Trotskii' reads 'Trotsky' and 'Aleksandra' is replaced by 'Alexandra'.

I am grateful to Malcolm Anderson, Genia Browning, Barbara Heldt, Desmond S. King and Elizabeth Waters for their comments and advice. I thank them for generously investing time in a manuscript that was not their own and for producing critical, supportive and amusing remarks when they were needed. They may not agree with the conclusions I have reached, and cannot be reproached for any errors of detail, or inability to generalise. Thanks are also due to Nigel Bowles, Alice Brown and Desmond S. King for permitting me to use their word processors after mine became allergic to this manuscript.

Finally, I am grateful to Peter Aeberli for arranging tranquil accommodation and space in Oxford in which to write, and to Deborah Borst for providing it. A most pleasing view from my attic desk across the Oxford canal at the bottom of the garden to Port Meadow beyond provided a delightful setting. A more dramatic view over the roof tops of Edinburgh to the hills of Fife kept me going through the final drafts, with the help of Mahler and Szymanowsky.

Introduction

Why, in a socialist state officially committed since 1917 to equality of the sexes, have we not seen a rigorous analysis of gender roles? Why is it that 'feminism' is condemned in the USSR as counter-revolutionary and denigrated as an example of bourgeois self-indulgence? Why are there no articles in Soviet economics journals critical of the situation in which women's average earnings are only two-thirds of men's, let alone serious proposals for rectifying this? Why is it that the concept of 'parenting' enjoys more popular coinage in the capitalist USA than in the USSR where childrearing in the 1980s continues to be seen by many as the mother's responsibility with support from the state, rather than the concern of the father as well? And why has the extremely low number and profile of Soviet women in key decision-making bodies such as the Politburo, Secretariat, Central Committee party departments and Council of Ministers not been defined as a serious problem by Soviet leaders?[1] Moreover, why when we pose these questions in the USSR, do many Soviet women in factories, offices and universities either look at us with quizzical sympathy as they dismiss their importance, or laugh good-humouredly with us, all the time making clear that they just do not see the world this way?

Study of the content of Soviet ideology on women from 1917 until today helps us to answer these questions by examining the main concepts, propositions and concerns through which the *'zhenskii vopros'*, or 'woman question', has been interpreted, projected and officially packaged in the USSR. Issues which are defined as important for women's lives in different periods of Soviet history must be examined to see the ways in which they have been presented, and the kind of controversy which they caused.

Continuities and changes in ideological lines on women and the space permitted for discourse and debate about female roles in different historical periods are largely ignored in the existing literature. Since the late 1960s Western scholars have directed their attention at the extent of Soviet women's subordination in politics, in the paid work force and in the home. Research has focused on the degree to which women enjoy equal citizenship rights with men (Dodge, 1966; Sacks, 1976; Atkinson *et al.*, 1978, Lapidus, 1978). Various explanations for sexual inequality have been proposed. Some historians draw attention to the impoverished material situation of the young Bolshevik state which could not easily provide social services to ease childcare and housework. Others emphasise the resistance to women's liberation within Bolshevism itself. Many revolutionaries paid lip-service to equality of the sexes, but simultaneously found it hard to cope with in their personal lives. Strong opposition existed generally in the population, particularly among rural women and men. The cultural values of peasant households, which had firm roots in the nineteenth century, resisted change (Vucinich, 1968). The material and attitudinal prerequisites for equality of the sexes were lacking in 1917, even though equality was embodied in law and it was wholeheartedly supported by some Bolsheviks and thousands of women (Hayden, 1976, 1979; Farnsworth, 1978; Stites, 1978; Clements, 1985). The uneasy existence from 1919 to 1930 of the department for work among women (*otdel po rabote sredi zhenshchin*), or the *Zhenotdel* as it came to be known, reflects this combination of commitment and hostility to women's liberation (Hayden, 1976, 1979; Stites, 1978).

Economic changes following the Revolution drew more women into the labour force and out of the home. They were channelled either into traditionally female and low-paying sectors, such as clothing and textiles, or else into the bottom end of job hierarchies in new fields. Western social scientists have generally concluded that economic modernisation under state socialism had positive and negative results for women and also a differential impact on various categories of women (Scott, 1974; Sacks, 1976; Lapidus, 1978; Heitlinger, 1979; Wolchik and Meyer, 1985). Paid employment gave women opportunities to develop skills in a social setting and provided varying degrees of financial independence. But despite these new opportunities, women tended to concentrate in unskilled and low-paid jobs, rarely attaining top, decision-making posts.[2] This was partly because the state did not provide sufficient kindergartens for childcare; nor did it significantly weaken traditional gender roles. Thus one result of increased women's participation in the economy was the creation of a draining 'double burden' or 'double shift' for women.

A distinction between mobilisation and liberation may be drawn to account for this process. One convincing interpretation holds that women were perceived by leaders as an economic and political resource, but one to exploit rather than to liberate (Lapidus, 1978, p. 338). Another author maintains that the paradox between high female employment in the economy and low participation in decision-making elites can best be explained by the unwillingness of men to share power with women (Jancar, 1978, p. 9). Others identify several mutually reinforcing factors underpinning this paradox. These include: the lack of inclination on the part of many women to become involved in conventional politics due to the double burden, scarce time and low levels of confidence; the tendency of women to study the humanities − an inappropriate preparation for manage-ment in industry and agriculture; the widespread belief among some women that politics is 'dirty' and 'men's work'; male resistance to women's political aspirations; and male networks which effectively screen women out (Jancar, 1978; Moses, 1978a; Buckley, 1981b; Sternheimer, 1983).

Related to the above factors are two essential issues of power-sharing and socialisation. The first poses the question of how much effort a male leadership is likely to devote to supporting women for top jobs or expend on making gender issues a high priority. The issue here is whether male leaders are likely to define the promotion of equality of the sexes as in their own interest (Buckley, 1985). This is especially important given the authoritarian nature of the Soviet state which prevents the formation of autonomous women's organisations (Browning, 1987). The second issue focuses attention on the persistence of traditional gender roles in the USSR and attributes these, in part, to socialisation processes which convey conservative cultural values.[3] For example, many Russian proverbs and Muslim sayings degrade women and are still cited in popular culture.[4] Contemporary Soviet children's books depict girls as passive and unadventurous and boys as active, determined and assertive. Many Soviet sociological and pedagogical studies proceed from the assump-tion that women are soft and gentle, and best suited to caring and nurturing, whereas strong and determined men are not (Rosenhan, 1978; Attwood, 1985, 1988).

A wide range of interrelated factors is relevant to a systematic understanding of the position of women in Soviet society. A multidisciplinary analysis of history, cultural settings, the nature of political leaderships, economic and social relationships and the policies designed to transform them, the changing content of ideology and the topics of intellectual debates, is essential to grasp the complexities of changes and continuities in women's lives. Whilst the flow of research which began in the mid-1960s continues to build up a solid Western literature on women's social, economic and political roles, much less attention has been paid to Soviet ideology on women and debates about female roles. The aim here is to fill this gap.

Objects and arguments

This is a book about the political construction of Soviet ideology on women. Its object is to trace the content of ideology from the Russian Revolution to the late 1980s, attempting to account for consistencies, changes, silences and fresh emphases in arguments about female roles. The main contention is that the policy priorities of successive Soviet leaders, and the economic, political, social and demographic pressures on them, have been major influences on Soviet ideology on women. Evidence suggests that ideological lines on women's lives under socialism, the nature of debate about them, and the images of women propagated by the state, have been tailored to the needs of different periods of Soviet history, as defined by their political leaderships.

This book rests on the premise that Soviet ideology on women has been inspired by far more than the Marxist classics. But ideology's starting point was nevertheless rooted in nineteenth-century theoretical tracts, and in subsequent developments in them. By 1917 Marxists had developed preliminary thoughts on the emancipation of women, the meaning of equality and the nature of the family. The young Bolshevik state began with commitment to these ideas and to the liberation of women. Loyalty to the Marxist classics has been reiterated since Lenin's death by Stalin, Khrushchev, Brezhnev, Andropov, Chernenko and Gorbachev. However, the arguments on women that the Bolsheviks inherited from Bebel, Engels, Marx and Lenin have since been extended, adapted, qualified and variously packaged to suit the policies of different periods.

Whilst material conditions have often affected ideology, it is the leadership's interpretation of those conditions at a given time that influences their relevance to ideology. Material circumstances alone do not mould ideology. Past ideological platforms can have a constraining effect on how much a line can change. Innovations in theory affect ideology too. In addition, the results of intellectual debate can feed into ideology; and how pliable or taut ideology is at a particular time can in turn influence the extent of intellectual debate.

Definitions and assumptions

We define ideology as a political belief system which is composed of interrelated ideas. These ideas offer a theoretical explanation of reality and defend a preferred political order, either past, present or future. Pursuit of these ideas gives rise to an action programme or strategy to put them into practice through political and social action.[5] Liberal democratic systems can embrace competing ideologies within their political frameworks, and these ideologies may be associated with different political parties. The Soviet state from its inception denied non-communist parties the right to exist and gave one party the right to rule and to interpret doctrine. Thus, 'armed with Marxism–Leninism' the CPSU today executes its 'leading and guiding' role.[6] Soviet ideology is thus officially constructed 'from above'.

Commitment to an ideology entails adherence to the doctrine's interpretation of reality, as understood by the holder, and support for the policies, programmes and strategies deemed appropriate to bring about its goals. This does not preclude debate and dissension, even in the USSR, about what is 'appropriate' at a given point in time. Nor does ideological commitment imply that policy is always drawn up in one-party systems for purely ideological reasons. The link between programmes and strategies on the one hand, and broader normative goals on the other, may not always be precise and obvious, or even exist. Specific policies may be promoted, packaged and justified with ideas that are not easily reconcilable with Marxism–Leninism, or with what Franz Schurman has called 'pure ideology'. 'Practical ideology', or what others may prefer to see as propaganda, may not appear consistent with 'pure ideology' (Schurman, 1968). Classical Marxism is abstract and does not offer detailed policy guidelines; and it is not always clear what, in practice, consistency would entail. And often 'practical ideology' is geared to produce a particular political result, as defined at a party Congress. Thus, the ongoing construction of ideology is nourished by the moment, even if many of its concepts and arguments stem from the past.

The significance of official Soviet ideology may vary according to historical context, political system, leadership, level of economic development, issue or situation. Ideology is neither constantly shaped by, nor reducible to, external determinants – ideology interacts with other factors. Thus ideology at different times can inspire policy, be seriously modified itself by policy, qualify policy, be ignored by policy or even jar with policy. The impact of ideology on society is neither constant over time nor uniform across issues and situations.

Some strands of ideology, moreover, may prove to be more durable than others. Certain ideological arguments may be persistently championed, while others may fall fallow, never to be cultivated further. Some themes or emphases ripen in particular circumstances and are given special attention, but become anachronistic in a different setting. Completely new arguments may be incorporated into the existing corpus of ideas, thereby serving to graft fresh notions on more established ones. Official ideology is therefore dynamic. Leaders can use it, develop it, mould it or ignore it to fit their own policy priorities, whether or not these policies are directly inspired by ideology.

Some have suggested that the 'true' spirit of Marxism is violated by these additions and subtractions; others have argued that it is creatively extended by them. Either way, the content of ideology matters because arguments put forward by Soviet official ideology are not only promoted through propaganda and political socialisation processes, but have implications for policy-making and discussions about policy in academic journals and the press. The content of official ideology and its theoretical parameters can limit the extent of debate about policies, just as policy priorities can influence which elements of ideology are emphasised or played down at a particular time. Ideology can affect the extent to which a given policy is normatively 'acceptable' and similarly policy can force ideology into a strait-jacket. Ideology can be of minimal relevance, or at other times take on the status of an independent variable and play a more directing role. Ideology can also mix with a blend of intervening variables and become one of many factors that affect political outcome.

The relevance of ideology to different policy areas must be analysed against a background of empirical research. We should not confer various characteristics on ideology in *a priori* style, but should look both *at* and *behind* the content of ideology. Only once this has been done in various policy areas, will it be possible to account for similarities and differences in the way in which ideology has been used. Since this book focuses on one area of policy, it discusses just a small part of a potentially much larger picture. Conclusions drawn here about the use of ideology may not therefore apply across policy areas.

Although in particular periods similar patterns may obtain across policy areas, for example in the lively debates in the 1920s, or the relative silence under Stalin, or the limited reassessment under Khrushchev, or the more realistic appraisals during the Brezhnev years and the widening of discussion under Gorbachev, this remains a question for detailed empirical investigation. The nature and ideological content of debate is likely to vary according to the nature of the topic. Similarly, the timing of shifts in line is affected by many factors. Therefore, ideological patterns are unlikely to be identical for the woman question, national question, the writing of official history or the relevance of genetics to agriculture.

Ideology and the study of Soviet politics

Many of the points made in the debate on Soviet ideology which raged in the West in the 1960s were abstract speculations rather than generalisations carefully reached after reading the source materials. Although Soviet primary sources do not speak for themselves and should not be taken at face-value, they are vital starting points. Only once Soviet official documents, scholarly journals, academic books, dissertations, newspapers and magazines have been read, can the debates, lines and themes of different periods be identified.

Those who proclaimed, in the 1950s and 1960s, the 'end of ideology' seemed particularly reluctant to base their views on a systematic analysis of primary sources. Charges were made that Marxist ideology had been revised, displaced, relativised, rational-ised, eroded, fictionalised or falsified. But these charges against it were rarely substantiated by concrete evidence. The ideological treatment of specific policies was not delineated. There was no suggestion that different policy areas might receive different handling by ideologists nor that ideology could be eclectically used by leaders. At best, ideology was characterised as an *ex post facto* justification of policy. It was the afterthought of policy-makers or a device used to approve, defend and praise their actions. Ideological justification provided a protective shield of legitimacy.

Ideology may indeed be used in this way but ideology is not just a tool selectively and cynically used to bolster any politically agreed policy. This shallow view of ideology obscured *inter alia* the important observation that even if Marxist ideas played a diminishing role in policy-making, references to official ideology permeated the lives of Soviet citizens, even those who criticised it in private. Official ideology is the 'language game' of the Soviet system (Wittgenstein, 1968). From nursery school through kindergarten, secondary school and university, it pervades education. It is taught and reinforced in the Young Pioneers and Komsomol. Political meetings in the workplace prevent citizens from ignoring Soviet Marxism. The system of KGB informers deters deviation from it in public.[7] Television, radio, films, newspapers, magazines and books frequently cite or reflect ideology. Hoardings on the streets and posters in factories and libraries proclaim its glories. Public holidays celebrate it and museums and exhibitions applaud it. To varying degrees citizens internalise it and tend to use it in different ways depending upon who is participating in the conversation. Some are highly cynical about elements of ideology and others embrace it with varying degrees of enthusiasm.

Ideology and methodological problems

The scholarly neglect of ideology in analyses of Soviet politics, as well as in the broader field of empirical political science, is partly related to problems of definition, measurement and validity. Ideology is a persistent, suggestive and ambitious concept, but it is unclear and various meanings have been given to it. Many writers have bewailed the diverse and conflicting uses to which it has been put, and its umbrella nature under which so many different interpretations have been subsumed (Minar, 1961, p. 317; Converse, 1964; Barnes, 1966; Lichtheim, 1967; Sartori, 1969; Christenson *et al.*, 1975). Because of this, writings on the concept have been fragmented rather than cumulative – the literature has been described as 'cold and murky' waters lacking in precision and clarity (Putnam, 1971, p. 615).

This murkiness is partly due to the concept's wide appeal to sociologists, historians, philosophers, economists and psychologists as well as political scientists. Within political science it is used at the individual, group and systemic levels of analysis in connection with mass and elite behaviour and with system performance (Buckley, 1981a). The concept of ideology also risks being thoroughly ideologised (Geertz, 1964; LaPalombara, 1968). It is a term with 'evil connotations' and a 'nasty reputation' (Jansson, 1959). Indeed, the normative content and pejorative overtones evoked by the concept were starkly revealed in the 'end of ideology' debate. For Raymond Aron, the 'end of ideology' heralded the death of passionate fanaticism; for Seymour Martin Lipset, it was the end of red flags and May Day parades; and for Edward Shils, it meant the return of civility and the ebb of unpleasant expressions of romanticism in the form of Marxism and National Socialism (Shils, 1955, 1958; Aron, 1968; Lipset, 1968). If the concept is to be used effectively in social science research, it must shed its evocative and politicised connotations. This applies particularly to analyses of the uses of Marxist ideology in state socialist systems.

While an assortment of definitions may be found in the theoretical writings on ideology and in empirical research on political belief systems in liberal democracies, analyses of state socialist systems have not produced such a wide variety. When scholars working in this field discuss political beliefs, they are generally referring to the official ideology, that is, to current interpretations of Marxist–Leninist doctrine. Ideology is viewed as a particular set of political ideas, officially sanctioned by a ruling political elite. Thus, the focus is on how ideology is formulated 'from above'. Despite this narrower focus, there is agreement neither on definition nor on the roles played by ideology in political socialisation, policy formulation and policy implementation. This is due not simply to the methodological difficulties involved in devising empirical referents for the effects of ideology on citizens and on policy. More important, there has been no access to a random sample of citizens to survey their attitudes, nor to a sufficient number of policy-makers willing or able to give frank accounts of the decision-making process. Complex concepts are hard to use in empirical research in good conditions and the problem of whether conclusions based on them are valid is ever-present (Hempel, 1952; Sartori, 1970). But when examining policy-making in the USSR and citizen's views of it, we lack these good conditions, despite some improvements in recent years.

Ideology and theoretical approaches

Although empirical work on ideology has been scant, ideology has been variously considered in theoretical approaches to the study of socialist systems. In fact, the degree to which the role of Marxism in the USSR has been a fashionable topic, has to a certain extent depended upon prevailing conceptual frameworks. At a time when the totalitarian approach enjoyed widespread currency, many subscribed to Merle Fainsod's view that 'in the Soviet state there is no real escape from the long arm of ideological control' (Fainsod, 1963, p. 300). The Orwellian characterisation that 'Orthodoxy means not thinking – not needing to think. Orthodoxy is unconsciousness' fitted well with this view (Orwell, 1951, p. 57). For Hannah Arendt, totalitarianism connoted 'total domination' and ideology was a weapon in this domination.[8] In her estimation, leaders such as Stalin and Hitler were bewitched by the 'inherent logicality' of ideologies (Arendt, 1958, p. 472). Carl Friedrich and Zbigniew Brzezinski similarly described it as a powerful ingredient in totalitarian systems and as a set of ideas, capable of adaptation, to which leaders attached considerable importance. They considered ideology to be one of six defining features of the 'totalitarian syndrome' (Friedrich and Brzezinski, 1965, p. 21).[9] The totalitarian approach, therefore, considered ideology an independent variable. Ideology was used to determine the goals and direction of society.

Subsequent theoretical approaches were, in part, reactions to the inadequacies of the totalitarian approach and its inability to account for changes in the Soviet system. These approaches either conceived of ideology as a dependent variable or ignored it. In theories of convergence and development, ideology was not regarded solely as a guide to action; ideology itself was modified by economic and political change. It could lose the primacy accorded to it during periods of revolutionary change as revolutionaries were replaced in positions of power by managerial modernisers (Tinbergen, 1961; Berliner, 1964; Kautsky, 1968; Lowenthal, 1970; Meyer, 1970). In the 'group approach' scholars analysed the policy process in a system which the totalitarian approach had earlier dismissed as a homogeneous and static monolith. They recognised that 'occupation' groups and 'opinion' groups could exert different pressures on policy makers (Lodge, 1969; Skilling and Griffiths, 1971; Solomon, 1983). A growing understanding of the complexities of the Soviet state and of different sets of professionals acting within the system undermined credibility in the 'totalitarian syndrome'. Developing out of the group approach, 'elite analysis' further marginalised discussions of ideology. Ideologues were just one group of political actors, in an increasingly heterogeneous leadership (Donaldson and Waller, 1970; Farrell, 1970; Fleron, 1970, 1973; Donaldson, 1972; Welsh, 1973). Underplaying the outputs of policy-making and neglecting the authoritarian 'leading and guiding role' of the CPSU, the group approach bypassed questions of the authoritative use of official ideology in presenting policies. As approaches to studying state socialist systems became more varied, ideology was removed from the limelight that the totalitarian approach had accorded it.

The 'functions' of ideology

Once displaced from conceptual approaches ideology received little attention apart from in a set of exchanges about its 'functions' which commenced in the scholarly literature in the 1960s.[10] David Dinsmore Comey, for instance, regarded ideology as performing 'masking', 'authenticating' and 'directive' functions. As mask, it veiled the true nature of society. As authenticator, it provided a psychological bridge between doctrine and policy, frequently quoting Marxist texts to justify policy, even when no logical connection between the two existed. As director, it served as a guide for the selection and implementation of policy (Comey, 1962).

Moving away from emphasis on the directive role of ideology, Alfred Meyer suggested that ideology served four main functions: it provided a language of politics, a code of communication, a legitimising device for policies and a form of self-legitimation for leaders (Meyer, 1966). Another author, Daniel Bell, estimated that ideology had one central function – that of propagating *partiinost'*, meaning 'party spirit' or 'party mindedness' (Bell, 1965). These writings provoked a series of reflections in the 1960s and 1970s on the role of ideology (Daniels, 1966; Joravsky, 1966; Chambre, 1967; De George, 1968).

Study of the content and use of Soviet ideology

From the 1950s to the 1970s, discussions about Soviet ideology were either integral to, or derived from, particular theoretical approaches to state socialist systems, or the result of conjecture about the role of ideology at an abstract level. Conclusions were not based on case studies. Perhaps if they had been, discussion would not have revolved so heavily around the question of whether ideology was 'determining' or 'determined'. Like most dichotomies in political science, this one obscures many nuances of relevance (Bill and Hardgrave, 1973, pp. 50–7).

It was not until the 1980s that the examination of Soviet ideology became more firmly rooted in case studies (White and Pravda, 1988). Discussions now focused on the complexities of the evolution of official ideology and the nature of its impact on different policy areas. Evidence suggested that official ideology had a particularly 'determinant influence' in the early post-revolutionary period, a 'predispositional influence' in labour and welfare policy, but not in foreign policy, and a diffuse 'environmental influence' over political language and the form of Soviet policy toward Eastern Europe (Pravda, 1988). Close scrutiny of different policy areas meant that, at last, conclusions had a sound empirical base and that preliminary comparisons could be drawn across policy areas.

In a similar spirit, the purpose of this book is to tackle the manageable and limited task of examining changes in official ideology in one area. To this end, five analytically distinct periods have been distinguished; from the Revolution to 1930; from 1930 to the death of Stalin in 1953; from 1953 to the removal of Khrushchev in 1964; the Brezhnev years from 1964 to 1982, followed by the brief incumbancies of Andropov and Chernenko; and the Gorbachev leadership from 1985 to 1988. Even though the emphasis of ideology may shift within historical periods, and despite the persistence of certain ideological positions over time, these five periods nevertheless enjoy distinguishing ideological features.

The heritage of Marxist ideas on women and the conditions leading up to the main events of the Russian Revolution are examined in Chapter 1. The circumstances in which the new Bolshevik state was established are important since these provided the setting in which Marxist arguments were moulded, the 'woman question' interpreted and policy on women formulated. The first chapter also discusses various arguments on women put forward from 1917 to 1930. During these years, the woman question provoked a lively debate about domestic labour, maternity pay, civil marriage, divorce, women's organisations, equality and sexuality. Particular attention is given to the writings of Alexandra Kollontai and Inessa Armand since these Bolshevik women were keen to promote and extend Marxist arguments on women. In 1919, Armand was arguing that 'if the liberation of women is unthinkable without communism, then communism is unthinkable without the complete liberation of women' (Armand, 1975, p. 86).

Chapter 2 examines developments in the theory and practice of early Soviet women's institutions and discusses the opposition that they faced. It looks at the *Zhenotdel* and the women's clubs, delegates' meetings and red tents that it promoted. One early question for Soviet ideology in the 1920s concerned the role of women's organisations under socialism. According to Marxist theory, class not gender was the key social division, and socialist organisations served the interests of both working men and women. Practical problems, however, required that special attention was paid to raising the political consciousness of women. For some purposes women were seen as a separate group from men.

Chapter 3 explores how for over 20 years serious discussion about women's issues was largely silenced because the woman question was declared 'solved' and equality of the sexes achieved. The lively debates of the early 1920s were replaced by a heroic literature which extolled the virtues of stakhanovite women, or shock workers, who overfulfilled production quotas. This literature also contained praise of the wives of stakhanovite men for supporting the efforts of their husbands in economic production. Discourse about production and output displaced earlier themes of liberation, equality, sexuality and domestic labour. If the latter topics were mentioned at all, they tended to be defined in terms of the former. In these years critical thought about the meaning of revolution for changes in female roles was replaced by hollow assertions that women had already been successfully liberated.

The absence of debate about female roles lasted until the post-Stalin years. Chapter 4 appraises how and why women's issues were moved back onto political agendas by Khrushchev. At the 20th party Congress in 1956 Khrushchev regretted the relative absence of women from prominent posts in the state and party. He later suggested that different groups had different needs and should be treated accordingly. In Khrushchev's view, women constituted one such group with distinct characteristics. Because of this, the contribution of women's organisations to socialism was reappraised and the *zhensovety* (*zhenskie sovety*), or women's councils, were set up in order to cater to the needs and interests of women.

Chapter 5 shows that, in the mid-1960s under the leadership of Brezhnev, the woman question was freshly declared 'unsolved' and inequality of the sexes officially recognised. Attaining equality of the sexes was now viewed as a complex and protracted process. It was argued that legal or 'formal equality' had been won, but 'factual equality', or 'equality in life', had yet to be attained. In 'developed socialist' society the lives of women were complicated by 'non-antagonistic contradictions', freshly identified by theorists. The female 'double burden' or 'double shift' of a day's work in the labour force followed by domestic chores was presented as a pressing non-antagonistic contradiction.

The unresolved status of the woman question made possible a wide-ranging discussion of how best to tackle its economic, domestic and political aspects. This commenced in the late 1960s, reached a highpoint in the 1970s and continued into the 1980s. Comprising 51 per cent of the labour force by 1970, Soviet women were a vital resource in production and reproduction. Sociologists, economists, demographers, lawyers and journalists all reflected upon the significance of the female double burden for socialist construction and offered competing suggestions on how to ease it. But the 1960s and 1970s were not the 1920s. Male–female relations, competing definitions of equality, sexuality and the transformation of the family were not high on the list of priorities. The prominent questions included: How can women best combine their roles in production and reproduction? What changes should take place in the lives of women to ease their dual role? Should work schedules for women be altered? Should women be encouraged to produce more children? Will more domestic appliances help? How can social services improve women's lives? Yet despite this channelling of discussion, different viewpoints were nevertheless expressed. Notwithstanding the ideological silences which persisted, the parameters of discourse widened.

After the 26th party Congress of 1981 the focus of discussion sharpened. Certain topics were removed from the agenda, such as the significance of part-time labour and the gravity of declining birth rates, as these now had official solutions. Solving the woman question was more explicitly tied to demographic policy. Although the limits of debate became firmer, and narrower in policy terms since the woman question was specifically connected to demographic policy, the woman question paradoxically broadened at the theoretical level. It was now linked to a range of issues including social integration, social homogeneity, the role of trade unions, housing policy and the development of democracy, which in the past had not all been so explicitly brought together. New interrelationships befitting the 'totality' of the 'organic social system' of developed socialism were being delineated by theorists.

Chapter 6 shows that the interconnectedness of issues has continued under Gorbachev. His policy of *perestroika*, which translates as 'reconstruction' or 'restructuring' is wide-ranging, and entails changes in economy, politics and society. Attempts are being made, amid opposition from different sectors of society, to promote broad changes in the USSR and the lives of women are not exempt from these. *Glasnost'*, which means 'publicity' or 'openness', is one of the means to the end of *perestroika*. It has prompted publicity about the weaknesses of Soviet socialism and with this has come more exposure of the difficulties faced by Soviet women in their daily lives. At the 27th party Congress in February 1986, Gorbachev mentioned the need to expand opportunities for young mothers to work part-time and to provide more vital social services, such as kindergartens. He also gave his support to the promotion of women into top jobs, which he reiterated with stronger commitment at the 19th All-Union Conference of the CPSU in June 1988. In addition, Gorbachev revitalised the *zhensovety* as channels for reaching women and for promoting *perestroika*. An All-Union Conference of Women which took place in January 1987 was convened explicitly to discuss the implications of *perestroika* for women and what shortcomings needed to be tackled by the *zhensovety*.

In the late 1980s the poor promotion record of women is more freely acknowledged and previously forbidden topics such as high infant mortality rates and the existence of prostitution are no longer ignored. Not all topics, however, are 'open' and there are ideological limits to *glasnost'*. Kollontai's theme of the transformation of the family unit is still out of ideological bounds, as is criticism of pro-natalist policies. It is acceptable to talk about part-time labour for mothers, but not part-shifts for fathers. Aspects of traditional gender roles continue to be reinforced rather than challenged. Some believe that women should stay at home in order to reproduce and thereby help to boost the birth rate and also soften the blow of future unemployment resulting from a more efficient economy; others object on the grounds that women want to work to be part of the collective, need to work for financial reasons and should work in order to develop their creative potential. Current writings on women pull in various directions, often reaching different conclusions. What binds them is a focus on the impact of Soviet policy on women's lives. Whereas many of the arguments about women voiced in the 1960s, 1970s and early 1980s concerned the implications of women's lives for the state, in the late 1980s the emphasis is shifting to include more discussion of the effects of social and economic policy on women. Thus, the issue of how socialist woman should live her life is again contentious. *Glasnost'* has spurred the growth of a range of ideas from the seemingly feminist to the highly traditional.

The case study of over 70 years of Soviet literature on women throws up a particular pattern of how official ideology has inspired some policies, been inapplicable to others, or been modified, moulded and extended to suit prevailing economic, political, cultural and theoretical priorities. The central questions are: how does the treatment of the woman question differ in different periods of Soviet history? What concepts are used and what arguments have been put forward? What is the scope for debate? How do innovations in ideology broaden or restrict the latitude of debate? What is the relationship between arguments about female roles and broader changes in Soviet ideology? What appears to be the relationship between the content of ideology and policy? And why have women's organisations been active in some periods of Soviet history and not others? While answers to these questions do not provide definitive arguments about the role of ideology in the USSR, they nevertheless show how it is used. This approach also helps us to grasp why there has not been a proliferation of theories about gender in the USSR and why feminism is castigated as misconceived and ideologically unsound.

Notes

1. Readers who are unfamiliar with Soviet political institutions could usefully consult: Mary McAuley, *Politics and the Soviet Union*; Ronald J. Hill, *Soviet Union: Politics, Economics and Society*; Gordon B. Smith, *Soviet Politics: Continuity and*

Contradiction; David Lane, *State and Politics in the USSR*; and Jerry Hough and Merle Fainsod, *How the Soviet Union is Governed* (McAuley, 1977; Hill, 1985; G. B. Smith, 1988; Lane, 1985; Hough and Fainsod, 1982).

2. Women were employed in industry before the revolution too (Bobroff, 1974). By 1885 they made up slightly over 22 per cent of all factory workers in European Russia. In Moscow at this time 47 per cent of tobacco industry workers were women and 31 per cent of textile workers (Glickman, 1978, p. 66). In 1887 27 per cent of workers in the Russian Empire in the chemical industry were female (Sacks, 1976, p. 15).

3. While official Soviet ideology is one element within socialisation processes, it would be a mistake to view the two as synonymous. Socialisation in the USSR is much broader and includes the passing on of cultural values and traditions. Ideology, too, serves more than political socialisation. It provides a system of ideas which can guide policy and be modified by policy.

4. Traditional sayings include: A hen is not a bird, a woman is not a person; long hair, small mind (Stites, 1978, p. 3).

5. This definition is not restricted to Marxist ideology, but is conceived to embrace all ideologies – Marxist, Anarchist, Social Democratic, Fascist or other. It is close to Reo Christenson's definition which similarly suggests that ideology offers a theoretical explanation of political order coupled with a strategy to attain it 'a belief system that explains and justifies a preferred political order for society, either existing or proposed, and offers a strategy (processes, institutional arrangements, programs) to its attainment' (Christenson *et al.*, 1975, pp. 5–6.

6. Article 6 of the 1977 Soviet Constitution (Fundamental Law) of the USSR states:

    The leading and guiding force of Soviet society and the nucleus of its political system, of all state organizations and public organizations, is the Communist Party of the Soviet Union. The CPSU exists for the people and serves the people.
    The Communist Party, armed with Marxism–Leninism, determines the general perspectives of the development of society and the course of the home and foreign policy of the USSR, directs the great constructive work of the Soviet people, and imparts a planned, systematic and theoretically substantiated character to their struggle for the victory of communism (Finer, 1979, pp. 149–50)

7. *Glasnost'* under Gorbachev has allowed for a freer expression of ideas in public, as demonstrations in Azerbaidzhan, Armenia, the Baltic republics and elsewhere illustrate. It would, however, be premature to suggest that the secret police has lost its role as deterrent in all situations.

8. Arendt did not offer a tight definition of 'ideology', but a rich array of connotations.

9. The totalitarian syndrome 'consists of an ideology, a single party typically led by one man, a terroristic police, a communications monopoly, a weapons monopoly, and a centrally directed economy' (Friedrich and Brzezinski, 1965, p. 21).

10. Two earlier classics on Soviet ideology are Barrington Moore's *Soviet Politics – The Dilemma of Power* and Henri Chambre's *Le Marxisme en Union Sovietique*. For a discussion of these and other works on Soviet ideology, refer to Stephen White, 'Ideology and Soviet politics' (Moore, 1950; Chambre, 1955; White, 1988).

1 Marxism, Revolution and Emancipation in the 1920s

Soviet ideology on women is grounded in the writings of August Bebel, Friedrich Engels, Karl Marx and Vladimir Ilich Lenin.[1] The works of these men provided the ideologically acceptable tracts on the woman question for the new Soviet state in 1917. Since then they have been the theoretical foundation and springboard for further arguments about women in the workforce, at home and in politics. In addition, they have furnished a mine of quotations for statements about Soviet goals and policies concerning women. Although what is taken from this corpus of ideas at any given point in time and what is ignored may vary to suit political priorities of the period, these Marxist texts nevertheless remain sources for inspiration, policy, official line and ideological justification.

This chapter thus begins by presenting the central ideas of the Marxist texts on women in society. It then moves on briefly to trace the nature of Russian Tsarism, the factors which made revolution likely, and the precarious circumstances and problems of the new Soviet state. Having described the historical setting, it examines the new legislation and policies which affected women's lives and discusses the contributions of Inessa Armand and Alexandra Kollontai to Marxist theorising on women.

Remarks about the broader context of political change are necessary, especially for those readers who are not students of Soviet politics and history, since the interpretation and development of ideas, as well as the formulation of policies inspired by them, take place in historical settings which influence their direction and affect the importance accorded to them. The goals of key political actors as well as new political circumstances affect ideas, legislation and policies.

Given the background of socialist writings, it would have been hard for the new regime not to support equality of the sexes. Bebel, Engels, Marx and Lenin had suggested, if only briefly, the direction in which policies should move. The early years after the revolution were a time when Marxist ideology on women stimulated policy and law. Legislation established civil marriage, easy divorce, abortion services, maternity pay and childcare facilities – as Engels and Lenin had advocated. The principles of equality of the sexes and equal pay for equal work were enshrined in law. But then the content of these policies, debate about them, and how they were finally implemented, were in turn affected by the norms and values embedded in the social structures at which they were directed. The Russian 'cultural filter' threw up various responses to the new policies, often leading to arguments which were unanticipated by policy-makers.[2] For example, peasants objected to the payment of alimony because it could seriously damage the running of peasant households. Suspicion of women's liberation and political aversion to it also provoked various forms of hostility.

Despite the immense difficulties of the new Soviet state, progressive legislation for women was kept on the political agenda showing that commitment to Marxist ideology in a revolutionary situation produced both debate and legislative change. Upheavals and uncertainties did not exclude but seemed to stimulate lively discussions on a range of women's issues – domestic labour, abortion, marriage, divorce, maternity, sexuality and women's organisations. Armand and Kollontai, in particular, enriched Marxism by reflecting upon these topics and upon the more general question of the relationship between women's liberation and socialism.

Marxist ideology, however, was not the only source of thinking among policy-makers and citizens about women's place in society. A range of factors was relevant including specific reactions against Tsarist law and the Church, the increase in female unemployment after 1921, the health hazards of abortions, concern about the negative results of sexual freedom, the practical implications of paying alimony, the desire to remain in secure family units, the pervasiveness of traditional ideas about gender roles, and fears that 'bourgeois feminism' would flourish and divide the working class. The political frailty of the new regime also made political survival far more pressing than the promotion of sexual equality. Limited financial resources put constraints on how many ideological promises the new leaderships could meet.

Marxist ideas on women: Bebel, Engels, Marx and Lenin

Like many earlier political thinkers who discussed, if only peripher-
ally, the position of women in society and polity, Bebel, Engels and
Marx related their arguments to the central themes of human nature
and private property. According to Marxist theory, and consistent
with the claims of liberals such as Mary Wollstonecraft, Harriet
Taylor and John Stuart Mill, women's natures were distorted and
disguised by the circumstances in which they found themselves.
Human nature was not immutable, but moulded by environmental
conditions, one of which was property ownership (Wollstonecraft,
1978; Mill and Taylor, 1870).

Marx and Engels maintained that the nature of individuals
'depends on the material conditions determining their production'
(Marx and Engels, 1969, p. 7). Character and mode of life reflected
the individual's place in economic production. Human nature was
shaped by the prevailing mode of production, be it feudal, capitalist,
socialist or communist.[3] As the inevitable progress from feudal
economic relations to communist ones took place, the opportunities
for warping or maturing human nature would vary. Individual self-
determination and freedom were viewed as possible only under
communism. Marx stressed that human beings could be distinguished from other animals by their creativity, which gave them the
ability to act upon or change their environment. Although individuals
had a fertile and many-sided potential, what they became and which
aspects of their broader potentialities were developed and which lay
dormant, depended upon the nature of society. Human nature could
be cramped or enriched depending upon the structure of society and
the individual's place in it.

The greater part of Marx's writings focused on the mechanisms of
capitalism, its effect on the lives of the working class and its eventual
breakdown. Marx contended that propertyless proletarians who
created surplus value for the capitalist entrepreneur became alienated and abstract individuals, robbed of real life content. Their
labour lost 'all semblance of self activity' and 'only sustained their life
through stunting it' (Marx and Engels, 1969, p. 66). Instead of being
an end in itself, work became a means to another end – survival.
Under capitalism, the contradiction between the forces and relations
of production was at its sharpest and the worker sank to the level of a
commodity. The potential of human nature was stifled and could not
be realised within the capitalist mode of production.

Human nature, argued Marx, could only be developed under communism, an economic system in which self-determined activity was compatible with material conditions of life. Alienation was not possible because there was no private property, no surplus value and no exploitation of one class by another. Like Charles Fourier before him, Marx also suggested that the nature of the relationship between men and women was an excellent gauge of the degree of humanity attained by society (Fourier, 1971; Meyer, 1978, p. 86). In his earlier works, in which he was much more preoccupied with Feuerbachian questions of 'essence', Marx claimed:

> From this relationship one can therefore judge man's whole level of development. From the character of this relationship follows how much *man* as a *species-being* as *man*, has come to be himself and to comprehend himself; the relation of man to women is the most *natural relation* of human being to human being. It therefore reveals the extent to which the human essence in him has become a *natural* essence – the extent to which his human nature has become natural to him. (Marx, 1975a, p. 296)

Alienated, 'unnatural', inhuman, behaviour of men towards women, that is, behaviour channelled by the economic dictates of society, and not by the choice of free individuals, warped the relationship between the sexes.

Marx did not elaborate upon this theme. He did not offer a systematic theory of gender relations because the central focus of his work was on the *raison d'être* of the capitalist mode of production. He was concerned to analyse its historical emergence, its mechanics and repercussions. Fuller comments on the changing relationship between women and men were provided by Bebel and Engels.

Like Harriet Taylor and John Stuart Mill, Bebel pointed out that so-called 'female' character traits such as the desire to please others have nothing to do with the intrinsic nature of women *per se* (Bebel, 1971, p. 118). Rather, such qualities resulted from the pressure of social conditions. According to Bebel, there were 'checks' and 'obstructions' which hemmed women in, and forbade them to do those things which men were allowed to do. The rights and privileges which men enjoyed exercising were a 'blot' or 'crime' when adopted by women (Bebel, 1971, p. 79). Bebel suggested that since females were irrationally brought up themselves, they could not rear others rationally.

As a result of their subordinate position, Bebel contended, women looked upon marriage as an institution for support, while men perceived it as a business relationship. Such a state of affairs continued only so long as capitalism endured. Like Marx, Bebel claimed that the overthrow of the capitalist mode of production would result in positive changes in the relations between the sexes. In Bebel's words: 'all social dependence and oppression has its roots in the *economic dependence* of the oppressed upon the oppressor' (Bebel, 1971, p. 9). Female oppression at the hand of men was one expression of this social dependence. Without a radical change in the social conditions which fettered women and blocked their development, women's emancipation was not possible. Without equality of the sexes there could be no 'emancipation of humanity' (Bebel, 1971, p. 6). For Marx and Bebel, the nature of the relations between women and men was dynamic, rather than static as it was for thinkers such as Aristotle, Schopenhauer and Nietzsche (Aristotle, 1862; 1943; 1973; Schopenhauer, 1891; Nietzsche, 1977).[4] It could change for the better, according to Bebel, not with the attainment of the 'bourgeois goal' of equal rights for women and men, but only with the 'removal of all impediments that make man dependent on man; and consequently, one sex upon the other' (Bebel, 1971, p. 118). The key to women's liberation rested in economic self-determination, in a system in which ownership of the means of production was not concentrated in the hands of a capitalist class. A prior condition was that women had to participate in the labour force *en masse* if they were to become the equals of men. As Engels put it:

> To emancipate woman and make her the equal of man is and remains an impossibility so long as the woman is shut out from social productive labour and restricted to private domestic labour. The emancipation of woman will only be possible when woman can take part in production on a large, social scale, and domestic work no longer claims anything but an insignificant amount of her time. (The Woman Question, 1975, pp. 10–11)

Female participation in the labour force, however, was not enough to guarantee liberation. It had to take place in a system devoid of profit – only through socialised industry, or common ownership of the means of production, would the exploitation of the many by the few cease.

An additional disadvantage of capitalism for Marxists was the institution of 'bourgeois marriage'. According to Bebel, bourgeois marriage was the result of bourgeois property relations; it was defined by private property and the right of inheritance, and amounted to marriage by compulsion (Bebel, 1971, pp. 1·6). Engels similarly argued that because the bourgeois family was based on capital and on private gain its main function was to produce heirs of undisputed paternity: monogamy was necessitated by a concentration of wealth in the hands of individual males. Bourgeois man's determination to leave his wealth to his own children rather than to the community enforced monogamy on wives. Hence, the foundation of the double standard that adultery was accepted for men, but not for women. Engels suggested that 'in order to guarantee the fidelity of the wife, that is the paternity of the children, the woman is placed in the man's absolute power; if he kills her, he is but exercising his right' (Engels, 1968, p. 497). Bourgeois marriage, according to this view, amounted to institutionalised prostitution as a result of a business arrangement.

Monogamy, however, did not have to be a degrading relationship. Engels recognised it as a 'great historical advance', but one marred by property relations (Engels, 1968, p. 503). Engels believed that under capitalism mutual love between a woman and a man was possible, but only among the proletariat. Because the working class did not own property they did not need heirs. This meant that the domination of men over women was superfluous because 'there is no stimulus whatever here to assert male domination' (Engels, 1968, p. 508). These remarks indicate that Engels lacked a general theory of gender relations. Engels and Marx both neglected the possibility that forms of domination could arise which were not the result of economic arrangements. They did not explore the dynamics of the superstructure under capitalism to see how it could construct, perpetuate and reinforce gender roles. Marx and Engels believed that the ruling ideas of every epoch are those of the ruling class. From this we would expect that the superstructure of capitalism carried images of female and male roles, which were, to some extent, adopted by the working class. Engels' ideal of harmonious love in proletarian families lacked empirical evidence because female subordination was widespread in nineteenth-century, working-class families and not restricted to bourgeois families. In addition, neither he nor Marx reflected seriously about the issues of sexual attraction, passion, exhilaration, anxiety and emotional commitment which fascinated nineteenth-century novelists such as Dostoevsky, Tolstoy and Turgenev. Sensitive women like Alexandra Kollontai considered that these concerns had to be included in discussions of emancipation.[5]

The Marxist tradition maintained that bourgeois woman was in a position of subservience to her husband. Her status was analogous to the proletariat in capitalist production, just as her husband's position was analogous to the bourgeoisie. She was simply a commodity to be 'bartered away'. From this it followed that the family was based upon 'the open or disguised domestic enslavement of the woman' (Engels, 1968, p. 510). The salvation of women thus lay in the termination of the bourgeois family. This could only come about, according to Bebel, Engels and Marx, through socialist revolution.

Most of the comments of Marx and Engels indicated that socialist woman and later communist woman would be the negation of bourgeois woman. This theme was on an abstract plane and did not contain concrete policy proposals but merely stressed that the family and male–female relations would inevitably be transformed once private property had been abolished. After socialist revolution freedom in marriage would come about, for then 'no other motive' than mutual affection would remain (Engels, 1968, p. 516). Engels pointed out that under socialism, monogamy would lose all characteristics which were previously imbued in it through property, namely male dominance and the indissolubility of marriage. He claimed that 'if only marriages that are based on love are moral, then, also only those are moral in which love continues' (Engels, 1968, p. 517). Whether or not Engels and Marx envisaged that the institution of the family would disappear under communism remains controversial. Engels' writings on communism give credibility to the view that the family would remain:

> The equality of women thereby achieved will tend infinitely more to make men really monogamous than to make women polyandrous.
> But what will quite certainly disappear from monogamy are all the features stamped upon it through its origin in property relations; these are, in the first place, supremacy of the man, and, secondly, indissolubility. (The Woman Question, 1975, p. 75)

The institution would remain to be freely entered and freely left: people would be spared the 'useless mire of divorce proceedings' by uncomplicated divorce procedures (Engels, 1968, p. 517). Marx and Engels both assumed that communism would devalue the family as society's basic economic unit, since the family represented the cornerstone of capitalist, not communist economies. Engels argued that:

With the passage of the means of production into common property, the individual family ceases to be the economic unit of society. Private housekeeping is transformed into a social industry. The care and education of the children becomes a public matter. Society takes care of all children, irrespective of whether they are born in wedlock or not. (Engels, 1968, p. 511)

Thus kindergartens and creches would be essential to women's liberation. The precise role of the state in childcare, however, remained unclear.

For Marx and Engels socialism would provide the conditions under which, from each according to their abilities to each according to their work, could operate. Under communism, from each according to their abilities to each according to their needs, became possible (Marx, 1968, pp. 324–5). How these two maxims could be implemented remained unclear due to a derivative view of equality of the sexes. It was something which came about, or 'happened', as society was transformed.

Lenin's writings on women echoed the theoretical arguments of Bebel, Engels and Marx and devoted more attention to practical policy goals, related to the concrete tasks of agitating for revolution in Russia and then building socialism. Lenin firmly believed that women were oppressed under capitalism at work and at home and that only socialist revolution could free them. He gave full backing to the politicisation of women since he saw this as leading to both women's liberation and successful revolution. Indeed, without women's involvement in revolutionary activities, or support for them, political change was unlikely to come about. He observed that 'you cannot draw the masses into politics without drawing women into politics as well. For the female half of the human race is doubly oppressed under capitalism' (Lenin, 1977, p. 85). One necessary prerequisite of women's liberation was political action. Moreover, women's backing was no less vital than men's. For this reason Lenin was in favour of agitation among working-class women before 1917, so long as separate women's organisations were not the result. Similarly, after the revolution he appreciated the need for special political work among women.

Lenin was keenly aware of the practical difficulties of emancipating women in the new workers' state. Speaking in 1919 to the 4th Moscow City Conference of Non-party Working Women, he argued that a 'double task' was required. The first was 'relatively simple and easy' and concerned 'those old laws that kept women in a position of inequality'. 'Bourgeois legislation' which humiliated women, such as laws on divorce and on children born out of wedlock, had to be struck off the books and new laws adopted to guarantee women's rights. The Soviet state had already done this and Lenin proudly announced that in law 'apart from Soviet Russia there is not a country in the world where women enjoy full equality' (Lenin, 1977, pp. 68–9). Since 1902, in fact, Lenin had stressed the importance of 'complete equal rights for men and women' and paid more attention to this than Marx and Engels (Lenin, 1977, p. 9). He was convinced that women's liberation demanded the abolition of restrictions on women's rights and needed the legal protection of equal rights.

But the second task was much harder. Women were oppressed by 'household bondage' and this had to cease, although laws alone could not end it. In much greater detail than Engels, Lenin elaborated upon the daily effects of domestic labour and linked these to the scope of possible emancipation. He observed:

> Notwithstanding all the liberating laws that have been passed, woman continues to be a *domestic slave*, because *petty housework* crushes, strangles, stultifies and degrades her, chains her to the kitchen and to the nursery, and wastes her labour on barbarously unproductive, petty, nerve-racking, stultifying and crushing drudgery. The real *emancipation of women*, real communism, will begin only when a mass struggle (led by the proletariat which is in power) is started against this petty domestic economy, or rather when it is *transformed on a mass scale* into large-scale socialist economy. (The Woman Question, 1975, p. 56)

Making the same point at the Women's Conference, Lenin argued, like Marx, Engels and Bebel before him, that women's liberation required that women participate in 'common productive labour' and that public dining rooms, nurseries and kindergartens would enable them to do so. In keeping with this conclusion, he advocated the development of a system of canteens and gave a commitment to a network of childcare facilities. Thus Lenin offered a public solution to private household tasks. In addition, to ease the personal stresses of domestic life, he supported easy divorce, access to abortion and the distribution of information on birth control. Together these measures, promoted by the workers' state, would enable women to become involved in the economy and in politics.

Lenin encouraged women to take a greater part in administrative jobs, suggesting that participation in the running of factories and the state was essential to equality (The Woman Question, 1975, p. 61). Like Bebel, Lenin believed that women had to help themselves to achieve equality – which could only be ensured at their will and not through law alone. Theoretically, moreover, until working women conquered their oppressions and took advantage of their new rights, the proletariat could not enjoy its freedom.

Although Lenin believed that socialism represented an advance for women, he wisely cautioned that 'it is a far cry from equality in law to equality in life' (Lenin, 1977, p. 61). Female Bolshevik activists in the aftermath of 1917 understood this. Their arguments built on the foundation laid by Bebel, Engels, Marx and Lenin. And the revolutionary situation of 1917 and the 1920s provided a context in which their ideas could flower; but the colossal hardships of these years of starvation, disease and civil war, the precariousness of the new state, the conservative attitudes embedded in Russian society, and the lack of firm practical commitment on the part of many Bolshevik leaders to promote equality of the sexes, the unreceptiveness of working women and peasant women to it, as well as women's resistance to attacks on the family unit, worked against them.

The revolutionary context

Revolution in Russia was a protracted process of upheaval which led to fundamental change in political structures and the ruling political ideas. In early 1917 a radical transformation of the Russian political system began. The eventual Bolshevik seizure of power towards the end of 1917 was followed in 1918 by unrest, opposition and the threat of a general strike by workers. Until 1921, civil war – a continuation of the revolution – raged (Rosenburg, 1985; Mawdsley, 1987).

The structural reason behind the revolutionary rupture with Tsarist autocracy was the increasingly anachronistic nature of the Russian political system. Under nineteenth- and twentieth-century Tsarism there were no political institutions in which subjects could participate until the *zemstva* were set up in 1864 and the first Duma was elected in 1906. But these only gave limited opportunities.[6] Liberal notions of representation and citizenship were almost as alien to Nicholas II as populist, anarchist and Marxist ideas, all of which he dismissed as dangerous and destabilising.[7] He believed that as Tsar he was ordained to rule by God and that power was legitimately concentrated in his hands (Pipes, 1974a; White, 1979). The political legitimacy of Russian autocracy, however, was increasingly questioned. Tsarism and its policies generated hostility for different reasons among the peasantry, intellectuals, workers, the growing business community and finally even among members of the bureaucracy and military who had propped the system up when it faced opposition in 1905, but were unwilling to do so in 1917. Peasants wanted grants of land; intellectuals yearned for freedom of expression, a lifting of censorship and an end to the infiltration of their groups by the secret police; workers wanted better wages, improved conditions and the right to strike; those in business and bureaucracy wanted trade and an outward looking Russia committed to progress rather than one which looked back, with the Slavophiles, to its rural traditions for inspiration. Finally, the largely peasant army after 1914 wanted the slaughter of the First World War to end.

A range of critical political views existed in the nineteenth century and into the twentieth which included anarchism, populism, Marxism and liberalism. Nineteenth- and early twentieth-century Russian political thought was rich and diverse (Venturi, 1960; Lichtheim, 1970, pp. 107–55; Berlin, 1979). Ideas, however, could not be easily or freely debated. Censorship meant that many intellectual writings and pamphlets had to circulate underground and until 1905 political parties could not legally be formed. After the failure of the movement to 'go to the people' in 1874 and 1875, members of *Narodnaia Volia*, or the People's Will, concluded that in these conditions political change could only come about through violent means (Lichtheim, 1970).[8]

From the early nineteenth century various forms of agitation indicated discontent and a desire for political change. These included the Decembrist Revolt of 1825, the spread of underground study groups in student circles in the 1860s, the movement to 'go to the people' of the 1870s, peasant revolts and workers' strikes of 1902 and the failed revolution of 1905. But these events did not provide the catalyst for fundamental political change nor indicate the form, timing and pace that it would eventually take. In retrospect, it is evident that crucial to the trigger of revolution was the overwhelming war weariness and the deprivations that war entailed. In March 1917 there was a swell of spontaneous opposition to Tsarism. It was not organised by the Bolsheviks, many of whom were either living abroad or confined in prison in Russia, or scattered throughout the country.

The Bolshevik party did not play a vanguard role of leading the working class; it was not the united, tightly-organised conspiratorial group that Lenin had described in *What is to be Done?* (Lenin, 1970, vol. 1, pp. 119–270; Rabinowitch, 1978). Leading Bolsheviks were not expecting revolution, any more than the liberals were.

The First World War drained Russia of resources and hunger was widespread. In early 1917 in Petrograd women took to the streets and demonstrated for food. Over 70,000 metal workers went on strike and as the days passed protests escalated (Florinsky, 1971, p. 222; Rosenberg, 1985). Eventually the government ordered the troops to fire on demonstrators; but they mutinied. Workers then called a meeting to set up the Petrograd Soviet. Military authority was transformed 'from below' and transferred to elected committees of soldiers and sailors.

Amid serious political opposition, Nicholas II abdicated and nominated his brother to succeed him. The intensity of political unrest was such, however, that a Provisional Committee of the Duma did not overwhelmingly support the preservation of the monarchy and Tsarism as a system effectively disintegrated (Florinsky, 1971, p. 224). Nicholas's brother refused to become Tsar and the task of running the country was placed in the hands of a Provisional Government. This arrangement was conceived as a temporary measure to be superseded by a popularly elected Constituent Assembly. From March to November two power centres existed: the soviets, which had been set up 'from below', and which were spreading to other cities, towns and villages, and the Provisional Government approved 'from above' by a committee of the Duma.

The Bolsheviks did not initially enjoy majorities in the soviets: the bulk of the seats were held by Social Revolutionaries and Mensheviks.[9] But as the year progressed, popular support for the Bolsheviks in Petrograd increased and in November, at Lenin's exasperated urging, they seized power in a *coup d'état*, overthrowing the Provisional Government. From July to October the Bolshevik promises of 'bread, peace and land' had become overwhelmingly attractive to soldiers, workers and peasants alike. In January 1918 the new Bolshevik leaders allowed the elections to the Constituent Assembly to go ahead. But they won only one-quarter of the seats and dissolved it.

The key to the failure of the Provisional Government was its continued support for the war. On 1 July it ordered a large-scale military offensive, which quickly failed (Hough and Fainsod, 1982, p. 48). When troops streamed away from the front to save their own lives and in the hope of joining in the land seizures rumoured to be taking place, the Government warned that desertion would be met with the death penalty. Although in 1917 Russia was ripe for the disintegration of Tsarism, the circumstances were not especially favourable to the construction of a workers' state. Rapid economic decline, grave food shortages and deepening insecurity fuelled outbreaks of unrest. Crises of production and distribution prompted many urban workers to leave the cities for the countryside to look for basic necessities. Some who remained demonstrated for food and jobs, only to be met with rifle fire. In 1918 the Bolsheviks placed two factory districts of Petrograd under martial law and banned all meetings (Rosenberg, 1985).

The Bolshevik dilemma of power

The Bolshevik leaders faced the difficulty of coming to power in unpropitious circumstances which made fulfilment of their promises extremely difficult. Their inability to meet basic demands led to criticism among erstwhile supporters, such as the metal workers of Petrograd. As new rulers in an extremely fragile political context, the Bolsheviks considered that they had to hold on to power at almost any cost. As early as November 1917, they shut down all rival newspapers and in December set up the Cheka, or secret police. By June 1918, the Bolsheviks had expelled the Mensheviks and Social Revolutionaries from the soviets and the new state became authoritarian and run by one party. Growing discontent and protest necessitated force and repression which were justified in the name of the noble end of communism. The danger to the revolution increased after 1918 in the civil war in which White Armies, with limited help from British, French, American and Japanese military intervention, fought Trotsky's Red Army.

The Bolsheviks requisitioned food from the countryside to feed the Red Army. In response, disgruntled peasants hid their grain. Once grain had been extracted from the peasants by force, they retaliated by sowing less which resulted in serious food shortages. The coercion and centralised control of so-called 'war communism' made the new state unpopular. The years 1918 to 1921 were punctuated by strikes, factory resolutions condemning the Government, peasant hostility and the revolt of sailors at the Kronstadt naval base. The sailors called for soviets without communists and commissars and in response Trotsky sent in troops and put the revolt down.

The consolidation and expansion of the revolution by agitation and coercion continued into the 1920s. Bolshevik rule was finally established in Belorussia in 1919, and in the Ukraine, Azerbaidzhan, Armenia and Georgia in 1920 and 1921. Most resistant were the Muslim areas of Central Asia which eventually became the Soviet republics of Tadzhikistan, Uzbekistan, Turkmenia and Kirgizia. Here fighting continued into the late 1920s (Pipes, 1974b; Rywkin, 1982, pp. 20–44).

With the civil war over in European Russia, Lenin instituted the New Economic Policy (NEP) in 1921. Markets were allowed to develop for many commodities and some denationalisation took place, although not for large industries. For Lenin, NEP was a necessary mixed transitional system, conceived to revive the economy. Its critics, however, feared it was the route to the restoration of capitalism and the abandonment of communism. These critics watched with concern as rich 'Nepmen' made profits whilst unemployment, particularly among women, increased (Dobb, 1978, pp. 125–76; Nove, 1972).

There were therefore immense practical and theoretical difficulties for a small Marxist party trying to run a state in which production was geared to war, food and fuel were in short supply and opponents were prepared to resort to force. Moreover, the proletariat of capitalist states did not come to their aid. According to Marxist theory, a capitalist economic base was a prerequisite for successful socialist revolution. Despite Russia's own economic boom in the 1890s, industry was concentrated on ' "islands" in a vast agricultural sea', with over 85 per cent of the population living in rural areas (Dobb, 1966, p. 36). Without 'permanent revolution' argued Trotsky, without the spread of socialist revolution to Europe, the Russian revolution was doomed. Its success depended upon 'the efforts of proletarians of several advanced countries' (Trotsky, 1974, pp. 186–233).

On top of these extreme difficulties, came Lenin's first stroke in May 1922 and his death in January 1924. Stalin then demonstrated the importance of the post of General Secretary of the party, with its power to appoint party officials, in consolidating his role as leader. He also used the 1921 Decree on Party Unity to purge those allegedly guilty of factionalism. Stalin engineered a purge of Trotsky and the so-called left-wing deviationists on the grounds that they were setting up a divisive faction within the party. Against Trotsky, Stalin argued that since other revolutions had not taken place and Russia was isolated in a hostile world, the dictatorship of the proletariat would have to be consolidated in one country. There was no choice. A base would then exist for the defeat of imperialism in all countries. He then charged Bukharin and those of the 'right' with factionalism and attacked their support of a continuation of NEP when he decided to push ahead with central planning. Gradually Stalin removed, by purges, his real and imagined enemies.[10]

Revolutionary ideas and women's liberation

The revolutionary ideas that had been unleashed in 1917 continued for a while to flourish (Keep, 1968, pp. 180–216). Debates took place on how best to build a socialist economy and the meaning of revolution for education, the arts and the liberation of women. Thus, the revolutionary situation of 1917 and the following decade provided the stimulus and opportunity for lively discussions of women's emancipation that already had roots in Russian political ideas. The rupture with Tsarism offered also a context for the pursuit of equality in practice.

Thoughts on women's emancipation did not, of course, begin in Russia in 1917. Female subordination and the need for liberation was a theme in the liberal and radical traditions of the nineteenth and early twentieth centuries. Liberal and radical perspectives and the political practice associated with them, have already been discussed by others (Stites, 1978; Edmondson, 1984). Promoting education for women, giving them skills for employment and fostering notions of independence from fathers and husbands were the overriding concerns of nineteenth-century female philanthropists such as Anna Filosofova, Nadezhda Stasova and Mariia Trubnikova. These women were liberals who were in favour of modest legal reforms. They were philanthropic, privileged women aiding the less fortunate by encouraging various forms of self-help through institutions such as the Society for Cheap Lodgings and the Sunday School Movement.[11]

Philanthropists were dismissed with the denigrating term '*aristok-ratka*' by female radicals and nihilists of the nineteenth century. Arguing against small deeds performed within the system, the radicals hoped for sweeping social and political changes. Inspired by the spirit of personal emancipation of Chernyshevsky's *What is to be Done?*, a small number of radicals lived in communes, eschewed traditional female roles, refused to attend balls if they came from the upper classes, and wore plain, dark woollen dresses.[12] But the radicals did not offer a full-blown theory of woman's subordination, nor any action programme for combatting it. Their focus fell on freedom from the yoke of traditional families and on individual liberation.

In the period after the failed revolution of 1905, the main advocates of change in women's lives were female liberals and socialists. Some liberals came together in the All-Russian Union for Women's Equality. Their political demands included a constituent assembly, suffrage for men and women, sexual equality before the law, equal rights for peasant women in land reform, co-education, and reform of the laws governing prostitution (Stites, 1978, pp. 199–200). Others gathered in the Women's Progressive Party which, unlike the Union, rejected cooperation with men on the grounds that it inevitably meant a subordination of women's issues to other political objectives. The Party proposed a constitutional monarchy, liberalisation of divorce, equal rights in education and an end to militarism. Liberal women who found both the Union and the Progressive Party too political for their taste preferred to work through the Mutual Philanthropic Society (Stites, 1978, p. 202).

The 'bourgeois' ideas of these 'liberal ladies' came under attack from socialist women. Kollontai saw the liberation of women as integral to socialist revolution and considered the existence of an independent women's movement as politically shortsighted. She believed that women should belong to the Russian Social Democratic and Labour Party (RSDLP), and not to women's groups which could not generate sufficient support for the genuine emancipation of women. When the First All-Russian Women's Congress eventually took place in December 1908, after having been postponed since 1902, Kollontai's contribution attacked the notion of a general women's movement on the grounds that working women and middle-class women had different class interests.[13] Women's emancipation, she contended, was part of broader social changes and linked to them.

The Congress stimulated enthusiasm for change among women, but it was met with criticism, ambivalence and tepid interest by bureaucrats and political parties. Although the League for Women's Equality became active after 1909, its membership of under 1,000 was negligible. Despite the existence of women's organisations between the upheavals of 1905 and the revolution of 1917, they were relatively weak and women's issues did not enjoy political prominence, except among the small numbers of liberal women seeking 'equal rights' and among the social democratic women who attacked the inadequacy of the notion and rallied for socialism (Stites, 1978, p. 227; Edmondson, 1984).[14]

Formal equality: From Tsarist denial to early Bolshevik legislation

Calls for the franchise, equal rights, more enlightened marriages and independence for women challenged the patriarchal principles of Tsarist family law. According to the 1836 Russian Code, a wife was 'obliged to obey her husband as the head of the family; to abide with him in love, honour and unconditional obedience; to render him all satisfaction and affection as the master of the house' (Atkinson, 1978, p. 33). A woman needed her husband's approval in order to work or study. If the husband moved abode, his wife was obliged to follow him.

Voting rights were granted in 1905 when the Duma was set up, but women were given inferior status. The right to vote was tied to property ownership and since many more men than women were property owners, the franchise was linked to gender as well as class. Women who owned property had the right to vote but it had obligatorily to be exercised through male relatives. If no male relatives existed, these women could not vote (Atkinson, 1978, p. 32). Although a draft law granting equal civil and political rights was drawn up, the Duma was dissolved in July 1906 before it could be approved. A minority of women from the upper classes owned and inherited property, but this had little relevance for the vast majority of women.

The revolution brought women and men vastly expanded formal rights. Equality before the law meant that civil and political rights which had previously been denied now, in principle, existed for all, with the exception of the old 'exploiters' who were disenfranchised. The precarious political position of the new Bolshevik state did not prevent the codification of law concerning women. Labour law, for instance, established the equal rights of men and women to insurance in cases of illness and recognised a right to maternity leave with financial support of full-pay for eight weeks before and after birth. A minimum wage for employees in Soviet institutions was also set and applied to both sexes. Similarly, female and male workers enjoyed the right to an annual holiday with pay. The principle of equal pay for equal work was adopted and this specifically included 'women performing work identical with men in quantity and quality' (Dmitrieva, 1975, p. 13).[15] Labour laws at this time may have been formal declarations, not respected in practice, but they established a foundation for changed patterns of behaviour. Equal rights to education were also established. Women's political rights were made clear in the first constitution of 1918 which granted women and men the right to vote and to be elected as deputies to the soviets.

Restrictions on divorce were quickly lifted (Matveev, 1978, pp. 94–5). Article 1 of the Decree on the Introduction of Divorce in December 1917 simply stated that 'a marriage is to be annulled when either both parties or one at least appeal for its annulment' (Schlesinger, 1949, p. 30). This radical change meant that mutual consent was not a precondition of divorce. It could be granted at the request of either spouse.

A Code of Laws concerning the Civil Registration of Deaths, Births and Marriages came into existence in October 1918. Marriage was cast as a civil rather than a religious union and 'not to be contracted unless the mutual consent of the parties to be married is obtained' (Schlesinger, 1949, p. 33). The principles of the legislation on divorce, already mentioned, were reiterated in Article 87, which stated 'the mutual consent of husband and wife, as well as the desire of one of them to obtain a divorce, may be considered a ground for divorce' (Schlesinger, 1949, p. 34). The ease with which divorce could be obtained was a reaction to the harsh restrictions of Tsarist law and an attack on the Orthodox Church. So was Article 104 of the 1918 Code which declared 'change of residence on the part of one of the married parties does not oblige the other to follow' (Schlesinger, 1949, p. 36). Woman's freedom of movement and choice of abode was no longer legally tied to the wishes of her husband.

Emancipation from restrictions was the sentiment which underpinned new Bolshevik legislation. This even extended to the choice of surname. According to Article 100, 'Married persons use a common surname (the matrimonial surname). On the registration of marriage they may choose whether they will adopt the husband's (bridegroom's) or wife's (bride's) surname or their joint surnames', thus ending the automatic imposition of the male's name on his wife (Schlesinger, 1949, p. 35). The same applied to divorce. Article 102 instructed that:

> When a marriage is dissolved by divorce, the petition for divorce must state by what surname the married parties wish to be known thenceforth. In default of agreement between them on this question, the divorced husband and wife shall be known by the surname by which each of them was respectively known before their marriage. (Schlesinger, 1949, p. 36)

New laws thus offered the freedom of new choices.

Partners were also unable to restrict each other's property rights. Article 106 stated that 'married parties may enter into any property relation permitted by law. Agreements by husband and wife intended to restrict property rights of either party are invalid' (Schlesinger, 1949, p. 36). Again, the aim was to deter a spouse from controlling or curbing the rights of wife or husband. The law upheld the freedom from control by the 'other'.

New inheritance laws were a reaction against past practices which had permitted the exclusion of daughters altogether, or gave them a much smaller share than sons. A law of November 1922 restricted inheritance to direct descendents, the surviving spouse and dependent, destitute and incapacitated persons. Articles 419 and 420 also laid down that, in cases when people died without making a will, 'the inheritance is shared out in equal parts per capita' among the legally entitled.

Whilst the emphasis of the laws of 1918 fell on rights, duties were inevitably included. Articles 107 and 108 obliged spouses to support their partners in marriage if the latter lacked the means of subsistence and were unable to work. This also applied after the dissolution of a marriage. Duties involved in the raising of children were radically reformed. Fathers of children born in or out of wedlock were liable, according to Article 143, to share expenses connected with pregnancy, birth and child maintenance. Article 162 stipulated 'the duty of maintaining the children devolves equally upon both parents, while the amount of the maintenance paid by them is defined in accordance with their means' (Schlesinger, 1949, p. 40). Children from non-registered marriages were also granted the same rights as children of registered ones. The status of 'illegitimate' was removed by Article 133 which instructed that, 'actual descent is regarded as the basis of the family, without any difference between relationships established by legal or religious marriage or outside marriage' (Schlesinger, 1949, p. 37).

Although these articles show a commitment to changing relations within households, the Bolsheviks were not united in their views about the family and this legislation was controversial. Some communists feared that new laws could give rise to personal irresponsibility and domestic instability and some held rather traditional views about woman's place in society. They were also concerned about the implications of the new abortion law.

Abortion policy

The Decree on the Legalisation of Abortions of 1920 permitted 'such operations to be performed freely and without charge in Soviet hospitals, where conditions are assured of minimising the harm of the operation' (Schlesinger, 1949, p. 44). The right to abortion conformed to the general pattern of lifting restrictions on women, but this was not the main reason behind it. Nor was the right inspired by a commitment to a woman's right to her own body. The main motive was to end backstreet abortions. The decree began by stating that the incidence of illegal abortions was increasing in Russia and in the West and that punishment of the women and doctors involved did not deter the 'evil'. Women were portrayed as victims of 'mercenary and often ignorant quacks who make a profession of secret operations'. The sad result was that 'up to 50 per cent of such women are infected in the course of operation, and up to 4 per cent of them die' (Schlesinger, 1949, p. 48). Anyone other than a doctor was 'absolutely' forbidden to perform the operation. The new law was not universally supported. Although lobbied for by women in the *Zhenotdel* on social grounds, many in the medical profession spoke out against it, and the party considered abortion undesirable and to be deterred.

A particularly large number of articles on abortion appeared in 1926 in women's magazines such as *Rabotnitsa* (Working Woman), *Rabotnitsa i Domashniaia Khoziaika* (Working Woman and House-wife) and *Delegatka* (Woman Delegate). Some doctors, such as L. Chatskii, argued that abortion was detrimental to health whether performed legally in properly regulated conditions or illegally in unsanitary ones (Chatskii, 1926, p. 3). The editors of *Rabotnitsa i Domashniaia Khoziaika* then invited readers to respond to Chatskii's article, arguing that he presented a medical point of view which did not pay attention to the problems of daily life. Other articles suggested that women did not think seriously enough about the implications of the operation and warned that as a consequence of abortion they could become infertile and age rapidly (*Rabotnitsa i Domashniaia*

Khoziaika, no. 1, November 1926, p. 3). Articles in *Rabotnitsa* and *Delegatka*, consistent with the party line, called for a struggle against abortion (Semashko, 1926, p. 17; Otradinskii, 1926, pp. 15–16).

Taking a stand against the critics of abortion, the journal *Kommunistka* (Communist Woman) underlined the social problems and personal pressures which made abortion necessary. It also described the inadequacies of the abortion service. The story of one working woman's life was cited to illustrate both of these points. The woman recounted how 'for 2 weeks I went to the abortion commission and stood in a queue from 4 in the morning until 3 in the afternoon ... and they refused me'. *Kommunistka* commented that already having three children, the youngest of whom was just over a year old, the woman felt she could not cope with another. She had no alternative but to pay 30 roubles for an illegal abortion (*Kommunistka*, no. 9, September 1928, pp. 48–9). *Kommunistka* also reported that of 2,137 requests for abortions, 447 were rejected.[16]

These same competing arguments were reiterated by gynaecologists at a conference on abortion in 1927 in Kiev. Dr B. A. Bebderskaia stressed that 'in fighting abortion our first task is to combat secret abortion and the quack'. By making abortion legal, Soviet socialism was combating quackery, unlike capitalist countries where 'the prohibition of abortion merely results in increasing the number of secret abortions' (Schlesinger, 1949, p. 182). Other participants expressed how harmful legal abortions were. The People's Commissar of Health in the Ukraine, D. I. Yefimov asserted that 'the biological and psychological injury done to the female organism by abortion is so obvious that no special proof is needed' (Schlesinger, 1949, p. 183). Against this Dr V. V. Selinsky criticised the 'hypocrites' and 'socially short-sighted' who dwelt only on infections, perforations and nervous disorders resulting from abortion. He implored 'open your eyes to the facts of real life, to the socio-economic conditions under which women have to live and to bestow life upon new human beings!' (Schlesinger, 1949, p. 186). He reflected that, 'it will be easier, I take it, for the individual woman to endure some abortions than to follow one little coffin after another to the cemetery and to bury her youth and vigour with them there' (Schlesinger, 1949, p. 186). As well as being sensitive to the social difficulties of producing children, Selinsky, unlike many men of the 1920s, appreciated the importance of women deciding their own fates for themselves and determining their own sex lives. He remarked:

No one of us men would accept a decision by some commission as to the social interest in his being married or not. Do not prevent women from deciding for themselves a fundamental issue of their lives. Woman has a right to a sexual life as freely realised as that of a man. In order to remain completely fit from the social and biological points of view, she ought to be able to satisfy that need as normally as does a man. We need no mass-produced class of spinsters, which would be merely harmful to the community. Unquestionably abortion is an evil; but as yet we have no substitute for it. (Schlesinger, 1949, pp. 196–7)

Abortion was therefore a controversial topic in the new Soviet state and in the 1920s there were open disagreements about the issue, not an automatic subservience to the party line.

Despite the practical reasons behind the legalisation of abortion, it was nevertheless part of a package of revolutionary legislation for women passed in the first three years of Soviet rule. Male dominance, superiority and control were no longer enshrined in law. The difficulty was, in practice, that male dominance continued to be helped by women's fears of the changes brought about by the revolution. Peasant women, in particular, were upset by Bolshevik criticisms of the traditional family because to them the family meant security; so they clung to it. The fate of women without men was made uncertain by social customs. For example, the commune put pressure on both widows and the wives of absent soldiers to surrender their allotments. Married women wanted to keep their husbands for their own survival (Clements, 1985, pp. 161–5). Lack of education and high levels of illiteracy among women made it hard for them to obtain skilled jobs. After 1921 rising unemployment hit women in the towns especially hard. Social customs, traditional attitudes, fear, instability and unemployment created a situation which made it hard to take advantage of the possibilities offered by the legislation.

A formidable task remained for women to become aware of the new rights, let alone take advantage of them in a conservative, predominantly peasant society, resistant to them. The appropriate attitudes and institutional infrastructure to support the legislation were missing, illustrating Lenin's remark that 'equality in law is not yet equality in life' and his observations on the topic of equality of the sexes, 'scratch a communist and you find a philistine'. Many male communists had an almost visceral reaction to the restructuring of gender roles. Notions of 'women's work', female subordination to men and dependence on them, died hard. Many women did not seek independence but wanted the emotional bonds and security of the family unit to be preserved, especially at a time of turmoil. To peasant women the destruction of the family meant a threat to personal survival and a challenge to the way in which villages were run. To many, women's liberation meant insecurity for both women and men.

The 1926 marriage law
The 1926 Code of Laws on Marriage and Divorce, the Family and Guardianship was adopted due to concern about the implications, for women in unregistered marriages, of the 1917 and 1918 laws. Since 1918 unregistered marriages had increased in number. Although the 1918 law had specified paternal duties toward children, these were not always performed. The spread of *de facto* marriages was accompanied by increasing insecurity for women for a number of reasons connected with economic policy, social policy and male behaviour. The NEP which had begun in 1921 had led to a sharp increase in unemployment for women and if a husband left his *de facto* wife, she could not be sure of securing assistance from him. In these years the number of abandoned children grew in number and 'fathers frequently threw their wives out when a child was born and denied both of them support' (Stites, 1978, p. 367). Government cutbacks after 1922 also affected the provision of childcare facilities for mothers and children. This meant that homeless women could not always find places for themselves and their children in a mothers' home or a children's home.

The People's Commissar of Justice observed, 'the wife in a *de facto* marriage enjoyed no rights' (Schlesinger, 1949, p. 85). This was an overstatement since the earlier legislation had indicated that 'no difference is to be made between relationships established inside and outside marriage' (Schlesinger, 1949, p. 41). The problem was that, although fathers were legally responsible for supporting the children of *de facto* unions, 'full protection' for these children was not always forthcoming. The 1926 Marriage Code granted registered and unregistered marriages equal legal rights and emphasised the obligations that came with them: it was hoped that this would guarantee financial support for women after the breakdown of partnerships. Article 3 of the law also attempted to encourage a switch from *de facto* to *de jure* marriage by allowing for retrospective registration.

Anxiety about the weak position of women in unregistered marriages was fuelled by an apparent growth in promiscuity and polygamy. Lax sexual behaviour was criticised by some as an 'undesirable phenomenon' which reflected a 'vagueness of relations' rather than deep commitment. In this context it was declared:

> There are not a few cases, whether in divorce or marriage, where we have a firm and formal marriage, and at the same time find that quite undisturbed relations are being maintained with a non-registered husband or wife. The project opposes these vague relationships by introducing responsibility for *de facto* marriages and making it a duty for non-registered couples to clarify their relations. The project is consistent with its principles, for we are developing the protection of the weaker party, which is the woman and child and combating the levity and vagueness with which some look upon marriage. (Schlesinger, 1949, p. 114)

Consistent with the attempt to inject propriety into sexual relations, Article 6 informed that it was unlawful to register marriages 'between persons one or both of whom is or are already married either with or without registration' (Schlesinger, 1949, pp. 154–5).

Irresponsibility in relationships was attacked because it meant that women could be deserted without financial support; moreover, women's contribution to the household within marriage would count for nothing. It was reported that:

> We find a number of cases among them where a worker's wife, or housewife, runs the whole house, looks after the upbringing of the little children and thus participates in the common household, but does not receive anything for her pains after the divorce because the husband – the worker – keeps everything. (Schlesinger, 1949, p. 116)

To avoid this result, Article 6 of the 1926 legislation moved away from the principle of a segregation of property to that of a community of property. It stated that 'property which belonged to either husband or wife prior to their marriage remains the separate property of each of them. Property acquired by husband and wife during continuance of their marriage is regarded as their joint property.' Article 11 emphasised that Article 10 applied to the property of those in *de facto* unions too.

Because *de facto* marriages now had greater legal recognition than before, *de facto* couples could acquire registered divorces. A registered divorce was easily obtained and did not require mutual agreement on the part of the couple. All that was necessary to obtain a divorce was an application from one person to the Civil Registry Office. Officials would then inform the spouse on a postcard that divorce had taken place.

During the year before this new Code became law, there was

extensive coverage of the draft law centring on the contention that women and children were the weak parties in unregistered marriages and in need of protection. As one supporting letter printed in a woman's magazine put it, 'the law defends a woman and her child. . . . Today woman has become politically conscious, and Soviet legislation stands up for her' (*Delegatka*, no. 4, February 1926, p. 7). Another backed the law on the grounds that 'the registration of marriage is necessary because we still have a lot of citizens lacking political consciousness, especially among the peasants' (*Rabotnitsa i Krest'ianka*, no. 3, 1926, p. 22).

Sophiia Smidovich, head of the *Zhenotdel* after Kollontai from 1922 to 1924, pointed out that the new legislation served the 'child question' (*detskii vopros*) as well as the 'woman question' (*zhenskii vopros*). She believed that the growing number of homeless children made legislation pressing (Smidovich, 1926, p. 47). Others suggested that the new law would help to combat promiscuity. A letter to the magazine *Working Woman and Housewife* declared that 'we must struggle against disgraceful sex lives just as we fight against alcoholism. The state must demand that every citizen register her marriage' (*Rabotnitsa i Domashniaia Khoziaika*, no. 6, November 1926, p. 1). In a similar vein, others argued that only registered marriages were proper and criticised women in *de facto* unions for being frivolous and flighty (*Delegatka*, no. 1. January 1926, p. 11). Maintaining that the state had a duty to promote registered marriages, one letter contended that 'marital relations are not the private affair of a man and woman. Society and the state must regulate them. If we wish to show our young people that marriage involves cleanliness, tidiness and honesty, then we must recognise only registered marriages' (*Rabotnitsa i Domashniaia Khoziaika*, no. 6, November 1926, p. 1).

Objections to the law were several. Some critics suggested that both women and men should be financially responsible for children. One citizen wrote:

> I see it this way: once a woman has the same rights as a man, both should pay for the child. For example, one working woman said to me, 'it is your child, pay for it or go and sit in jail'. (*Delegatka*, no. 1, January 1926, p. 11)

Many men writing in this vein voiced concern that women would abuse the law in an attempt to extract money from past lovers. Urban men tended to prefer the more relaxed status quo since it worked to their advantage. Rural men protested that payment of alimony would disrupt the *dvor*, the communal household around which the peasant economy ran, since members would collectively be responsible for one man's alimony. A letter to *Delegatka* complained that, if a judge made a young man pay alimony for eighteen years, 'for the peasant *dvor* this is an enormous sum' (*Delegatka*, no. 4, February 1926, p. 7). Another asked what if a man had lived with two or three women and then became an invalid or died, would all the women demand something, resulting in the village cow going to one and the cart to another? He concluded that 'to the peasant this law is entirely unfavourable. . . . Several women will abuse the law. I suggest we do not adopt it' (*Delegatka*, no. 1, January 1926, p. 11).

At the other extreme, those on the left of the party argued for an end to alimony altogether. Kollontai advocated the setting up of a General Insurance Fund with the implication that individuals would no longer be responsble for their own children. Instead, the burden would be shifted to the collective and workers would make payments to the fund on a graduated scale. Kollontai saw the fund as providing for those who would otherwise not receive alimony since in the short term the country could not offer a comprehensive welfare system. Kollontai also wanted freedom from state restrictions in personal unions and freedom for partners to define the nature of their relationships. In keeping with this, she argued that individual couples should draw up their own contracts specifying the nature of their economic responsibilities towards each other. Those who supported Kollontai's plan supposed that it would be easier to adminster a fund than track down large numbers of men evading alimony payments (Golubeva, 1926, p. 53). Her critics, however, accused her of promoting personal sexual irresponsibility (Farnsworth, 1978, pp. 149–60).

The 1926 Code of Laws failed to protect women. Divorce increased rapidly and women continued to suffer from it. In Leningrad the number of divorces rose from 5,536 in 1926 to 16,006 in 1927 (Stites, 1978, p. 370). A survey of the Vyborg district showed that 70 per cent of separations were unilaterally initiated by men and only 7 per cent by mutual agreement. In Stites' estimation 'even in the early 1920s armies of deserted and destitute women filled the streets of Soviet towns. By the end of the decade the situation was crying out for correction' (Stites, 1978, p. 371). Legislation of 1936 attempted just this, as Chapter 3 shows.

Marxist theorising on the woman question in the new Soviet state: Armand and Kollontai

It was against the backdrop of these laws of 1917, 1918, 1920, 1922 and 1926 and in a context of political turmoil in the early years of Bolshevik power that attempts were made to extend Marxist theorising on the woman question. The writings of the first two directors of the *Zhenotdel*, Inessa Armand and Alexandra Kollontai, were particularly important in this respect.[17]

Like Bebel, Engels and Marx, they believed that women's liberation was only possible under socialism. But like Lenin they realised that liberation would not automatically 'happen' or even 'be guaranteed' by a change in the economic substructure or through legislation. Several additional changes had to take place in the family, domestic labour, maternity, childrearing and sexual relations. The starting point after revolution was legal changes, but these were not sufficient. Special institutions were needed to reach, enlighten and mobilise women.

Socialist revolution and legal change

Armand praised the new laws, made possible by the revolution, for laying the foundation of women's liberation.

> For the first time in many centuries, for the complete liberation of woman from the most deeply-rooted form of her slavery – from family bondage, which lay on her shoulders like a heavy burden and in practice deprived her of the opportunity to be completely equal and completely free. (Armand, 1975, p. 62)

While commending Soviet power for providing 'complete civil and political equality' and for offering women 'the opportunity to build a new life of their own', Armand added that 'this is not enough' (Armand, 1975, pp. 62–6). Without reconstructing the entire fabric of family life and social patterns, Armand argued, 'woman will not be free' (Armand, 1975, p. 66). Radical changes in family life were necessary because 'the age-old family structure is the last fortress of the old order, of the old bondage'. Armand implied that social relations could not be transformed just because the revolution had taken place, property had changed hands and women proclaimed equal with men. Rather, to end the old order she stressed 'it is necessary to demolish this fortress' of the family (Armand, 1975,

p. 69). The nature of relationships had to be transformed for liberation to be possible.

Writing in 1919, Armand emphasised that women's lives would not automatically change with newly won political rights, but only through the active pursuit of change by women themselves. Her appeals for the political involvement of women implied that liberation was a process that took on a new form after the revolution. She observed that 'working woman just a year ago received complete political and civil equality, and only now is beginning to free herself from the second form of her oppression, from family and domestic slavery' (Armand, 1975, p. 69). Women's liberation had to be promoted, cultivated and nourished by political action under socialism. Part of this action had to be directed at transforming the family.

The family and domestic labour

The reorganisation of domestic labour and childrearing were seen by Armand and Kollontai as fundamental to the transformation of the family. Like Lenin, they suggested that private domestic work should be replaced by communal kitchens, dining rooms and laundries. But going one step further than Lenin, Kollontai maintained that housework would be unnecessary under socialism:

> The individual household is dying. It is giving way in our society to collective housekeeping. Instead of working woman cleaning her flat, the communist society can arrange for men and women whose job it is to go round in the morning cleaning rooms. (Holt, 1977, p. 255)

In a similar vein, Armand called for 'new household forms, new ways of upbringing' (Armand, 1975, p. 69). She praised Soviet initiatives for organising public dining rooms in keeping with her vision, but regretted that 'there are not enough of them'. For domestic life to change, communal eating had to be organised throughout the country. She concluded that 'it is necessary for working women themselves to take on this task' (Armand, 1975, p. 67). The suggestion here is that without their special efforts, it would not be achieved. Armand felt an urgency – 'all this should not be done in some distant future, but immediately, now' (Armand, 1975, p. 67). Women's liberation had to be incorporated in the construction of socialist society right from the start. The implication was that the prerequisites of liberation must be actively sought. Without special efforts by women, their liberation could be neglected; and without women's liberation the achievement of socialism would be compromised.

Armand viewed changes in domestic life as both specific to women's liberation and an integral part of socialist construction. She therefore extended the logic of Marxist arguments by asserting that the success of female self-determination and socialism itself were connected to the socialisation of domestic labour and childcare. If the old forms of the family remained with traditional female roles in domestic labour and childrearing, 'it is impossible to create a new person, impossible to construct socialism' (Armand, 1975, p. 69). Yet Armand realised that immediate action would not bring immediate results. The transformation of domestic life, she cautioned, 'takes time' (Armand, 1975, p. 69). Trotsky, too, was aware that domestic life could not be altered instantly; political equality was 'one problem and the simplest'. More difficult, according to Trotsky, was achieving 'industrial equality' in factories, mills and trades unions and 'doing it in such a way that the men should not put the women to disadvantage'. 'An infinitely more arduous problem' was attaining equality in the family, and, he warned, 'all our domestic habits must be revolutionised before that can happen'. Trotsky could identify therefore which aspects of equality were more readily attainable than others, and hold the view that the fate of political, economic, social and domestic equality were inextricably interlinked: without fundamental changes in domestic labour 'we cannot speak seriously' of equality of the sexes 'in social life or even in politics' (Trotsky, 1970, p. 21).

Trotsky, like Armand, wanted immediate action. But he noted that due to 'the scarcity of material resources . . . actual success will not be as rapid as we would have wished' (Trotsky, 1970, p. 30). Armand, too, was sensitive to the harsh conditions of daily life and their constraint on progress. She vividly described them as follows:

> Every working woman and peasant woman suffers and so do their children: there is little bread, insufficient firewood, not enough shoes, little soap and few clothes. . . . Children do not go to school because there is no heating or no boots. (Armand, 1975, p. 89)

Problems of basic living were acute. Reflections upon the theoretical implications of domestic chores and the meaning of equality was for many an irrelevant exercise, merely intellectual issues for a tiny group of women. In Trotsky's view, hard conditions and meagre resources were not the only barrier to progress. He regretted that 'inertia and blind habit hold sway with such force as in the dark and secluded inner life of the family' (Trotsky, 1970, p. 30). Such habits could be eased by laundries, restaurants, sewing workshops and public education. Through these facilities the bond between husband and wife could 'be freed from everything external and accidental' and come to depend 'on mutual attachment'. Genuine friendship and attraction between the sexes, stripped of the slave status of women, could in turn give rise to 'inner stability, not the same of course, for everyone, but compulsory for no one' (Trotsky, 1970, p. 26). Although Armand, Kollontai and Trotsky all recognised that extensive and fast changes in family relations were hard, they believed them ultimately to be possible due to the broader context of political and economic changes in which they were taking place.

The dominant Marxist view of family life in the 1920s held that its nature changed according to the mode of production. As Kollontai put it: 'the form of marriage and of the family is thus determined by the economic system of the given epoch, and it changes as the economic base of society changes' (Holt, 1977, p. 225). With the dictatorship of the proletariat 'the material and economic considerations in which the family was grounded cease to exist'. Women were no longer economically dependent on men, and responsibility for childcare shifted to the collective. Thus the family 'ceased to be a family' because it was stripped of past economic functions and responsibility for children. As a result, 'the family unit shrinks to a union of two people based on mutual agreement' (Holt, 1977, p. 226). As an institution of the superstructure the family unit could alter its form, congruent with changes in the substructure.

Maternity

The reorganisation of family life not only affected the nature of relations between woman and man, but also the bond between mother and child. Kollontai illustrated how socialism changed maternity for the better by contrasting the predicament of working-class and middle-class mothers under capitalism. In Kollontai's view, maternity enslaved working women in capitalist society because factory walls separated women from their children. Contrasting the motherhood of Masha the lady and Masha the working woman, Kollontai painted the following picture:

> Masha the lady amuses herself with the baby and then goes out visiting, goes shopping, or to the theatre, or to a ball. There is someone at hand to look after the baby. Motherhood is amusing, it is entertainment for Masha the lady.
> For the other Mashas, the working women – the dyers, weavers,

laundresses and the other hundreds and thousands of working-class women – motherhood is a cross. The factory siren calls the woman to work but her child is fretting and crying. How can she leave it? Who will look after it? She pours the milk into a bottle and gives the child to the old woman next door or leaves her young daughter in charge. (Holt, 1977, p. 131)

Kollontai argued that working women did not have the time or opportunity to look after children well, but instead spent the day worrying about them. Working-class mothers were also likely to be employed in poor working conditions which made them ill. These sick working mothers often bore unhealthy children, exposed to damp and crowded working-class housing.

Socialism guaranteed communal methods of childrearing and prompted more human relations between mother and child. Women at work would not have to fret about unattended children at home, and children would benefit from being part of a community of children. Kollontai believed that without communal childcare working mothers would not be liberated or enjoy healthy relations with offspring. In keeping with these arguments, the new Soviet state introduced maternity grants for women and began, with difficulty, to provide childcare facilities.

The argument that socialism would not be constructed without the socialisation of domestic chores and childcare, and that women could not be liberated without them, widened the boundaries of Marxist discourse. Socialist economic relations were viewed as necessary but not sufficient for women's liberation and for socialism.

Gender roles, socialisation and sexuality

Although the question of domestic labour was broached by Armand, Kollontai, Lenin, Trotsky and others, gender roles and socialisation into them were not critically examined. The main emphasis of their writings fell on a collective or social solution to domestic labour rather than a radical restructuring of gender roles. This meant that women would lose their domestic burden to social agencies and men would assume no new domestic roles. The relationship of women to domestic work was to change by the reduction of the time devoted to this work. Gender roles, their implications for male–female relations, and the mechanisms through which women were subordinated to men were not extensively analysed.

The omission was serious because it meant that the various forms of female subordination existing under socialism were not seen as topics to be addressed. Male behaviour in the home, for instance, was not analysed; nor were the condescending ways in which men often spoke to women nor the range of oppressive ways in which they interacted with them. Admittedly, male roles in Muslim households came under some scrutiny and their 'feudal' characteristics were condemned. But male behaviour patterns in peasant households, in urban settings and in communist families were not studied in depth. According to the Bolsheviks, male behaviour itself was not at fault, but the feudal and capitalist systems of the past which gave rise to exploitative relations between classes and individuals. Thus, an analysis of gender roles had no central place because class relations not gender were conceived as the determining factor. Indeed, in Kollontai's estimation one mistake of the bourgeois feminists was to view men rather than the system as blameworthy.

Without a systematic analysis of gender roles, deep-rooted problems could not be identified, isolated and tackled in practice. The various subtleties of domination ranging from the use of language to expectations of daily behaviour were not studied. These were considered non-topics and kept off political agendas.[18] The way political discourse is couched affects which questions are framed and which practical strategies follow from them. If male roles are not seen as a serious problem, then strategies will not be devised to change them.

Kollontai's short stories, however, touched on gender roles by making clear what sort of male roles were unacceptable and in need of change. In the story *Sisters*, Kollontai described the breakdown of a marriage in which the husband, a NEPman, regularly came home drunk, no longer discussed politics and society with his wife as he once had, showed no sympathy for her threatened unemployment and finally brought home a woman with him one night when drunk. The man accused his wife of 'woman's foolishness' when she attempted to discuss the decay of their relationship. He claimed that she threw 'feminine hysterics' when he became aggressive and tried to prevent her from leaving him (Holt, 1977, pp. 220–1). Being entirely self-centred he contrived reasons why she, in fact, was always to blame. Although Kollontai was pointing out the dangers of NEP, she also portrayed the personal anguish of unions which lacked mutual respect. But Kollontai did not go beyond observations on the need for independence and dignity to present a systematic view of the prerequisites of liberation or a social scientific breakdown of various forms of sexual subjection. She did not advocate ways of dealing with male aggression and violence or useful responses to disdain and neglect. Nevertheless, the description in her stories of several emotional states illustrated several ways in which individuals could stifle their partners and deny the other respect, personal space and sensitive commitment.

Kollontai did not use the terms 'sexism', 'male chauvinism', 'personal politics' or 'consciousness raising', adopted by Western feminists of the 1960s and 1970s. However, she attempted to link changes in the nature of relations between the sexes to broader social transformations. Even before the revolution Kollontai had wanted to develop the thinking of Fourier, Marx and Engels and open a discussion on 'the confused knot of personal relationships', 'the riddle of love', 'sexual crisis', 'sexual dramas' and 'fleeting passion'. She observed that the question of the relations between the sexes 'is a mystery as old as human society itself' and saw no reason why such 'mysteries' should be ignored (Holt, 1977, pp. 237–49). She was impatient with conservatives and socialists alike in their treatment of the 'sexual problem'. Conservatives wished to re-establish the old foundation of the family and with it the oppression of women. Socialists, she lamented, at a time ripe for analysing the topic:

> assure us that sexual problems will only be settled when the basic reorganisations of the social and economic structure of society has been tackled. Doesn't this 'putting off the problem until tomorrow' suggest that we still haven't found that one and only 'magic thread' that promises to unravel the tangle. Shouldn't we find it now, at this very moment? (Holt, 1977, pp. 237–8)

Kollontai believed that the 'sexual crisis' was assuming a profound and threatening character since peasants and workers, as well as the old bourgeoisie, were now confronting changing patterns of daily life. She argued that:

> The problems of sex concern the largest section of society – they concern the working class in its daily life. It is therefore hard to understand why this vital and urgent subject is treated with such indifference. This indifference is unforgivable. (Holt, 1977, p. 239)

She scorned the relegation of 'sexual matters' to the realm of 'private matters' which were 'not worth the effort and attention of the collective' (Holt, 1977, p. 239). Kollontai did not expand upon the unhelpfulness of using the distinction between 'public' and 'private' spheres to merit inattention to the latter, but her preliminary remarks on the matter led some Marxists to engage in a tentative critique of the exclusion of so-called private matters from the public domain. Sex-life was not a purely private matter, but an activity which was linked to issues of self-expression, liberation and oppression. The precise nature of these linkages had yet to be established.

It was important to Kollontai that individuals did not fall into the trap of clinging on to old sexual codes just to prevent loneliness when they should be changing the nature of their sexual relationships, 'basing them on the creative principle of friendship and togetherness rather than on something blindly physiological' (Holt, 1977, p. 240). Coming to terms with sexuality required a 'radical re-education of our psyche' and a revolutionary situation was the best time to pursue this. For Marxists to tackle all dimensions of the woman question, they had to expand their horizons. 'Couldn't one say', probed Kollontai, that:

> while great social and economic changes are in progress, the conditions are being created that demand and give rise to a new basis for psychological experience? ... Another class, a new social group, is coming forward to replace the bourgeoisie with its bourgeois ideology, and its individualistic code of sexual morality. The progressive class, as it develops its strength, cannot fail to reveal new ideas about relations between the sexes that form in close connection with the problems of social class. (Holt, 1977, pp. 245–6)

The time was ripe to discuss the dynamics of sexuality. The question was, how best to go about it?

Kollontai began by criticising the 'crude individualism' of relation-ships whereby individuals sought their own spiritual and physical pleasures through their partner without paying attention to the needs and desires of the other. Individualistic behaviour had to be replaced by the 'simplest rule of life – that another person should be treated with great consideration' (Holt, 1977, p. 241). New concepts were needed to 'teach us to achieve relationships based on the unfamiliar ideas of complete freedom, equality and genuine friendship' (Holt, 1977, p. 241). These ideas, however, were unattainable so long as extreme individuality and the cult of egoism persisted. Their realis-ation was also distant while 'two characteristics of the psychology of modern man' endured. These were the idea of 'possessing' one's partner and the belief that the two sexes were unequal in worth 'in every way, in every sphere, including the sexual sphere' (Holt, 1977, p. 242). Kollontai believed that these pervasive and retrograde attitudes produced a double standard of morality and a profound inequality between the sexes that made genuine friendship impossible. As inferior to men, women were appropriately subordinate and not supposed to be independent. This meant that behaviour could be acceptable or unacceptable depending upon the sex of the actor. Through radical change Kollontai hoped that the 'potential for loving' would increase. However, without combating egoism and challenging the beliefs of possession and inequality, the psyche of a human being would be incapable of loving, but remain distorted.

Many Bolsheviks were critical of, or shocked by, Kollontai's thoughts. In particular, they condemned her writings on 'wingless eros' and 'winged eros'. Kollontai used these terms to distinguish between physical sex without love – 'wingless eros' – and sex rich with emotion – 'winged eros'. She pointed out that during revolution 'winged eros' was too distracting for revolutionaries since it consumed their inner energy. By contrast, the relatively undemanding 'wingless eros' satisfied sex drive and allowed concentration on political activity. With the construction of Soviet socialism under way 'wingless eros' failed to satisfy psychological needs in a period of calm (Holt, 1977, pp. 277–8). While suggesting the superiority of 'winged' over 'wingless' eros, Kollontai explained how the latter fitted a particular period of history. Sex was vital to the 'preservation of health' and was one element in 'the full and correct satisfaction of all man's needs'; sexual activity was healthy and sexual restraint was not (Holt, 1977, p. 229). This did not mean that any form of sexual activity was desirable but merely that sex was relevant to liberation and needed to be discussed in order to sort out how. Many, however, preferred not to discuss it and not to link it to human needs under socialism.

Sexuality had not been a topic for theoretical discussion which had interested Marx and Engels and they did not incorporate it into their remarks on the position of women. In the *Origin of the Family, Private Property and the State*, Engels did refer to reproduction, but did not reflect upon the significance of sexuality. Lenin was not convinced that theoretical work on sexuality was particularly relevant to Marxism or useful to revolution. Klara Zetkin alleged that Lenin had believed that preoccupation with sexuality was counterproductive since it detracted from more important questions of political activity and stupified the proletariat. She claimed that Lenin once remarked 'I mistrust those who are always absorbed in the sex problem, the way an Indian saint is absorbed in the contemplation of his naval' (Lenin, 1977, pp. 101–7). Lenin regretted the 'glass of water theory' which held that under communism satisfying sexual desire was as simple as drinking water. He dismissed it as un-Marxist and antisocial and commented that a 'plethora of sex life yields neither joy nor strength. On the contrary, it impairs them. This is bad, very bad, indeed, in the epoch of revolution' (Lenin, 1977, p. 107). Lenin's letters to Inessa Armand written in 1915 convey a similar disapproval about excessive reflections on such a 'bourgeois' topic (Lenin, 1977, pp. 38–42).

Kollontai did not share Lenin's rejection of sexuality as a topic for Marxists. Discussion of it was not bourgeois self-indulgence because she believed that the private sphere or personal life could itself be political. She was also suspicious of the argument that once economic and social structures had been reorganised, problems of sexual relations would finally be resolved.

Against 'bourgeois feminism'

Although Kollontai, Armand and other Bolshevik women championed equality of the sexes and discussed the theoretical and practical implications of work, marriage, divorce, and sexuality for women, they drew a strict distinction between themselves and 'bourgeois feminists'. Before the revolution Kollontai repeatedly exhorted working-class women to be active as socialists in order to promote revolution, rather than work for the narrow reformist goals of bourgeois feminists. Prompted in 1908 by the forthcoming First All-Russia Women's Congress, Kollontai wrote *The Social Basis of the Woman Question* in which she derided the 'host of truly noble and charming nameless heroines' with their 'individual acts of charity' (Kollontai, 1984, p. 26). She criticised these bourgeois feminists, like the 'repentant gentlewoman' of the 1870s, for pursuing the modest goals of philanthropy, education for women, and legal reform. For Kollontai the political rights sought by bourgeois feminists were insufficient since they left capitalism intact. Only through socialist revolution could working women and men be freed from oppression. The feminists, she charged, incorrectly, identified men as the immediate enemy since they enjoyed rights and privileges and condemned women to bondage and obligation (Kollontai, 1984, p. 33). But this was entirely misconceived.

The interests of working women were much closer to working men than to middle-class women. As Kollontai put it, 'the woman worker is bound to her male comrade worker by a thousand invisible threads, whereas the aims of the bourgeois woman appear to her to be alien and incomprehensible' (Kollontai, 1984, p. 33). Kollontai rejected the notion of a universal 'woman question' and in response to the call of the feminists for unity stated 'a sober examination of reality reveals that this unity does not and cannot exist'. In Kollontai's view, the 'victory of the women's cause depends on the victory of the common proletarian cause' (Kollontai, 1984, pp. 34–5). Although specific issues, such as domestic labour and childrearing, affected women directly, more general political arrangements affected their solution.

Armand made similar points. After 1917 she stressed that 'working women have no specific women's tasks, no special interests separate from the interests of the whole proletariat' (Armand, 1975, p. 67). Here Armand, like Kollontai, pitched her argument at a general theoretical level. However, she was acutely aware of the practical difficulties in encouraging women's liberation and of important differences in the lives of men and women. The scale of change necessary to achieve liberation was clearly immense and Armand recognised that 'it demands the most profound restructuring of all social relations and the greatest revolution in all attitudes and understandings' (Armand, 1975, p. 106). She added that if Soviet women thought that they were now entirely emancipated and fully equal, then they were deceiving themselves.

Women's organisations
Before the revolution Kollontai's and Armand's belief that the fate of working women was inextricably bound with that of working men rendered separate women's organisations politically counter-productive. Feminist organisations were seen to detract from class struggle, divide the working class and foster bourgeois feminism. This view received Lenin's backing in his statement 'we derive our organisational ideas from our ideological conceptions. We want no organisations of communist women' (Lenin, 1977, p. 110). Scepticism among communists about the political worth of women's groups and mistrust of their goals derived from this argument.

But by the end of 1918 Armand and Kollontai were backing women's institutions with vigour. They believed that specific difficulties faced by women in the Soviet state could best be dealt with through women-only organisations. Lower levels of political participation among women than among men required special treatment. Since revolution had successfully triumphed, these organisations would serve the revolution, not bourgeois feminism, because they existed in a socialist state pursuing socialist goals.

Armand put the case in the following terms. Working women freed themselves from centuries of oppression by joining in the political struggles of the working class, by overthrowing capitalism and by building socialism. Before the First World War some working women were politically active, but the level of women's involvement in proletarian struggle was relatively low when compared with that of men. After the war their political activity increased, but women still suffered from low political consciousness (Armand, 1975, pp. 36; 53–4; 64). Women-only organisations could tackle the roots of this. Armand advocated commissions for agitation and propaganda among women under the umbrella of the party with two main goals in mind: political education of working women to draw them into the party by organising meetings, party schools and propaganda groups; and women's commissions to involve working women in constructing the new life. In particular, Armand recommended concentration by women on new forms of household organisation and new ways of rearing children to be promoted by women's participation in the work of the soviets, factory committees and trade unions (Armand, 1975, p. 72).

Women's reluctance to engage in political activity and high levels of illiteracy were cited as reasons for women's commissions, but Armand also pointed out that despite the vital work of the party and soviets among the proletariat, these institutions had devoted inadequate attention to women. She deplored the tiny number of women in the party, soviets, factory committees, trade unions and at the front. She inferred that the methods used to mobilise the working class were successful with men, but 'it is evident that the working women must be approached in a different way' (Armand, 1975, p. 71). She considered that this could partly be explained by historical circumstances. Women had been burdened by traditional family chores which made participation in broader social life and politics difficult, held back the political development of women, and also contributed to the growth of 'several psychological characteristics' which had to be taken into account by propagandists if women were to be politicised (Armand, 1975, p. 71).

Armand implied that women formed a group within the working

class with their own specific characteristics. She did not make this point explicitly because the prevailing Marxist notion was that working women and men had identical interests; at most, these differences were the product of 'vestiges of the past' from oppressive political and social systems. Therefore, strategies were needed to cope with women's political backwardness at a specific stage of historical development. Women's institutions were needed only on a temporary basis to meet a short-term problem (Armand, 1975, p. 71).

The specificity of woman's predicament, then, needed attention. Women, however, did not constitute a homogeneous category. Although Armand did not use this terminology, she pointed out that peasant women, in particular, suffered from the extremely conservative and inward-looking values of the countryside which had barely been touched by the revolution and where organisational work was weak (Armand, 1975, p. 60). Arguing against critics of special work among peasant women, she pointed out that peasant men had been drawn into the Red Army and enjoyed the advantage of tuition in special political schools, an opportunity women lacked. Additionally, a large percentage of those who were illiterate in rural areas were women, whereas illiterate men tended to be old (Armand, 1975, pp. 94–8). Although the interests of peasants and workers officially coincided in the new Bolshevik state, the problems of transforming the lives of the peasantry were more difficult and the task of remoulding the lives of peasant women was enormous.

Like Armand, Kollontai reached the conclusion that general propaganda 'had proved insufficient' to motivate women to defend the revolution. This was an acute problem since the majority of urban and rural women 'looked with fear upon communists and Soviet power' judging them to be godless destroyers of ancient traditions and 'heartless people who wished to take children away from their mothers and hand them over to be brought up by the state' (Kollontai, 1984, p. 163). Kollontai contended that the starvation of the early years of Bolshevik power accentuated the 'blind resentment' of women which they instilled in other family members. The low political consciousness of women meant that they were expressing anti-Soviet views. She observed, in an opinion which was identical with Lenin's, that 'in the interests of communism it was necessary to win over the women workers and turn them into defenders of Soviet power'. Therefore 'a special approach had to be found' (Kollontai, 1984, p. 163). Although on a theoretical level Lenin maintained that the interests of men and women were indivisible, in practice he advocated 'systematic work' with the specific purpose of 'rousing the broad masses of women, bringing them into contact with the Party and keeping them under its influence' (Lenin, 1977, p. 110). To ignore women's lack of interest in politics, their 'backward psychology' and 'narrow scope of their activities' would be 'absolutely silly'. Against critics of propaganda targeted at women, Lenin retorted 'this is not bourgeois "feminism"; it is a practical revolutionary expediency' (Lenin, 1977, pp. 110–11).

Although the core of Bolshevik ideology resisted special groups for women, the practical need to confront the low level of women's involvement led to support for special women's organisations, so long as they were not separate from the party. Women had to be educated and mobilised to fit the goals of the party and be kept under party guidance and control. In order to reach women various institutional forms were established ranging from women's commissions and the *Zhenotdel*, to delegates' meetings, women's clubs, conferences and red tents.

Conclusion

Despite the hardships of the early Bolshevik state and notwithstanding the way in which the Marxist tradition had couched the woman question, extensions were nevertheless made to theoretical writings, in particular those concerning domestic labour, maternity and sexuality. These developments failed to flower in subsequent decades, as Chapter 3 shows. Soviet practice confirmed Armand's wise observation of 1919 that 'the path to this emancipation is long and thorny' (Armand, 1975, p. 106).

Notes

1. August Bebel (1840–1913); Friedrich Engels (1820–95); Karl Marx (1818–83); Vladimir Ilich Lenin (1870–1924). The ideas of Nadezhda Krupskaia and Klara Zetkin are also relevant to this discussion, but have been omitted for reasons of space. For further details, refer to Richard Stites, *The Women's Liberation Movement in Russia* (Stites, 1978).
2. 'Cultural filter' is a concept used by Moshe Lewin. Through it Lewin wishes to convey the notion that social systems have their own specific and complex cultures which respond to policies handed down 'from above'. The cultural filter can be

unreceptive to policies, redefine them and turn them into something which was initially never intended by policy makers (Lewin, 1985).

3. For an introduction to historical materialsm consult William H. Shaw, *Marx's Theory of History* (Shaw, 1978).

4. Aristotle argued that women by nature were not fit to rule, but instead to be ruled (Aristotle, 1862, 1943, 1973). Schopenhauer portrayed women as 'big children' and contended that nature intended them 'for the propagation of the species' and thus 'they are not destined for anything else' (Schopenhauer, 1891, p. 112). According to Nietzsche, 'everything concerning woman is a puzzle, and everything concerning woman has one solution: it is named pregnancy'. Nietzsche claimed that women existed for men, pregnancy and children. Where the joy of men said 'I will', the joy of women said 'he will'. The highest attainable achievement for a woman was to produce a 'Superman' (Nietzsche, 1977).

5. See, for example, Fyodor Dostoevsky's *The Brothers Karamazov*, Tolstoy's *Anna Karenina* and Turgenev's *First Love* (Dostoevsky, 1988; Tolstoy, 1988; Turgenev, 1982). For a critique of portrayals of Russian heroines by male writers, refer to Barbara Heldt's *Terrible Perfection* (Heldt, 1987).

6. The *zemstva* were organs of local self-government concerned mainly to develop roads, sanitation and education. They levied taxes and employed professionals such as doctors and teachers to supplement the activities of the bureaucracy. The bulk of the population was excluded from political involvement in them. Although not to be dismissed as unimportant, the *zemstva* failed to provide a channel for the political mobilisation of the peasants and enjoyed extremely limited power.

   Of greater, but unrealised, political potential was the Duma, or legislative assembly. After the strikes in 1905 and land seizures, Nicholas II allowed the Duma to be set up in the hope that it would help to appease his critics. But the Duma was a concession that the Tsar had been reluctant to grant. His aim was to keep it as impotent as possible. Initially it enjoyed the limited privilege of discussing laws and advising the Tsar. The pressures of continued political unrest led Nicholas to concede that no law could be passed without the Duma's approval. But his gesture was half-hearted since he wanted a weak Duma in which the gentry was over-represented.

7. Nicholas II was Tsar from 1894 to 1917. He was preceded by Alexander III (1881–94), Alexander II (1855–81) and Nicholas I (1825–55).

8. Thousands of young people decided to 'go to the people' in 1874 with the vision of enlightening the peasants and spurring revolutionary change from the country-side. The peasants reacted with suspicion and hostility (Lichtheim, 1970, pp. 145–7; Venturi, 1960, pp. 469–506).

9. The Mensheviks formed in 1903 at the Second Congress of the Russian Social Democratic (Labour) Party. The RSDLP split into two main factions – Bolsheviks and Mensheviks. Leading the Bolsheviks, Lenin argued for a tight, conspiratorial, underground party to be run along the lines of 'democratic centralism'. Iulii Martov, supported a more open mass party which became the Menshevik wing of Russian Social Democracy. The Socialist Revolutionary Party (whose members are frequently referred to as SRs) was committed to revolutionary change through the peasantry.

10. For discussion of Stalin's consolidation of power, refer to Isaac Deutscher's *Stalin* and Jerry Hough's and Merle Fainsod's, *How the Soviet Union is Governed* (Deutscher, 1966; Hough and Fainsod, 1982, pp. 110–46).

11. The Society for Cheap Lodgings was set up in 1859 and aimed to provide poor families, particularly single parents and their children, with somewhere to live. It also established dressmaking workshops, communal kitchens and a school for working mothers. Pursuing a related goal through the Sunday School Movement,

female philanthropists tried to recruit women without education, since the schools offered free adult education to all social classes. This was one response to an education system which until the 1850s denied most women a secondary education. Another response was the organisation of the Alarchin and Lubianka evening classes for women. Here professors instructed mainly upper-class women with a view to preparing them for higher education (Stites, 1978, p. 77).

12. In the 1870s women such as Sofiia Perovskaia followed Petr Lavrov's idea of the 'repentant noble'. Perovskaia travelled on foot, slept on floors and conducted propaganda work in factories (Stites, 1978, p. 131). The radicals spent the 1860s reflecting upon the meaning of personal emancipation and the 1870s trying to bring it to the peasants and workers (Lichtheim, 1970, pp. 144–7). Some, including Perovskaia and Vera Figner, initially opposed violence as a means to political change, but eventually resorted to it as the only route to take in a situation of repression.

13. Kollontai's contribution was read in absentia (Stites, 1978, p. 216).

14. According to Linda Edmondson, the women's movement came to a halt in 1908 when the All-Russian Union for Women's Equality collapsed. Whereas the woman question was an issue for debate in the 1860s, it lost this status in the aftermath of 1905 (Edmondson, 1984, pp. 53–4).

15. Four days after the Bolshevik seizure of power the eight-hour day was decreed. This applied to male and female labour. Night shifts and work underground for women were forbidden because it was believed that women needed protection from harmful working conditions.

16. Elizabeth Waters of Australian National University has pointed out that it was difficult for the hospital system to cope with the demand for abortion in the early 1920s because so many women came forward. Abortion commissions were set up to decide who should have the free government service. The most needy and those with large families were given preference. A government abortion service requiring payment was also set up at the same time and private clinics were allowed.

17. Alexandra Kollontai was born in St Petersburg in 1872. She was an independent thinker from an early age and read widely as a girl. She married at her parents' wish in 1893 but in 1897 left her husband to study in Zurich. She became a Marxist and upon returning to Russia engaged in socialist agitation in St Petersburg. She was not at this time a Bolshevik. From 1905 to 1917 Kollontai wrote various pieces on the 'woman question'. Her writings on women as well as her political activity was pitched against the 'bourgeois feminists'. After the revolution Kollontai continued her work among women in the Zhenotdel. There are several sources for more detailed biographical information (Clements, 1979; Farnsworth, 1980; Porter, 1978; Stites, 1975, 1978, pp. 246–69).

Inessa Armand was born in Paris in 1874 into a theatrical family. She was reared by an aunt who was employed as a tutor by a Russian–French industrialist in a house situated near Moscow. Inessa married into this family at 18 years of age and had five children. However, she left her husband after falling in love with her brother-in-law. Inessa Armand was a liberal during her married life and she then worked with a charity organisation which helped prostitutes in Moscow. She later joined the Social Democrats in Moscow and became active in socialist work. Inessa became a close friend of Lenin's. She was first director of the Zhenotdel until her early death from cholera in 1920 (Podliashuk, 1973; Stites, 1978, pp. 254–6).

18. This same observation has been made about Lenin's conception of the party which kept vital questions of democracy and the meaning of politics off the agenda (Polan, 1984).

2 Women's Organisations: Bolshevik Theory and Practice

The 'long and thorny path' to women's liberation under Soviet social-ism began with fresh legislation on equal rights. New laws, however, did not guarantee the place for women in social production or politics that Bebel, Engels, Marx and Lenin had advocated. Nor did revolution bring the widespread reorganisation of domestic labour that Armand, Kollontai and Trotsky considered essential for women's liberation and socialism. Revolution may have ushered in a new political system, but it could not transform social structures overnight nor remove the all-pervasive assumptions about gender that character-ised nineteenth- and early twentieth-century Russia. For the goals of Marxist ideology on women to be met, a special praxis had to be developed. For patterns of behaviour to change in keeping with the vision of the 'new communist person', Armand and Kollontai believed that women's organisations should reach, enlighten and liberate women.

Praxis had to address the problem that the pre-conditions of libera-tion were lacking. Most women were illiterate, lacking in skills, sub-ordinate to their husbands, and living in rural, inward-looking, religious villages. Urban working-class women were easier to mobilise into politics than peasant women, but in the minority. Rural women in Russia were more accessible than Muslim women of Soviet Central Asia, where social structures were not sufficiently disintegrated to be ripe for re-fashioning (Massell, 1974). Praxis therefore had to vary across the vast Soviet land mass.

Socialist practices to promote women's liberation had to respond to existing social structures, unpopular economic policies and changing political circumstances – conditions which made it difficult to bring about the changes in women's lives that ideology envisioned. Despite the euphoria about socialist revolution among female revolutionaries, their achievements in 'work among women' were constrained by the historical setting in which they found themselves. Although Armand and Kollontai dreamt of radical changes in domestic life, the instability of the Civil War from 1918 to 1921 and the insecurities caused by increases in unemployment from 1921 to 1929, led many families to cling for security to familiar patterns of daily life. Scarce resources also made it hard for the regime after the Civil War to provide sufficient public dining rooms and kindergartens to make a restructuring of the family feasible (Waters, 1988).[1] The canteens, kindergartens and nurseries that were available were often too costly for workers to afford (Hayden, 1979, pp. 310–11). In addition, party leaders failed to encourage radical changes in home life. Their first priority was to win women's support for the Bolshevik revolution, not to redefine domestic labour. The growth of private enterprises under NEP and unemployment then forced women activists into the defensive stance of trying to protect women's right to work that had been decreed in 1917. Economic stringency at this time also caused *Zhenotdel* funds to be cut back and led to reductions in staff (Hayden, 1979, pp. 181–6).

By the end of the 1920s, primacy was placed on drawing women into the work-force to supply essential labour for industrialisation. The productionist emphasis of Bolshevik policy placed a high priority on 'output' and 'plan fulfilment'. The Soviet Union had to develop its economic base before it could build socialism and provide adequate welfare policies. According to Marxist theory, socialist revolution would take place in capitalist societies with developed economies.[2] Russia had not fitted this expectation; its leaders were committed communists but lacking the socio-economic means to shape a communist society. Industrialisation and modernisation became the means to the communist end, but aspects of ideology became displaced in the process (Lowenthal, 1970). Topics such as domestic labour, the transformation of family life, the nature of male–female relations and female self-determination were far less important than the presence of women in the work-force and their support for the economic plan. The subordination at work of women to men was not important for male leaders, but the fact that they were active in the labour force and contributing to the foundations of socialism.

Although female activists in women's organisations were dedicated to changes in the public and private spheres, an increasingly centralised and bureaucratised political system encouraged them to focus on recruitment into the workplace and class war. Their diaries and articles, however, show a sensitivity to a range of problems affecting women's lives, and a commitment to revolutionising life at home, which the priorities of the regime made hard to address.

In the mid-1920s power struggles within the Soviet leadership also sucked women's organisations into factional disputes and campaigns against Stalin's opponents. Those who campaigned appropriately rose in the *Zhenotdel* hierarchy and tended to pay more attention to the interests of the party than to problems affecting women. By 1927 women's organisations came to be viewed by many women, particularly those in rural areas, as 'agents of Soviet power' to be resisted (Hayden, 1979, p. 323).

Economic policy, subordination to a centralising party, and power struggles, were not the only factors influencing the process of liberation. Chauvinistic attitudes among male communists and the frequent lack of support from party committees for women's organisations affected the possibilities for work among women. So did women's resistance to new roles.

This chapter looks at the theory and practices of women's organisations against this backdrop and asks the following questions: How were women-only organisations justified ideologically under socialism? How were the organisations established, what were their goals and activities, and to what extent were they successful? How much support did party congresses give them? What was the nature of opposition to them?

While several authors have discussed the role of the *Zhenotdel* and its changing priorities (Massell, 1974; Hayden, 1976, 1979; Stites, 1978, pp. 329–45; Heitlinger, 1979, pp. 57–63), few have focused on the range of agitation and propaganda work conducted by delegates' meetings, women's clubs, red tents and red tea shops, or linked their practice to ideological goals (Massell, 1974; Hayden, 1979; Rorlich, 1986).[3] The object here is to describe these different organisations, assess their significance for women's liberation and discuss the hurdles they faced. The fate of early women's organisations is important because subsequent official thinking about women's liberation is, in part, based on it.[4]

The ideological dilemma: Gender versus class or class serving gender?

In the 1920s, the relevance of women's organisations to socialist construction was controversial. The last chapter showed that even staunch supporters of women's institutions repeated the official line that the interests of working women and men were identical and therefore that no separate organisations for socialist women were necessary. At an abstract theoretical level of historical materialism, it was class that defined interests, not gender. But at a practical level, differences between the sexes were evident. Men were more politically active than women in the conventional sense of party membership and holding positions of authority. Illiteracy rates among women were higher, as Table 2.1 shows. A lower level of education coupled with traditional domestic roles and childrearing made it harder for women to be recruited into the work-force and mobilised into politics. The long-term interests of the sexes were not necessarily different and there was not an inevitable contradiction between organisations based on gender and an ideology in which class was the key social division; rather, for the successful construction of socialism, certain unnecessary differences between the sexes had to be eradicated. A flexible ideology could justify the temporary existence of women's organisations which were special, but not separate or independent from the party.

Despite controversy about the legitimacy of women's organisa-

Table 2.1 Literacy in the Soviet population – percentage literate in the 9 to 49 age group

Year	Both sexes			Men			Women		
	Urban and rural	Urban	Rural	Urban and rural	Urban	Rural	Urban and rural	Urban	Rural
1897	28.4	57.0	23.8	40.3	66.1	35.5	16.6	45.7	12.5
1920	44.1	73.5	37.8	57.6	80.7	52.4	32.3	66.7	25.2
1926	56.6	80.9	50.6	71.5	88.0	67.3	42.7	73.9	35.4
1939	87.4	93.8	84.0	93.5	97.1	91.6	81.6	90.7	76.8

Source: TsSU (1972) *Narodnoe khoziaistvo* SSSR 1922–1972, *iubileinyi statisticheskii ezhegodnik (Moscow, statistika)*, p. 35

tions, there was formal agreement voiced at party congresses that their broad ideological aims were to reach, teach, mobilise and politicise female members of the working class and peasantry, deemed relatively backward in their political consciousness when compared with men. Those aspects of women's lives which retarded their political awareness had to be countered. Once more women became active in the labour force and in politics, women's organisations would be redundant. The *raison d'être* of women's institutions was based on the immediate practical need for women to catch up with men in their political consciousness. New strategies had to be developed that would succeed in making women aware of their class interests where more conventional approaches had failed. Politically conscious women would then be liberated and support the new socialist state. Women's organisations thus served both gender and class. Women were to be liberated through delegates' meetings, women's clubs and red tents, be taught the class basis of that liberation, and as a result come to support Soviet power since they would see that it served their own interests. Kollontai argued that:

> A special method of work among women had to be developed in order to force them to understand and appreciate what their position should be and which power best guaranteed women's interests – the dictatorship of the proletariat, or a return to the rule of the bourgeoisie. (Kollontai, 1972, p. 164)

Consistent with this, Kollontai viewed remote areas which lacked women's organisations as disadvantageous for the Bolshevik state. Here the 'mistrustful and passive attitude among the mass of women to the revolution and to Soviet power' persisted (Kollontai, 1972, p. 166).

Kollontai had first called for a special party apparatus to work among women in 1906. Her support for women's organisations was not new, and her arguments in favour of them after 1917 may have been carefully tailored to the priorities of the regime in order to make them 'ideologically legitimate' and more persuasive. The Bolsheviks had, in fact, already been compelled to take an interest in women's organisations because in early 1917 they 'were springing up, either spontaneously or through the organising efforts of their political opponents'. Their spread, combined with the practical need to gain more support for the revolution, led to the formation in 1917 of a women's bureau by the Petrograd committee of the Bolshevik party (Hayden, 1979, pp. 88–93).

The *Zhenotdel*: goals and structure

Official commitment to institutions designed specifically to conduct work among women after the Bolshevik revolution began in December 1918 when the Central Committee created commissions for propaganda and agitation among women. They were set up by party committees in the *guberniia*, towns, districts and *uezds*.[5] In 1919 work among women assumed a higher political status and became directed by the *Zhenotdel* (*otdel po rabote sredi zhenshchin*), the Women's Department of the Central Committee Secretariat, which issued directives to other *zhenotdely* (*zhenotdels*) which were set up by lower level party committees.[6] The *zhenotdely* were horizontally subordinate to the party committee at their own administrative level, which set them up (or had taken them over if they were a women's group already in existence) and vertically responsible to the *zhenotdel* at the administrative level above. So a district level *zhenotdel* was responsible to the district party committee and the *guberniia* level *zhenotdel* (Emel'ianova, 1971, pp. 95–102; Chirkov, 1978, p. 56).

At the very apex of *Zhenotdel*, the director was accountable to the Central Committee of the Party. During the eleven years of its existence, the *Zhenotdel* had five directors. Inessa Armand held the post from 1919 to her death from cholera in 1920. Alexandra Kollontai was then in charge until 1922 when her unacceptable behaviour in the Workers' Opposition caused her to be 'removed' to diplomatic work in Norway.[7] Both of these women invested immense energy in the *Zhenotdel* and were strongly committed to it. They were followed by three women who were perhaps more willing to be amenable to the party leaders: Sophiia Smidovich from 1922 to 1924; Klavdiia Nikolaevna from 1924 to 1925 and Aleksandra Artiukhina from 1925 to the abolition of the *Zhenotdel* in 1930 (Chirkov, 1978, p. 55; Stites, 1978, pp. 323–34).

The goals of the *Zhenotdel* were regularly discussed at meetings and conferences of *Zhenotdel* leaders and also at party congresses. *Zhenotdel* leaders described their official work as a blend of general class-related tasks and specifically women's issues. For example, at the 4th All-Russian Meeting of the Heads of *Guberniia Zhenotdels* the broad aims of Women's Departments were defined as follows:

> In front of our departments stand two tasks – on the one hand to increase the independence and activity of the mass of women through the path of drawing them into the general work of the party and soviets, and on the

other to set up or develop projects stemming from the particular unfavourable conditions in which working-class women find themselves in the contemporary transition period. (Chirkov, 1978, p. 62)

It was formally agreed that the *Zhenotdel* had three main purposes: first, to expand the influence of the party over a large number of working-class and peasant women through enlightening them about politics and life; second, to draw these women into the party, trade unions, cooperative organisations and the soviets; and third, to liaise with other organisations, such as trade unions, to promote the construction of nurseries and public dining rooms since these were necessary for women's liberation (Institut Marksizma–Leninizma, 1984, vol. 3, p. 285). To cope with this broad brief, the administrative work of the *Zhenotdel* was broken down into three subdivisions and one sector: organisational–instructional work; agitation–propaganda; the press; and work among women of the East.

Organisational–instructional work entailed various tasks which included holding meetings with leaders of local organisations, such as trade unions, about questions of female labour; drafting suggestions about work among women for the *Orgburo* and *Secretariat* of the party; and placing female cadres throughout the *Zhenotdel's* structure and reviewing their progress.[8] This administrative and managerial aspect of the *Zhenotdel's* work was the closest to 'high politics' since it entailed contact with the *Orgburo*, *Secretariat* and the bureaucracies concerned with health, prostitution, food, welfare, education, insurance and trade unions. These links provided the opportunity for exerting some pressure on policy concerning women (Stites, 1978, p. 335; Kollontai, 1984, p. 165).

The 'agitprop' work of the *zhenotdels* in the *guberniias*, towns, districts, *uezds* and regions amounted to the promotion and direction of 'low politics' among women.[9] Delegates' meetings, women's clubs, red tents and other organisations were set up by the *Zhenotdel* and seen as crucial points of contact between female Bolsheviks and as yet politically inactive women. The *Zhenotdel* guided their work, provided them with some resources and supervised the training and retraining of women who worked in them. The *Zhenotdel* also promoted conferences and congresses of non-party women and organised coverage in the press of work among women.

The agitprop in which the *Zhenotdel* engaged extended beyond these non-party organisations. Women were frequently exhorted to join in short-term campaigns tailored to the political moment. During the Civil War, for example, the *Zhenotdel* encouraged women to support the Red Army by taking first-aid courses. Then as 'red sisters' they nursed the wounded (Chirkov, 1978, p. 156). The *Zhenotdel* also urged women to participate, either as teachers or students, in a general literacy campaign of the 1920s. The *Zhenotdel* sponsored brief 'women's weeks' in which agitprop among women was either initiated for the first time, or else stepped up. For example, when the *Zhenotdel* began its work in Kaluga it was launched by a women's week (*Kommunistka*, no. 10–11, March–April 1921, pp. 45–6). Women's weeks were also directed at particular political tasks. In connection with support for the Red Army there was 'The week of the red barracks' and also 'Help to the front'. Other campaigns included 'Week of help to the starving' and 'Week of the child' (Emel'ianova, 1971, p. 105).

The third subdivision of the *Zhenotdel* supervised publications. Its aim was to disseminate literature about work among women which was useful for agitprop and to organise the publication of women's magazines. In 1920 it launched *Kommunistka* (Communist Woman), the theoretical journal of the *Zhenotdel*, followed in 1922 by *Krest'ianka* (Peasant Woman) and in 1923 by a revived *Rabotnitsa* (Working Woman), which had started in 1914, resumed in 1917 but had been closed down in 1918 due to a shortage of newsprint (Hayden, 1976, p. 154). As the leading and guiding theoretical journal for work among women, *Kommunistka* discussed various aspects of the woman question, such as women and work, motherhood, the position of women in the countryside, the liberation of Muslim women, abortion and prostitution. It printed the conclusions reached at conferences of *Zhenotdel* leaders and passed on information about party policy affecting women. It also reported on the current work of *zhenotdely* in different parts of the country and recommended useful techniques for agitation and propaganda. More general articles on current political issues were included too, such as the needs of the Red Army, how to fight starvation, the state of the textile industry, decisions of Congresses of the Communist International and developments in the international women's movement. *Krest'ianka* and *Rabotnitsa* by contrast, were more popular magazines designed for a wider audience of women 'but not for the most advanced women – these would read the general press, rather for the less developed' (Chirkov, 1978, p. 83).[10] Their aim was to inform workers and peasants about the basic political problems of the day and of their newly won rights. *Zhenotdely* in the towns, regions and republics also published local women's journals such as *Delegatka* (Woman Delegate) in Moscow, *Rabotnitsa i Krest'ianka* (Working Woman and Peasant Woman) in Leningrad, *Krasnaia Sibiriachka* (Red Siberian Woman) in Siberia and *Sharg Kadyny* (Women of the East) in the republic of Azerbaidzhan (Kotelenets, 1977, p. 117; Sultanova, 1957, p. 4). The general pattern of these three main subdivisions of the *Zhenotdel* was repeated in the republics, but there, however, variations could be found and additional subdivisions were occasionally created to suit local needs.

Finally, the sector for work among women of the East supervised the liberation of women in Muslim republics, which posed special problems. Muslim women lacked rights in the home to a much greater degree than Russian and Ukrainian women. As children, girls could be sold as brides for a *kalym*, or bride-price, without their consent. Arranged marriages were the norm with gold or cattle being paid by the future husband, in an amount befitting the status of the girl's family. Women's lives were essentially circumscribed by the home where they were expected to obey and serve their fathers, husbands and brothers. They lacked education and in 1917 just 2 per cent of women in Soviet Central Asia were literate. Bolshevik power set out to challenge the customs permitted by the Koran and Shariat such as bride-price, polygamy and the infanticide of young girls.

In Soviet Central Asia and Transcaucasia the domestic situation of women was such that many of the agitprop strategies adopted in the rest of the country were either inappropriate or had to be supplemented. Inventive approaches had to be devised and fresh institutional forms developed for reaching a mass of severely restricted and isolated women. Work among Muslim women was also distinct due to the ferocity of local opposition to it. Women and girls were murdered by husbands, brothers and fathers for bringing shame on the family name by their acts of liberation. Tragically many Muslim women also committed suicide because once they had thrown off the *chadra*, *parandja* or veil, they were shunned by their family and found themselves unable to get work due to their lack of skills and few job opportunities. The options open to them were to work as prostitutes, put the *chadra* back on or commit suicide (Iman-Zade, 1954; Sultanova, 1957; Massell, 1974; Aminova, 1977).

So various forms of agitprop work were promoted by the *Zhenotdel* to reach non-Muslims and Muslims in both urban and rural areas.

These were designed to catapult women out of their political backwardness. In theory, each form of activity served a special purpose, which distinguished it from other forms, and was justified on particular ideological grounds. In practice, however, results were mixed and did not always match ideological expectations.

Formal party support for work among women

Party congresses throughout the 1920s gave their official blessing to the *Zhenotdel*. At the 8th Congress in 1919, for instance, party committees were urged to strengthen work among urban and rural women 'in the struggle for communism and socialist construction' (*Institut Marksizma–Leninizma*, 1984, vol. 2, p. 114). The message of the 9th Congress in 1920 was more pressing. Work among women was described as 'one of the urgent tasks of the moment and a necessary part of our general party work'. Women were needed to participate in the construction of a new society, but their own lives had to be changed first. It was therefore essential to reach them. The Congress called upon *guberniia* and *uezd* party committees and communist cells 'to pay the most serious attention' to work among women. Those committees which had not yet organised women's departments were exhorted to do so (*Institut Marksizma–Leninizma*, 1984, vol. 2, p. 267).

Progressively more time was devoted at Congresses, especially between 1922 and 1925, to the topics of 'Work among the Female Proletariat' and 'Party work among working women and peasants'. The 11th Congress held in the Spring of 1922, for instance, emphasised the importance of stepping up work among women in the transition period rather than slackening it (*Institut Marksizma–Leninizma*, 1984, vol. 2, p. 528). This was particularly vital during NEP since unemployment among women had increased and 'petit-bourgeois' ideas were widespread. The party had to reach women guided by its class perspective. The implicit danger here was for women to come together outside party structures and thereby foster bourgeois feminism.[11] The Congress also suggested that work among peasant women should be strengthened in order to boost the number of party cadres in the countryside (*Institut Marksizma–Leninizma*, 1984, vol. 2, p. 529). By 1922 women comprised 9.2 per cent of urban party members, but just 4.5 per cent in rural areas (Lapidus, 1978, pp. 209–10). The party wished to close the gap. The need to recruit more female cadres was echoed at the 12th Congress of 1923 and culminated in a call for more planned and systematic work among women. Resolutions from the Central Committee and *Orgburo* made the same points (*Institut Marksizma–Leninizma*, 1984, vol. 3, pp. 125–6; 138–40).

'The general political backwardness of working women' (*obshchaia otstalost' rabotnits*) was regularly cited as the main reason for expanding the work of the *Zhenotdel*. This point was made at the 13th Congress in 1924, which also noted that women were less quali-fied than men, earned less, and were not joining the party in suf-ficiently large numbers. More systematic work among women was therefore vital (*Institut Marksizma–Leninizma*, 1984, vol. 3, pp. 284–7). This was particularly the case in Muslim areas. Work among 'women of the East' was discussed at a Central Committee plenum of 1925 and the subject of a Central Committee resolution of 1927 (*Institut Marksizma–Leninizma*, 1984, vol. 3, p. 332; vol. 4, pp. 134–5). The general message was that flexible and special approaches to indigenous women had to be developed as thoroughly as possible. Despite the debates and disagreements that preceded the final resolutions and congress statements, the official and final party line was that the *Zhenotdel* should extend its work. Even as late as 1929, a year before the *Zhenotdel* was disbanded, a Central Committee resolution stressed the importance of mobilising women to help in the implementation of the First Five Year Plan. It called upon all women's departments to use their different institutional forms and methods to ensure that this was successful (*Institut Marksizma–Leninizma*, 1984, vol. 4, pp. 515–23).

Throughout the 1920s, then, the party reiterated its formal approval and support of the *Zhenotdel* and argued that its activities should be stepped up. The activities recommended, however, were tailored to the changing priorities of the regime set 'from above'. These did not necessarily coincide with the priorities of female revolutionaries and were not a response to demands pressed for by working women 'from below'. Agitation and propaganda work among women 'in the field' was conducted by delegates' meetings, women's clubs, red tents and other 'clubs in miniature'.

Agitprop among women: the practice of women's organisations

The ideological goal of women's organisations was to liberate women. Women, however, were not a homogeneous group. Muslim women in Uzbekistan suffered different disabilities from working-class urban women in Kiev or rural women living 200 miles north-east of Moscow. Thus the agitation and propaganda work among women sponsored by the *Zhenotdel* had to meet the needs of very different categories of women living in varied settings.

The most general form of agitprop among women was the delegates' meeting or delegates' assembly (*delegatskie sobranie*). These were praised by Armand as 'without doubt the most important organ of all our work'. She believed that delegates' meetings provided the best opportunity for exerting long-term influence on non-party women (Armand, 1975, p. 102). They were, however, less effective among Muslim women. It was left to the women's clubs (*zhenskii kluby*) to devise innovative approaches to winkle Muslim women out of the confinements of their private sphere, including individual visits to women at home, group discussions in public bathhouses, the setting up of women's schools, liquidation of illiteracy centres, women's workshops, women's shops and women's tea houses. Special conferences and congresses of 'women of the East' were also convened. Delegates' meetings were similarly unable to reach the nomadic women of Kazakhstan. Instead, special Red Tents moved with the nomads, trying to attract the attention of women and then propagandise the advantages of Soviet power. In order to make headway, careful attention had to be paid to indigenous customs and expectations.

Delegates' meetings: 'elections' and activities

The political activity of non-party women began by the selection of a *delegatka*, or female delegate, to attend delegates' meetings. In factories of over 300 workers one *delegatka* was chosen for every 25 or 50 workers, depending upon the republic, and initially for a period of three, four or six months, which was later extended after 1923 to one year (Samoilova, 1920, p. 26; Emel'ianova, 1971, p. 159; Guliev, 1972, p. 395; Kotelenets, 1977, p. 110). Handicraftswomen and wives outside the paid labour force were also mobilised as delegates. Town, district and *uezd zhenotdely* went about this by organising meetings of local women and then selecting appropriate delegates. In

Azerbaidzhan, for example, it became the practice to select one delegate for every ten housewives (Guliev, 1972, p. 395).

Although workers formally 'elected' their delegates, sources indicate that *Zhenotdel* activists picked out suitable women in advance and a list of names was then submitted to the primary party organisation for approval. Thus the selection of delegates in some towns and districts was effectively processed through a *nomenklatura* system.[12] However, the selection procedures varied throughout the new state. In many rural areas a list of candidates was posted for general discussion. Then a meeting was convened to make the final choice. In areas where traditions were hard to change and where the selection of *batrachi* or farm labourers was involved, men too were invited to attend selection meetings. But despite these variations in selection, the main aim of *Zhenotdel* activists was to see that women preferred by them were named as *delegatki*.

Once 'elected' to be a *delegatka*, a woman received theoretical instruction in discussion groups, gained practical experience in a government institution or social organisation and was encouraged to vote in elections for the soviets and become politically active. Different forms of activity catered to these three main tasks (Sokolova, 1926b, pp. 7–12).

For an introduction to theoretical issues, *delegatki* attended weekly or fortnightly delegates' meetings, directed by *Zhenotdel* activists and geared to political education. Discussions covered a wide range of topics which included 'The Communist Party and the working class', 'Basic tasks of the development of industry and agriculture', 'The role of the soviets, trade unions, cooperatives and Komsomol' and 'The union of workers and peasants'. Issues affecting women were part of the programme and focused on 'What does a trade union give to the working woman?', 'The position of working women in capitalist countries', 'The history of the women's revolutionary movement in Russia' and 'The work of the *Zhenotdel*'. But women's issues paled in number and significance compared with political themes (Sokolova, 1926b, pp. 7–9; Emel'ianova, 1971, p. 161; Kotelenets, 1977, p. 111; Chirkov, 1978, p. 94). This was consistent with the aim of delegates' meetings to provide a broad awareness of various issues of 'socialist construction' rather than concentrate exclusively on women's issues. However, in some regions more attention was almost certainly devoted to women's issues. In Iakutia, for example, topics included 'A Leninist Party and the Woman Question', 'What the October Revolution Gave

Women', 'Policies of Soviet Power Concerning Bride-Price and Divorce' – themes which catered explicitly for very traditional local conditions (Tomskii, 1969, p. 48).

The more practical study which the *Zhenotdel* designed for the delegates included excursions, research work and practical work experience in state and social institutions. The excursions went to factories, museums and law courts and were linked to general discussions on the state of Soviet technology, the protection of labour, the functions of shops and public dining rooms, and the significance of cultural work. These visits were organised through liaison between the *Zhenotdel* and the soviets, trade unions, cooperative organisations and the peasants, and workers, inspectorate (Chirkov, 1978, p. 95).

As part of their practical study, *delegatki* were divided into different sections where they explored particular topics in depth. Special topics included the work of the soviets (with particular attention to the protection of mothers and children, education, and work in collectives), the role of trade unions and the importance of cooperative organisations. Not surprisingly, there were variations across the country tailored to local needs. In Muslim areas, for example, sectors were also devoted to the topic of family life and household organisation.

The third area of practical study was work placement. For a period of two or three months, *delegatki* became apprentices or *praktikantki* in departments of local soviets, and after 1921 in trade union offices, the courts, hospitals and schools. Here they observed how work proceeded and became involved in one aspect of it. The object was for them to learn about socialist construction in practice, to identify problems, to develop a range of skills useful to the workplace and to be encouraged to move to jobs in soviet administration (Hayden, 1976, p. 158; *Kommunistka*, no. 8, August 1927, pp. 6–10). The broadening of placements after 1921 away from an automatic funnelling into the soviets came about after the Central Committee called for a greater involvement of women in economic construction and an extension of the practical work of delegates into the trade unions and other organisations to meet this goal. This call was a response to pressure in 1920 on the *Orgburo* from Kollontai, in her capacity as director of the *Zhenotdel*. She urged Soviet leaders to consider how the work of trade unions could profitably complement the activities of the *Zhenotdel* with women (Novikova *et al.*, 1984, p. 27).

Two practical results of this change in placement policy after 1921 were a diversification of the experience of non-party women in towns, and the mobilisation of rural women to be *praktikantki* in the soviets for the first time. By 1924 trade unions in the towns were organising 55 per cent of the delegates, the soviets were responsible for 34 per cent and 11 per cent came under cooperative organisations. In rural areas the corresponding percentages were 25, 63 and 12 (Chirkov, 1978, p. 96). Thus in the countryside the role of the soviets in work among women was not as great as in the towns and was outstripped by the activity of cooperative organisations.

Political participation was the third general area of activity for the *delegatki*. This embraced a range of pursuits from involvement in election campaigns and factory committees to the setting up of kindergartens and participation in *subbotniks*, or unpaid labour days.[13] Delegates also paid particular attention to homeless children after December 1921 and to those evacuated from regions where the problem of starvation was acute.[14] Delegates from the Urals, for example, helped to set up 22 children's homes in Ekaterinburg offering a total of 1,520 places (Kotelenets, 1977, p. 113).

The term of a *delegatka* was temporary. This was designed to instil political consciousness and work skills quickly and to ensure a high turnover of *delegatki* and *praktikantki* in order to educate and mobilise as many women as possible. *Zhenotdel* leaders hoped that even women who were not *delegatki* would be indirectly reached by them since, once elected, *delegatki* had to report back to their workplace on their experiences. This procedure was intended to influence the political development of a large number of women (*Kommunistka*, no. 1–2, June–July 1920, p. 32).

Delegates also reported to their counterparts in other districts, *oblasts* and republics. They discussed how to improve their work and held competitions for the best campaign. There were similar competitions for the best delegates' meeting in districts and *oblasts*. Through these mechanisms *delegatki* came into contact with a network of women and could compare their activities and problems (Chirkov, 1978, p. 97). In Muslim areas, swopping information about reactions against political work among women was common. At the first All-Azerbaidzhan delegates' meeting, for example, the topic of husbands killing their wives was discussed and commitment pledged to fight against it (Alieva, 1962, p. 31).

The end of a delegate's term was marked by a supposedly festive evening meeting attended by delegates, working women and men of the local community, and by representatives of the party and trade unions. Proceedings commenced with a speech on a current political theme and continued with a representative of the party organisation summarising the results of the year's work and giving prizes to the best delegates. At the end came an 'artistic part' of music or singing (Chirkov, 1978, pp. 97–8). Thus the delegates' term was structured 'from above' from beginning to end with the intention of communicating certain political lessons.

This pattern continued in the re-selection meetings. Upon the recommendation of the Central Committee of the party, fresh 'elections' to replace outgoing delegates took the form of mass meetings (Chirkov, 1978, p. 91; *Institut Marksizma–Leninizma*, 1984, vol. 3, p. 139). Elections not only served the immediate task at hand – selection of *delegatki* – but also aimed to involve the workers and peasants of the local community. Local campaigns frequently preceded the election to inform people of political events, attract them to the proceedings and draw them into the administration of the new state. The selection of *delegatki* was preceded by a speech on the current political situation of the Bolshevik state. After this, the most active *delegatki* who were coming to the end of their term gave an account of their work over the last year. Then came the selection of new delegates.[15]

In the Muslim areas of Soviet Central Asia and the Caucasus where the lives of women were particularly restricted, quite intense campaigns were conducted in the late 1920s in the run-up to 'election meetings'. Concerts and plays were put on, activists stepped up attempts to reach women in remote areas and groups of women were organised to throw off their veils. Speakers often addressed topics special to Muslim areas such as how delegates could fight against *kalym* or bride-price or how they could prevent girls from being given away as child-brides. Aminova reports that meetings sometimes drew large numbers of women and men. In Besharyk, situated in the Fergana district of Uzbekistan, one meeting attracted 2,000 women (Aminova, 1977, p. 68).

Delegates' meetings: ideological goals

Delegates' meetings were claimed to be the main form of systematic party work among politically backward women during the transition from capitalism to socialism. Along with a host of other non-party mass organisations, they were viewed as necessary tentacles of the party for passing on 'its will to the working class' and for converting the working class to the party. Through such 'driving belts', 'motors' or 'schools of communism', the party was joined to the people (Sokolova, 1926b, p. 6; El'darova, 1963, pp. 20–1; Chirkov, 1978, pp. 89–100). The dictatorship of the proletariat had to work through such organisations in order to be effective and build legitimacy.

Delegates' meetings were praised by Inessa Armand as facilitating 'a course of systematic discussions of a defined political nature' which served to raise women's political consciousness, prepare them for work, and draw some into government institutions (Armand, 1975, p. 102). In Samoilova's words they were 'practical schools' and 'laboratories' for the creation of communism (Samoilova, 1920, p. 26). There appeared to be a consensus among female activists that delegates' meetings were the core or pivot of all political work among women and a 'tried and tested' method (*Kommunistka*, no. 5, October 1920, p. 14; Rakitina, 1929, p. 38).

In their agitprop work delegates' meetings aimed to reach and educate as many women as possible and to encourage them to take an interest in politics, join the party and assume public responsibilities. Leaders of the *Zhenotdel* stated in 1921 that the official goals of delegates' meetings were to:

> Join around the Party, Soviets, and trade unions backward sections of working women and peasants, to involve them in the circle of social productive, professional and party interests, to teach them to conduct defined political work in soviet, party and professional construction and to make women workers and peasants active members of the party and workers in all social and state organs and institutions. (Chirkov, 1978, p. 90)

Women's magazines of the 1920s told readers how through being delegates they could familiarise themselves with the goals of the Soviet state and help the party to bring them about (Shitkina, 1926, p. 1).

Party Congresses throughout the 1920s reiterated these sentiments and gave the delegates' meetings an official stamp of approval. For example, at the 12th Congress in 1923 delegates' meetings were referred to as the 'most essential apparatus for uniting the party with the broad mass of non-party working women and peasants' (*Institut Marksizma–Leninizma*, 1984, vol. 3, pp. 125–6). A more detailed point of praxis was made in a Central Committee resolution of September 1923 which suggested that elections for delegates' meetings take place every September throughout the USSR. Such standardisation across the Union was viewed as a way of preparing women for participation in election campaigns for the soviets (*Institut Marksizma–Leninizma*, 1984, vol. 3, p. 139). Then in 1929 a Central Committee resolution called for the maximum adaptation of delegates' meetings to the task of mobilising women to take part in the implementation of the First Five Year Plan (*Institut Marksizma–Leninizma*, 1984, vol. 4, p. 515). According to party documents and articles in *Kommunistka*, delegates' meetings were essential to the successful liberation of women. However, the way in which liberation was discussed at party congresses shifted in emphasis as the decade progressed. In the early 1920s, liberation meant being educated about socialism, being aware of one's new rights as a woman, supporting the regime, taking a job in the labour force and perhaps joining the party; by 1929, liberation meant participation in plan fulfilment.

How successful were delegates' meetings?

Delegates' meetings certainly reached a large number of women and throughout the 1920s mobilised an increasing proportion of them. In 1922 there were 95,000 delegates, rising to 620,000 in 1927 and 2.2 million in 1932 (Chirkov, 1978, p. 93). Although in some areas they persisted throughout the 1930s and into the 1940s, 'regrettably no figures have survived' (Aminova, 1977, p. 71). Delegates' meetings also spread through individual republics, generally from town to town, then fanning out into rural areas and finally touching remoter parts. For example, the pattern in Dagestan, according to party archives, was as follows. The first election of delegates took place in October 1920 in Temir-Khan-Shure. This was followed in the same year by elections in Derbent. Then in 1921 *delegatki* and *praktikantki* were named in Makhachkala, the capital of Dagestan. By 1922 delegates' meetings were being set up outside the towns and after 1925 began to reach remoter parts. Again the figures reflect this expanding activity. By 1924 there were 998 delegates in Dagestan, 502 of whom were *gorianki*.[16] Three years later the total reached 3,187, which included 2,450 *gorianki* (Gasanova, 1963, pp. 42–3).

According to the criterion of access to women in different districts, delegates' meetings registered some successes. However, the percentage of women in the general population who were reached by them remained small. The 620,000 delegates of 1927 comprised only 0.9 per cent of the total female population. Moreover, in rural areas access fell far below the towns, especially in Muslim republics. In

Azerbaidzhan, delegates' meetings were organised in the larger rural centres only. This was 'due to the specific domestic conditions of Muslim women', which made access difficult, as well as to 'an insufficient preparation of local women workers' and the weakness of local Soviet institutions' (Guliev, 1972, p. 396; 398). *Kommunistka* regularly carried articles on the shortage of women qualified to conduct political work, which made the task slow and unsystematic (*Kommunistka*, no. 8–9, August–September 1922, pp. 27–8; *Kommunistka*, no. 16–17, September–October 1921, pp. 52–3). Many party committees were forced to admit that 'we do not conduct any work among peasant women due to a lack of personnel' (Emel'ianova, 1971, p. 107). Often a local *Zhenotdel* did not exist at all, or if it did, it frequently had only two workers. Some party committees also placed the setting up of women's departments and the organisation of delegates' meetings low on their list of priorities. For instance, out of thirteen *uezd* party organisations in Smolensk *guberniia* only two in 1921 were conducting work among women satisfactorily; work was 'inadequate and poor' in six and in the remaining five *uezdy* the desire to liquidate the *Zhenotdel* dominated (Emel'ianova, 1971, p. 107). Commitment to reaching women varied throughout the country (Liubimova, 1926b).

An official aim was to expose women to communist ideas. Clearly, thousands of women received instruction in Soviet ideology and Marxism but the extent to which women accepted Marxism cannot be ascertained from existing sources. They were exposed to it, but this did not necessarily mean that they came to see the world through its lens, or believe in its claims. A related task of the delegates' meetings was to rectify the extremely low female party membership. In Dagestan, for example, there were 1,066 communists in 1923, but only 49 were women. Of these 49, just five were *gorianki*. Then in 1924, 91 *delegatki* joined the party, including nine *gorianki*. What made this possible, according to one Soviet historian, was the 'preliminary training' provided by delegates' meetings (Gasanova, 1963, pp. 42–5). Yet while delegates' meetings may have helped to produce female communists who would otherwise not have joined the party, they cannot be seen as institutions which functioned as automatic conveyor belts into the party. Statistics suggest that most *delegatki* did not become party members.[17] Consistent with this, the 13th party Congress of 1924 pointed out how few women had joined the party during the Lenin Enrolment and regretted that 'insufficient attention' had been paid by party organisations to attracting women (*Institut Marksizma–Leninizma*, 1984, vol 3, p. 285). Although female membership of the party increased from 9.9 per cent in 1924 to 11.9 per cent in 1926, articles nevertheless pointed out that the percentage of female members was falling in some areas, or fell below expected targets.

In the Ukraine women were leaving the party, despite alleged increases in their political consciousness (*Kommunistka*, no. 12, June 1929, p. 45). Reports from Central Asia also revealed that most women refrained from joining the party and those who were members on occasion left it with defiance. Massell cites sources which show that some Muslim women after having unveiled at the end of the 1920s, claimed that they had been forcibly obliged to join the party against their will. They subsequently refused to carry out party assignments. Even highly active party members who had by choice become involved in the work of the *Zhenotdel* and delegates' meetings occasionally rebelled. One *Zhenotdel* leader in Central Asia apparently arrived at party offices for a membership check wearing her veil. When asked why she was so dressed, she retorted 'I feel like it; it's none of your business.' Thereupon she resigned from agitprop among women. These examples can be taken to illustrate either the reluctance of some women to be commanded 'from above', or the difficulty for Muslim women of breaking out of traditional patterns, or a blend of both (Massell, 1974, pp. 328–9).

Low levels of female involvement in politics extended to the soviets (*Kommunistka*, no. 8–9, August–September 1922, pp. 4–5). Admittedly the share of women on the soviets had increased from 18 per cent in urban areas and 10 per cent in rural areas in 1926 to 32 per cent and 27 per cent, respectively, in 1934 (Lapidus, 1978, p. 204). However, percentages obscured variations in participation across soviets. Articles pointed out that in some rural areas women's involvement in the soviets was, in fact, decreasing and as low as 4 per cent (*Kommunistka*, no. 10, October 1927, pp. 61–5; Polianskaia, 1933, pp. 6–9). Moreover, statistics could be deceptive. Just because a woman was formally a member of the soviet, it did not always follow that she carried out her responsibilities. One conference reported cases of peasant women deputies who were elected to the soviet, but who failed to turn up for meetings. Some deputies who did attend worked badly or thought themselves superior to their constituents and failed to listen to what they had to say (*Soveshchanie zhenshchin-delegatok XIV Vserossiiskogo i 5 Vsesoiuznogo S"ezdov Sovetov*, 1929). Calls were made for a careful monitoring by the *Zhenotdel* of women's deputies to make sure they were properly contributing to the soviets. By the end of the 1920s some thought that the *Zhenotdel* ought to accord this work with a higher priority than delegates' meetings (*Soveshchanie zhenshchin-delegatok XIV Vserossiiskogo i 5 Vsesoiuznogo S"ezdov*, 1929, p. 26).

Sources indicated that not all *delegatki* attended delegates' meetings. The Leningrad magazine *Rabotnitsa i Krest'ianka* reported that not all women completed their terms as *delegatki*, giving up either through lack of interest or due to an unwelcome reception they were given as *praktikantki*. Some delegates hesitated to go to meetings, or if they did arrive, they sat whispering not working (*Rabotnitsa i Krest'ianka*, no. 16, August 1926, p. 7). One working woman wrote to *Rabotnitsa* that 'I am not a delegate, but I attend delegates' meetings. They interest me. Those delegates who were selected by workers and who do not turn up amaze me' (*Rabotnitsa*, no. 16, August 1926, p. 17). Addressing the problem of absenteeism, *Delegatka* stressed that only women who were keen to learn and to be useful to society should be picked as delegates (*Delegatka*, no. 7, September 1923, p. 3). By 1927 attendance at delegates' meetings was sometimes as low as 40–60 per cent. This was still the case in 1929. Often women did not turn up because they were afraid to criticise factory leaders (Hayden, 1979, p. 286; 357).

Clearly some delegates were diligent. Unfortunately representative views of delegates about the value of their work are hard to acquire. Magazines of the 1920s did print success stories alongside failures, but how to interpret them is a problem. For example, one *delegatka* claimed that 'I have been a delegate for just four months. Already I am not what I was before. I recall with pain how I used to live a useless and aimless life.' Moving closer towards the heroic style of the 1930s, already evident in the second half of the 1920s, another *delegatka* pronounced 'Delegates' meetings are a school for me and I now see that I am going down a wide and bright road.' A third rejoiced that 'I came to understand the writings of Lenin at delegates' meetings. I joined the party' (*Rabotnitsa*, no. 16, August 1926, p. 17). While these statements may reflect reality, it cannot be overlooked that many may have said not what they believed, but what the party wanted to hear. Such sources should not be taken at face value. In this case, the most definite conclusion that one can draw is that some *delegatki* appeared to be much more enthusiastic than others.

Only a tentative assessment can be made of the extent to which delegates' meetings represented the interests of the women whom they mobilised. Politically conscious women directed 'from above' less enlightened women who were allegedly unable to recognise or articulate their own interests. The structured process of mobilising *delegatki* from 'election' to graduation was designed to meet political priorities determined by the party leadership. The process was not shaped around the suggestions of the *delegatka*. The party was involved in approving the selection of *delegatki*, defining the breadth of the experience of *praktikantki* and judging who were successful *delegatki* at the end of their term. There was, of course, room for variation and space for delegates to take initiative. Reality could not be minutely planned. But activities did have particular directions in mind. Moreover, what constituted 'success' was relative to the goals of the regime rather than to criteria established 'from below' by the women. Although the general concern was to promote the liberation of women, the issues upon which the *delegatki* concentrated did not prompt frequent reflection on the meaning of this liberation for individuals. At best, preliminary themes of not being constrained by marriage, by motherhood and by religion were addressed. Delegates' activities were tailored to economic and social construction rather than to individual concerns of self-confidence, self-expression or marital problems. In Uzbekistan, for example, delegates urged local women to tackle production tasks and to take part in the Spring sowing campaign (Aminova, 1977, p. 71). The reasoning behind this was that personal emancipation would follow from participation in social production. But then within a traditional context, recruitment into the labour force was, for many women, a radical change in their lives.

Can one reach firmer conclusions about the extent to which delegates' meetings involved women in socialist construction? During their period of tenure as *delegatki* women were mobilised into discussion groups and frequently sent into offices on apprenticeships as *praktikantki* as well. So according to official criteria they were pursuing socialist construction. In the short-term, at least, they were drawn into an aspect, or several aspects, of building a new society. They set up nurseries, heard cases in the People's Courts, worked for the soviet, campaigned to improve public catering, organised teams of women to pick cotton, helped other women to learn to read and engaged in a host of other activities. However, the extent of women's involvement was criticised by the 13th party Congress of 1924. Just because an increasing number of women were being drawn into the work of the soviets, trade unions and cooperative organisations, it did not follow that the percentage of active women was high. In fact, women's role in social construction was criticised as 'far from sufficient'. In order to remedy this, the party declared in 1924 that work among women was now a 'top priority' and pronounced that it was necessary to struggle against 'conservative attitudes toward women' (*Institut Marksizma–Leninizma*, 1984, vol. 3, p. 286). Indeed, in some Muslim areas, women *praktikantki* were turned away by the authorities they were sent to help because they did not want women working with them (Massell, 1974, p. 301).

Tackling extremely conservative attitudes towards women required an innovation and flexibility that delegates' meetings could not always provide. Delegates' meetings were mainly directed at working women, and were therefore less effective at reaching housewives in Muslim areas who led very confined lives. For this reason, delegates' meetings were less widespread in Soviet Central Asia. Here a different approach to mobilising women out of the home was provided by women's clubs.

Women's clubs: ideological goals

Women's clubs were intended to ease the transition between secluded home lives and taking the initial step into social production and political participation (Chirkov, 1978, pp. 100–1). Ideological justifications for them stressed that their special approaches to Muslim women were essential since the overwhelming majority of the 'people of the East' had not passed through the capitalist stage, and so the objective conditions for solving the woman question did not exist. In feudal or tribal environments, progress was necessarily slow and special agitprop techniques for them had to be developed (*Kommunistka*, no. 12–13, May–June 1921, p. 52; Chirkov, 1978, p. 46).[18]

Women in Central Asia and the Caucasus were in a more difficult predicament, according to Soviet ideology, than other women in the Soviet state due to factors of economics and nationality. Illiteracy preserved religious and domestic prejudices which enslaved women. (Kotelenets, 1977, pp. 124). Women therefore endured a triple oppression of class, nationality and family. First, women had suffered, like men, from class oppression before Bolshevik rule had freed them.

Second, years of oppression as members of various nationalities reduced their self-determination, even after revolution. Third, in family life women were subject to feudal–patriarchal relations. In fact, those living in mountain areas, such as Dagestan, were still enclosed in tribal patterns of life (Kuznetsova, 1979, p. 9). These could not be changed instantly by the Bolshevik revolution.

Since women's extreme isolation was tied to national customs, special work tailored to the 'specific characteristics of each nation (*natsii*), each people' was proposed and party work among Muslim women was defined by the special and distinct features of the nationality to which they belonged – Uzbek, Kazakh, Darghin or Rutul (Kuznetsova, 1979, p. 11). Solving the woman question was considered to be inextricably bound up with solving the national question (Sultanova, 1964, p. 32).

Clearly legal rights had not begun to solve the woman question among the many nationalities who had refused to implement them. Customs such as the abduction of young girls, the sale of daughters into marriage at 9 years of age and polygamy were hard to abolish by legislation. They were too deeply ingrained in society and sanctioned by religion. Instruments to bring about change, other than legal ones, had to be devised. According to the party line, 'in these conditions it was necessary to search for special and specific forms of work among women' (Kuznetsova, 1979, p. 12). Lenin's advice to party workers in the Caucasus was against using stock phrases in political work and criticised the mechanical transfer of examples of political practice from the centre to the republics. He suggested that tactics had to be modified to suit different conditions. Different nationalities and ancient traditions had left a deep stamp on women's consciousness which 'demanded great differentiation of forms and methods of work' and 'incessant political education' (Bil'shai, 1959, p. 173). A Leninist flexibility to praxis was required since without the appropriate approach towards them, women could not change their lives.

Women's clubs were portrayed as 'genuine preparatory schools for life and work' (Kuznetsova, 1979. p. 12). Their most basic task was to 're-educate' women into 'socio-class instincts' (*Kommunistka*, no. 5, May 1923, pp. 10–11). Their immediate twin goals to liberate women from slavery and to raise their cultural level by liquidating illiteracy, were linked in the minds of the editors of *Kommunistka* to broader goals of working among the whole population in order to eradicate ingrained notions of female roles. Ultimate success depended upon changing men's views of women as well as women's images of themselves.

Support was given to women's clubs in official party documents and at party congresses. For example, a resolution of the *Orgburo* in December 1924 on party work among women in the East, suggested that one way of making women more aware of their legal rights would be to develop a network of legal advice bureaux within women's clubs (*Institut Marksizma–Leninizma*, 1984, vol. 3, p. 318). A Central Committee Plenum of January 1925 supported the *Orgburo* resolution (*Institut Marksizma–Leninizma*, 1984, vol. 3, p. 332). Then in 1927 a Central Committee resolution 'Concerning the Tasks of Women's Clubs in the Soviet East' called upon oblast and republic party organisations to set up clubs in areas where strong traditions prevented women from joining the labour force and also to improve the quality of existing clubs. As in other areas of work among women, the Central Committee stressed the importance of a carefully planned and systematic approach which was in keeping with general party goals and simultaneously catered to local needs.[19] The resolution went on to suggest establishing sections within women's clubs such as healthcare, cultural enlightenment, legal advice and cells for the Komsomol and Young Pioneers. Whilst there was flexibility on the mix of sections within any particular club, production work and political education had to be included as core elements.[20] Through political education, women should become active both within and outside the club, liaising with the soviets and cooperative organisations (*Institut Marksizma–Leninizma*, 1984, vol. 4, pp. 134–5).

By 1927 it was clear that the party was trying more actively to involve general party institutions in the work of women's clubs. This was, in part, on an ideological level, to ensure a sound non-feminist class approach. It was also an attempt to rectify lack of party interest in the woman question.[21] By 1929 the Central Committee was calling with some urgency for considerable effort on the part of women's clubs and delegates' meetings in the mobilisation of women around 'all tasks standing in front of the party and soviets' (*Institut Marksizma–Leninizma*, 1984, vol. 4, p. 515). Propaganda emphasised that the need to mobilise women and men was now viewed as 'especially acute' since the First Five Year Plan had to be implemented and fulfilled, the defensive might of the country had to be strengthened and the battle with bureaucratic tendencies waged.

The activities of the Ali Bairamov Club in Azerbaidzhan

The first women's club was set up in Baku in 1920 by Dzheiran Bairamova (Kotelenets, 1977, p. 130).[22] It began by five or six women meeting in Dzheiran Bairamova's flat and then its numbers steadily increased to 100 by the end of its first year (*Otdel Rabotnits i Krest'ianok*, 1927, p. 16; Abilova, 1970, p. 8). Initially its size was small due to difficulties Muslim women faced in obtaining their husband's permission to leave home or in finding the opportunity to slip away undetected. Even those who attended, according to one member, did so 'with great difficulty' (*Otdel Rabotnits i Krest'ianok*, 1927, p. 16). The group, however, soon became too large to assemble in a flat and in 1922 was given a building for its work by the Azerbaidzhan Communist Party.[23] It then took the name of Ali Bairamov, after a local revolutionary (Radzhabov, 1975, p. 142). By 1926 its membership had grown to 1,600, reaching 2,268 in 1930 and 4,486 in 1935 (Chirkov, 1978, p. 103).

The Ali Bairamov Club recruited women by recommendation only, in order to 'ensure a class approach'. Members had to come from working-class families and relatives of 'the exploiting classes' were not considered (Chirkov, 1978, p. 101). Its work was divided into three sections: education, production and medical instruction. Education assumed special importance since only 2.7 per cent of girls in Azerbaidzhan attended primary school and 1 per cent of Azerbaidzhani women were literate (Radzhabov, 1975, p. 144). The first goal of the Club was to urge members to learn to read and write. 'Liquidation of Illiteracy' was viewed as a necessary precondition of both women's liberation and socialist construction. Women were encouraged to attend special schools within the Club for the liquidation of illiteracy and for the partially literate. Of the Club's 1,600 members in 1926, 210 were studying in the former and 232 in the latter slightly more advanced groups (*Otdel Rabotnits i Krest'ianok*, 1927, p. 17). The Ali Bairamov Club set up its own reading groups and extended this activity into political and cultural education. In these groups women read newspapers, women's magazines, pamphlets, stories and plays. Literacy and political education were also promoted by wall posters. Simple cartoons were used to convey political messages and to encourage women to read.

Women who could not easily visit the Club to learn to read were visited at home by young teachers. Thus much of the work was done on an individual basis catering to the very specific needs of one person. Activists within the Ali Bairamov Club also attempted to conduct political education on a one-to-one basis in homes. Nabat Efendieva recalls how:

> Together with other activists I went from house to house, where we conducted systematic conversations with women, attempting to talk simply and convincingly. Our main theme was how after the establishment of Soviet power a wide road was opened for women into work, culture and genuine freedom. (Radzhabov, 1975, p. 143)

The women were then invited to visit the Ali Bairamov Club, to chat with members and look around in the hope that thereafter they would attend regularly. Efendieva described this as 'painstaking agitation work' which could not be completed in days or weeks but required close attention for months and years (Radzhabov, 1975, p. 143).

The level of commitment of some activists was high. One said recently in an interview in Baku:

> We felt we were bringing light to women. We were 'cultural soldiers' fighting on a front in a real war. We were soldiers who had to bring light to the darkness. We freed women. But many nasty things were said about us.

The work of large numbers of 'cultural soldiers' was organised independently of the Ali Bairamov Club by school teachers and Young Pioneers; yet their pursuits overlapped. For instance, the Pioneers divided regions into 'fronts'. 'Soldiers' then had to find illiterate women and men on their front and visit them at home with the brief of stamping out illiteracy.

When recruited to the club, women gathered at a weekly meeting to hear talks and lectures about politics and healthcare. The topics addressed ranged from 'The Contemporary International Situation' to 'Hygiene', 'Venereal Disease' and 'Children's Illnesses'. These were followed by 'cultural enlightenment' through plays, concerts, singing and dancing (*Otdel Rabotnits i Krest'ianok*, 1927, p. 17; Tsetkin, 1926, pp. 299–309). Drama was used as an instrument for raising political consciousness – club members acted out scenes of their own liberation. A particularly popular drama of the period was *Sevil'* by the male playwright Dzhafar Dzhabarly. It portrayed the unhappiness, anxiety and personal progress of a Muslim woman breaking out of domestic confinement into the world of work (Dzhabarly, 1979).[24]

After preparation in the clubs, women were encouraged to participate in political campaigns to heighten their consciousness. One extensive and volatile campaign conducted in Muslim republics in 1928 and 1929 mobilised women to throw off the *chadra* and *parandzha* (different forms of yashmak) and veil.[25] During 1928 and 1929, 270,000 women in Azerbaidzhan threw off the *chadra*. Reaction and violence followed (Musaeva, 1964, p. 42; Massell, 1974, pp. 322–89).

Every aspect of the Ali Bairamov Club's educational work directly challenged the organisation of Muslim households. For example, its production section had the twin goals of enabling women to become more independent of their husbands by earning their own wages and drawing them into the construction of socialist industry and agriculture. To meet these goals the Club established its own four-year professional–technical school and organised courses to train dressmakers, weavers, telephonists, shorthand-typists and typesetters. The Club also set up its own independent textile factory. This began by seven women bringing their sewing machines from home. Soon their number grew to 35 (Abilova, 1970, p. 9). According to one source, 50 sewing machines were acquired by expropriating them from the bourgeoisie (*Otdel Rabotnits i Krest'ianok*, 1927, p. 19). As more and more orders for work were placed with the seamstresses, the small workshop grew to the scale of a factory which provided dormitory accommodation for its workers. By 1931, 1,500 women were working in what became known as factory No. 4 (Musaeva, 1964, p. 40). Still in existence after the closure of the Ali Bairamov Club in 1937, the factory was employing 15,000 workers by the 1970s (Abilova, 1970, p. 9).

A smaller number of women were trained to work with children, some of whom went into the countryside to run kindergartens. Of 30 who received this specialist instruction in 1926, 14 were given posts as kindergarten teachers (*Otdel Rabotnits i Krest'ianok*, 1927, p. 18). The Ali Bairamov Club also organised its own party cells and a women's party school, as well as Komsomol and Young Pioneer organisations for members' children to attend (Radzhabov, 1975, p. 143). Through these, strides were made to raise the political consciousness of women and children and to involve them in political participation. The Club produced four wall newspapers every month. Two of these were Komsomol papers and one was put together by the Young Pioneers (*Otdel Rabotnits i Krest'ianok*, 1927, p. 19). After visiting the Ali Bairamov Club, Klara Zetkin praised it as the *Zhenotdel*'s 'main fortress' in Azerbaidzhan where women were involved in 'diligent and creative work'. She concluded that the Club was 'the most successful means for bringing Muslim women together, educating them and preparing them for great social life' (Tsetkin, 1926, p. 299).

Like delegates' meetings, women's clubs grew in number during the 1920s. In 1922 a second club was set up in Baku, called the Ibragima Abilova Club (Radzhabov, 1975, p. 143). By 1932 there were 42 women's clubs in Azerbaidzhan (Musaeva, 1964, p. 44). They were set up in other republics too and by 1922 there were 22 clubs in the country as a whole. They increased to 27 in 1923, 57 in 1925, 87 in 1926, and 103 by 1930 (*Otdel Rabotnits i Krest'ianok*, 1927, p. 4; Kotelenets, 1977, p. 130). Their aims were broadly similar, as were their sections, but variations existed. Some were larger than others and offered a wider range of activities. Some were better organised than others and like the Nadezhda Krupskaia Club in Tashkent systematically followed up talks with relevant excursions: a lecture on electricity would be complemented by a visit to a hydro-electric station, for example (*Otdel Rabotnits i Krest'ianok*, 1927, p. 22). Some had legal sections and others did not (Chirkov, 1978, p. 102). Some involved men in their activities, such as putting on plays or organising sections of work, while others avoided this. Some found it hard to obtain financial backing outside the *Zhenotdel*, others did not (*Otdel Rabotnits i Krest'ianok*, 1927, pp. 20–35).

Many clubs modelled themselves on the Ali Bairamov Club. In some areas, however, this model was considered quite inappropriate. Instead, different forms of political activity emerged such as Houses of Dekhanki (*Dom Dekhanki*), red circles, red tents, women's shops and red tea houses. These are generally referred to in Soviet literature as 'clubs in miniature' and are seen as similar to, but distinct from, the network of clubs just discussed. Their distinctive characteristics stemmed from their environment and the sorts of women they were aiming to reach.

Clubs in miniature

Sensitivity to the political need to cater to the special characteristics and particular customs of different nationalities gave rise to a range of 'clubs in miniature'. Some, for instance, were set up in towns, but drew their membership exclusively from rural areas. The House of Dekhanki begun in Ashkhabad in 1925 falls into this category. Women came up from the countryside for about two weeks and lived in a hostel. Political education, the liquidation of illiteracy, reading aloud from the press, sewing and talks on hygiene were included in the intensive programme. Women were also taken to the local bathhouse to wash and be taught about cleanliness, how to feed a child and how to cope with children's illnesses (*Otdel Rabotnits i Krest'ianok*, 1927, p. 43). A nursery made it possible for women with children to attend. A minority of women stayed for as long as six months to train as organisers. They then returned to villages to set up red corners and schools for the liquidation of illiteracy (Kotelenets, 1977, p. 132; *Kommunistka*, no. 8, August 1926, pp. 57–8). Activists working in the Houses also visited the rural areas in their catchment area. Here they organised exhibitions, arranged for lawyers and doctors to give legal and medical advice, and set up red corners and literacy schools (Chirkov, 1978, p. 104).

Red corners and peasants' huts were other, although not very widespread, forms of club work. By 1930 there were just 364 of these (Chirkov, 1978, p. 104). They often lacked permanent activists and frequently emerged from within the local community or were sometimes set up by visiting activists or by peasant women who had undergone a brief training spell in a town. Women drawn into the red corners read aloud to each other from political literature, tried to overcome their illiteracy, sewed and knitted. Arrangements were also made for visiting speakers such as agricultural specialists and doctors to enlighten the women. Thus, red corners offered a mix of activities from social gatherings to education and political instruction (Kotelenets *et al.*, 1977, p. 132).

Clubs styled on the Ali Bairamov Club, the Dom Dekhanki, or red corners would have failed to attract the attention of nomadic peoples. So mobile clubs were devised, called red tents. These moved from place to place, staying for two to three months with one nomadic group before moving on to another. The first red tent was set up in 1926 in Kazakhstan. They then caught on among Buriat, Altai and Kulmych peoples. By 1930 there were 150 women's red tents (Kotelenets, 1977, p. 133). At a minimum, a red tent consisted of two workers – a director and a medical worker. Larger tents included a teacher, lawyer and agronomist.

Red tents are portrayed in the literature as 'big holidays' for nomads, offering regular distractions of singing, dancing and cinema (Chirkov, 1978, p. 106). The purpose of the tents was initially to provide social entertainment and then to move on to health education and some political work. The *Zhenotdel* recommended that the red tents focus in particular on questions of sanitation, health and production, relegating political and legal questions to second place. The official tactical aim here was to begin with topics of more immediate relevance to the daily lives of nomads in order to win their attention. Having secured trust, activists moved on to more complicated political education (Chirkov, 1978, p. 105). Another practical reason behind these priorities was the belief than many nomads needed instruction about hygiene and cleanliness. Commenting on the nomads of Buriat, Mongolia, one activist emphasised that they were 'the most backward' (*naibolee otstalym*) 'most prejudiced' (*naibolee sklonnym k predrassudkam*) and 'the most ignorant' (*naibolee temnym*) and reported that 'the Buriat do not wash their clothes, very rarely wash themselves, some never wash themselves, because they carry the prejudice that it is sinful to wash and to clean bedding and clothes' (*Otdel Rabotnits i Krest'ianok*, 1927, p. 40). Basic hygiene was therefore more important than political enlightenment.

Activists among nomads also organised sewing and cookery classes and most red tents had a sewing machine, milk separator and film projector. In addition, women were taught to read and write and information about the goals, laws and policies of the Soviet state was then passed on through conversations, lectures and reading groups. Komsomol and party groups emerged later. The tents also organised other institutional forms of reaching women, such as delegates' meetings and conferences (Chirkov, 1978, p. 106). Allegedly, nomads invariably asked the activists not to move the red tent on and pressed them to stay longer than planned (Chirkov, 1978, p. 106). This claim is hard to substantiate.

Another special approach to the education of women took place in women's shops. These were set up in 1925 in Tashkent and later in other parts of Uzbekistan and Azerbaidzhan. They were organised by shops' commissions which ensured that literate communists of the local nationality worked in them. Thus female communists sold goods to women-only shoppers and conducted political-educational work among them. For example, they read aloud from women's journals to shoppers and discussed questions of daily life. According to one commentator, in many rural areas 'women's shops were the centres of work among women' (Kotelenets, 1977, p. 133). The women's shop in Tashkent initially attracted 80–100 women, increasing to many more (*Kommunistka*, no. 7, July 1926, pp. 70–2; no. 9, September 1927, pp. 62–7).

Red tea houses for women played a similar role in the towns and villages of Uzbekistan. Initially, about every ten days women came together to drink tea, listen to the radio, chat, and study political literature. Women-only tea houses then opened in which women were taught to read and write (Kotelenets, 1977, p. 133).

Finally, a general form of political sponsorship of the countryside by the town existed. 'Political sponsorship' was not a club *per se*, but a form of work similar to that of a club, through a very different structure. 'Sponsorship commissions' were set up in primary party organisations in large enterprises in the towns. More politically advanced workers were then sent out to help more backward women in rural areas. Their aim was to explain to peasant women how socialist construction was relevant to them. The urban women talked about politics, distributed political literature, helped to set up nurseries and invited women to come to the town to look around factories and kindergartens in order to learn about socialist construction. Peasant women sometimes attended delegates' meetings in the towns and were taught how to organise them upon their return to the countryside. This process was reversed once the collectivisation of agriculture got underway in 1929 and 1930. The working women from towns then went to help set up collective farms (*Kommunistka*, no 3–4, March–April 1923, pp. 11–13; Chirkov, 1978, pp. 106–8).

Were women's clubs successful?

One problem which women's clubs all shared was in attracting women out of the home. Many clubs were hard to start because women would not join them. An activist from Tashkent reported that 'For the first days we waited in vain for visitors. But nobody came to the club' (*Otdel Rabotnits i Krest'ianok*, 1927, p. 20). An attempt to entice women by setting up a children's clinic within the club failed. Activists then went out to look for women who, after having been approached, slowly trickled to the door at a rate of two or three a day. Initially, however, they would not cross the threshold, having been forbidden by their husbands to enter.

Another activist in Kirgizia told a similar story. At the start she attempted to attract women by offering food and drink. As she described it 'I put on a large *samovar* and called out for people to come and drink tea, saying "come to the club, we'll drink tea and you will be fed"'. Nobody came because a rumour circulated that if the women turned up, they would be forced to throw off the *parandzha* and dance. These and other rumours kept women away. The activist began visiting individual homes; if she saw a woman eating or praying she went up to her and talked or prayed alongside. In her own words 'That way I succeeded in gathering several women. I explained to them that if they wanted to be club members, we could open a school for the liquidation of illiteracy and an advice centre' (*Otdel Rabotnits i Krest'ianok*, 1927, pp, 25–6).

Red tents were similarly hard to organise. One activist reported that she had to begin by gathering men together because the women would not appear. She then set up a school for the liquidation of illiteracy for 50 men. Only after she had done this did she manage to reach their wives and sisters by using the men as intermediaries to persuade female relatives to visit the tent. The red tent then worked in two shifts, the first one for men and a second for women (*Otdel Rabotnits i Krest'ianok*, 1927, p. 36). Initial success was indeed slow. But then progress was expected to be negligible and painstaking. The door-to-door approach of club activists was specifically designed to cope with these difficult circumstances. In the end, women were reached and mobilised. They were drawn out of the confines of their homes and some even joined the party.

The same points made above about delegates' meetings apply also to the women's clubs. Although some women did attend clubs, they were in the minority. Although women joined the party, the majority of club members did not. Like the delegates' meetings, the clubs suffered from opposition and condemnation both within and outside the party. Many male party members were reluctant in practice to support the clubs because of the social and personal results they were likely to produce. This especially applied to the campaigns of 1928 and 1929 which prompted women to remove the *chadra*. Many Muslim men subsequently left the party because they objected to policy towards women (Massell, 1974).

Within the community at large, the clubs were denigrated and violence used. One member of the Ali Bairamov Club recalled the events of the late 1920s, in an interview 50 years later. She stressed that:

> The years up to about 1933 were difficult. Komsomol members were killed, even Pioneers. Peasants killed them. Parents killed them. Many died. Opponents and critics called the Club a brothel. The mullahs collected believers together and propagandised against women. The situation in Soviet Central Asia was worse than in Azerbaidzhan since it was more backward. The violence was more fanatical. I was able to teach

women and throw off my chadra in 1928 because my husband let me. I was lucky!

Many such stories persist in political folklore. One oft-told story in Azerbaidzhan concerns the murder of Sariia Khalilova, who was a member of the Ali Bairamov Club, a worker in textile factory No. 4 and a mother of four. Various sources claim that her 'fanatical father' and brother killed her in 1930. One co-activist whom I interviewed alleges that 'they threw rocks at her for breaking feudal laws and then stabbed her eighteen times'. In admiration, she added:

Sariia Khalilova was a representative of the working class and an orator. It was impossible for her to stay outside the movement. She used to go from house to house teaching women to read. Her husband saw her doing this one day. So he killed her.

Her burial was followed by a large demonstration of working women against backward customs (Musaeva, 1964, p. 44).

The Clubs, then, did mobilise women and encouraged quite radical changes in domestic and social roles. In so doing, they were in some respects actively promoting in theory and in practice women's liberation and the construction of socialism. The short-term costs were enormous; liberation sometimes led to physical and psychological tragedy. Social attitudes did not accompany the pace of change in behaviour. Moreover, local women were not drawn into organisational work to the extent intended.

One aim of the clubs was to mobilise Muslim women and then draw them into agitprop work. Women of the indigenous nationality were not usually available to take on roles as activists and organisers since they were the very ones who needed to be mobilised by others. Frequently Russian women mobilised non-Russians. In Baku, for instance, most of the instructors placed in jobs by the *Zhenotdel* were Russian working women (Guliev, 1972, p. 390). The rules of Leninist praxis demanded that the special characteristics of each nationality be taken into account, but not all activists could have been fully aware of the details of the cultural tradition with which they were struggling, or as sensitive to customs as local women would have been. For example, one member of a *Dom Dekhanki* regretted that work among women suffered because the *Dom* lacked a sewing teacher who could speak the local Turkmen language. Lessons had to take place through an interpreter (*Otdel Rabotnits i Krest'ianok*, 1927, p. 43). Similarly in Dagestan, 'serious difficulties' were caused by activists' lack of knowledge of local languages (Gasanova, 1963,

p. 30). Likewise, work among Jewish women, according to one article in *Kommunistka*, was practically non-existent because agitprop in the Ukraine and Belorussia was conducted in Russian (*Kommunistka*, no. 10–11, March–April 1920, pp. 34–5).

It was hoped non-Russians would eventually become activists and organisers themselves. But once mobilised, non-Russians did not automatically progress to agitprop work. In an attempt to remedy this, special courses were designed by *Zhenotdel* workers to train Azerbaidzhani activists. But again only a small minority of women took part. Nevertheless, some moved up in political status from 'mobilised by Russians' to 'mobilisers of other Azerbaidzhanis' (Guliev, 1972, p. 390).

Like delegates' meetings, therefore, women's clubs did fulfil official goals in a limited way. Indeed, anything greater than modest success, given the nature of social conditions, was not feasible. The instant liberation of all women was impossible. Likewise, a massive influx of suddenly enlightened women into the party was highly unlikely. Nevertheless, the activists helped to trigger key changes in some women's lives in a context where traditional social relations were deeply embedded.

The activities of delegates' meetings and women's clubs were complemented by other forms of work among women such as meetings, conferences and congresses. These latter were not considered as important, but nevertheless had their place as 'means of agitation and propaganda of the idea of communism' and met the 'immediate task' of drawing attention to 'questions of the moment' (*Kommunistka*, no. 5, October 1920, p. 13).

Meetings, conferences and congresses of non-party women

In the first few years after 1917 meetings were organised in the factories, towns and districts. Their purpose was to inform workers of the current tasks of the party and to forge a link between the party and the masses. These general meetings were attended by working men and women, but men usually outnumbered women and more readily took the floor (Chirkov, 1978, p. 86). Because of this male prominence in mixed meetings, women-only meetings were subsequently organised and comprised much of the *Zhenotdel*'s early work. They were particularly common immediately after the revolution; for example, in the first three months of 1919, 529 meetings of working women were held in Moscow (Chirkov, 1978, p. 86).

Parallel to women's meetings were women's conferences. These were considered to be a 'higher level of organisation' than meetings and consequently as their role increased, the importance of meetings declined.[26] Non-party conferences for women, like such conferences for men and women, were viewed by Lenin as channels for gauging the mood of the people, attempting to influence them politically and spotting appropriate workers to co-opt into government work. From the perspective of the party, conferences were fertile instruments of propaganda and agitation among the broad mass of women. According to *Kommunistka*, the purpose of conferences was to draw working women towards questions of great practical significance for themselves and to prompt them to participate in the solution of these questions (*Kommunistka*, no. 5, October 1920, p. 13).

Women's conferences were organised by the *Zhenotdel* at *volost*, district and *guberniia* levels. Their practical aim was to gather non-party women and raise their consciousness to a more advanced level. At the beginning of the 1920s *guberniia* conferences took place several times a year. In just six months of 1920 there were 60 *guberniia* conferences and 853 at lower administrative levels (Kotelenets, 1977, p. 99). Then from March 1920 to May 1921 in 15 *guberniias* alone there were 151 *guberniia* level conferences, 202 at *uezd* level and 1,144 at *volost* level (Chirkov, 1978, p. 99).

Three general themes were usually discussed at conferences. The first covered current politics in the international arena as well as domestic developments. The second focused more specifically on the role of women in socialist construction in the particular *guberniia*, *uezd* or *volost* where the conference was being held. Topics here included the participation of women in the local soviets and their contribution to local departments of the workers' and peasants' inspectorate. The third general area of discussion concerned recent improvements in the position of women in society, such as the spread of kindergartens and their significance.

As well as attempting to raise consciousness through discussions, the conferences also organised practical work in the locality. Women inspected children's homes and hospitals, took part in unpaid labour days (*subbotniki*) and went on excursions. Sometimes commissions of women were nominated at the conference to help the local soviet in its work. So the same sorts of activities promoted by delegates' meetings and clubs were sponsored by conferences, albeit in a more limited way.

Inessa Armand described conferences of non-party women as 'one of the remarkable facts of our revolutionary reality' (Armand, 1975, p. 50). She contrasted the first conference of working women held in Moscow in May 1918 in which women, inexperienced in representing their workplace, 'took their first still timid steps' with a subsequent Moscow conference of September 1919 with its organised agenda of presentations on the current political situation, food supply, social security, the communist party and working women, religion and the nationality question. The mobilisation of women in support of the goals advocated by Soviet power was the common aim of all the conferences but immediate tasks varied according to locality and to the political moment. Thus the first non-party women's conference of April 1921 held in the small town of Derbent in Dagestan had different problems to contend with from the first such conference in Moscow (Gasanova, 1963, p. 39). Conferences, therefore, flexibly adapted their agendas to cope with regional diversities and politically pressing issues. Frequently on the agenda at conferences in Dagestan, for instance, were items related to the topic of 'Muslim women of the Soviet republics' (El'darova, 1963, p. 20; Gasanova, 1963, p. 34).

Congresses of non-party women were similar to conferences, but were generally larger and drew together women from a broader catchment area. The First All-Russian Congress of Women Workers and Peasants was a lively affair. Held in November 1918 before official support had been granted to special organisations for work among women, it discussed how women could best contribute to the Civil War and what work they could perform for the party and trade unions. Women were also informed of their rights under socialism and of the social services available to them. Calls were made at this congress for commissions of agitation and propaganda among women, which were subsequently heeded. As noted earlier, these commissions were precursors of the *Zhenotdel* (Hayden, 1976, p. 156).

Where Congresses drew women from more than one republic, such as the large Congress of Women of the Peoples of the East held in June 1921, local *zhenotdely* generally organised prior congresses within the republics in order to select their delegates to send to the larger affair (Sultanova, 1964, p. 57). Local women's departments set up special commissions in several towns with the sole purpose of preparing for it (*Kommunistka*, no. 7, December 1920, pp. 24–6; no. 8–9, January–February 1921, p. 57). The official aim of the Congress of Women of the Peoples of the East was 'to loosen untouched soil and to

interest and influence the broad mass of women in Soviet construction'. The intent was 'to educate women in the spirit of communism
and to harden them for stuggle with the enemies of workers' (*Kommunistka*, no. 7, December 1920, p. 25). Just as congresses organised
at the republic level named delegates to larger congresses which span-
ned republics, so conferences at lower administrative levels within
republics selected delegates to attend republic level congresses.

Congresses became a regular part of work among women. In Dagestan, for example, four congresses were organised between 1920 and
1925. The number of participants grew from 73 at the first congress
to 180 at the fourth (Gasanova, 1963, pp. 34–7; El'darova, 1963,
p. 21). As well as discussing general topics related to socialist
construction, serious local problems were addressed too. One which
stood out in Dagestan was the significance of the fact that almost 90
per cent of the population was suffering from malaria (Gasanova,
1963, p. 35). Similar spates of congresses took place in other
republics in the early 1920s with predictable regional variations
(Sultanova, 1964, p. 56).

Throughout the 1920s, conferences and congresses were convened
in the republics and at the All-Russian level to rally women to support
the regime and to encourage liberation. It is hard, however, neatly to
measure the impact that they had since they were at best convened on
an annual basis and were of short duration. Their work was supplementary to the activities of more permanent bodies that had weekly
or fortnightly contact with women, such as delegates' meetings and
clubs. Thus conferences and congresses were political reference
points as past and future big occasions, rather than ongoing mechanisms of mobilisation.

Opposition to work among women

Despite the official decisions and resolutions of party Congresses,
evidence shows that exhortations to set up women's organisations
were met with hostility, suspicion, derision, ambivalence, amusement
and non-action. Many party committees were reluctant to establish
their own women's departments. Several sources indicate that as soon
as the *Zhenotdel* was set up, opponents advocated its immediate
liquidation.

In some areas members of party committees openly criticised the policies of the *Zhenotdel*, closed them down and burnt their documents (Samoilova, 1921; Hayden, 1976; Aminova, 1977). For instance, *Nizhegorod gubkom* discussed the role of the *Zhenotdel* in 1921 and then decided to close it down. Other party committees, such as that of *Ivanovo-Voznesenskii guberniia*, liquidated the *Zhenotdel* and transferred its functions to the trade unions and organisations for political enlightenment (Emel'ianova, 1971, p. 109). Elsewhere party committees suggested that the responsibilities of the *Zhenotdel* be transferred to the party's agitation and organisation departments (Samoilova, 1920; Hayden, 1976; Aminova, 1977). In Turkestan, for instance, at the 5th Congress of the Turkestan Communist Party held in 1920, work among women was relegated to a subsection of the Agitation and Propaganda Department of the Turkestan Central Committee. Female activists had to appeal the decision in order to win back their previous more independent status (Aminova, 1977, p. 26). A second drive to liquidate the *Zhenotdel* began in late 1927 (Hayden, 1979, p. 351).[27]

Party secretaries often failed to mention the work of women's organisations in their speeches to conferences and congresses, even when they had previously been implored to do so by *Zhenotdel* activists (Liubimova, 1926a, p. 33). In fact, party committees often refused specific requests from the *Zhenotdel* with abuse. In response to a letter from one *Zhenotdel* activist asking for a desk and chair so that she did not have to stand all day, came the reply: 'Refused. You and your work are not worth the paper that your request was written on' (Liubimova, 1926a, p. 14). Other reports show that the local soviets and trade unions quite arbitrarily ignored communications from the *Zhenotdel* (Emel'ianova, 1971, p. 106).

Popular images were constructed, particularly in Muslim areas, which implied the *Zhenotdel* workers were either incompetent or immoral. Some men in the party allegedly tried to discredit and denigrate the *Zhenotdel* by drawing the distinction between 'good' and 'bad' women. The men claimed that since the clientele of the *Zhenotdel* included prostitutes, the *Zhenotdel* must be focusing its attention on 'bad' women. Apparently, they frequently asked *Zhenotdel* activists if prostitutes came to their meetings and added that if so 'how after this can I let my wife attend your meetings?' Some 'comrades' refused to defend the *Zhenotdel*, excusing themselves with the words 'what can be said about the work when all *Zhenotdel* workers are prostitutes?' (Liubimova, 1926a, pp. 13–14).

Employees in party and soviet institutions 'under various pretexts took great pains to prevent women from being drawn into political work and socialist construction' (Guliev, 1972, p. 397). The poor treatment of women's organisations by party members was, in fact, raised at the 9th party Congress by a female activist. In her speech she rebuked party members for picking any female comrade to organise women without concern for her suitability for the post. She observed 'when I raise this question at this serious Party Congress, it brings a smile to your faces, and this smile indicates an attitude toward the organisation of this work which will later affect its results' (Hayden, 1976, p. 160).

There was considerable conservative resistance among the Bolsheviks to new roles for women. But personal dislike of the *Zhenotdel* could be cloaked in ideologically legitimate statements that women-only groups might promote bourgeois feminism and thereby detract from class struggle. It is therefore hard to separate sincere belief that class not gender underpinned the revolution from other factors, such as traditional attitudes towards women, fear for the stability of the family, anxiety about women taking men's jobs or simple prejudice that women should not be involved in politics. Certainly fears of separatism were reiterated at party Congresses and discussed in the press, thereby contributing to the question mark that hung over women's organisations. Although the official party line supported the *Zhenotdel*, it was often laced with qualifications that the independence of women's organisations had to be curbed.

The spectre of 'feminist tendencies' constantly hung over women's organisations and three main arguments were presented in the 1920s on how best to contain these tendencies. The first held that since the *Zhenotdel* was organised within the party structure, it was accountable to party committees and was intimately associated with party work. These links with the party countered separatist tendencies. This defensive line of argument was used by activists, when justifying the existence of the *Zhenotdel*. It was also used by critics to suggest that women's organisations should be more closely supervised in order to guarantee their correct orientation.

A second argument was that women activists should be drawn out of women's organisations into more general party work in order to increase their qualifications. This was directed at particular *zhenotdely* when it was thought that 'considerably separate work' was being pursued among working women. The implication here was that 'feminist' activists should be removed from work among women. An extension of this argument was that party committees should take over the direction of *Zhenotdel* work entirely wherever it was considered unsatisfactory (*Institut Marksizma–Leninizma*, 1984, vol. 3, p. 125).

The third line of argument was that feminist tendencies were more likely in areas where party work among women was weak or non-existent. To contain feminism, it was therefore essential to set up more women's departments rather than ponder their likely pitfalls (*Institut Marksizma–Leninizma*, 1984, vol. 3 p. 125). Those in favour of an expansion of women's work found this an attractive argument.

The ideological slur of 'feminist tendencies' combined with opposition to work among women aggravated the defensive position that women's organisations had been forced into by the NEP. The issue of disbanding the *Zhenotdel* came onto the political agenda soon after it had been set up, before the *Zhenotdel* had time to demonstrate what it could achieve. Energy had to be used to justify the existence of the *Zhenotdel* and rebut arguments against it.

The call for liquidation prompted a swift reaction from women activists. In 1920, Samoilova contended that liquidation was quite untimely and meant stopping work among women at the very moment when it was most necessary. She stressed that incorporating work among women in other party departments would be pointless since in many areas these departments did not yet exist; where they did, they could not cope with the large amount of work that had to be done among women. Samoilova concluded that to separate the work of the *Zhenotdel* into agitation and propaganda, as some advocated, was like giving its head to agitation departments and its trunk to organisation departments. The two, she emphasised, were inseparable (Samoilova, 1920). She further argued that only those familiar with the psychology of women and the daily problems they faced could work with them. To transfer work among women to those who lacked experience in this field would be highly inappropriate (Samoilova, 1921, p. 5). Another early defence printed in *Kommunistka* argued that if special departments for women were not set up, less attention and energy would be devoted to mobilising women. Without the *Zhenotdel* there would be no centre for consolidating work among women. Without it, who would refine the techniques necessary to drawing women into socialist construction? (*Kommunistka*, no. 5,

October 1920, p. 13). According to this reasoning, the new regime could not afford to lack a women's department.

Arguments in favour of the *Zhenotdel* voiced in its own journal did not, however, deter opponents and were probably not even read by them. Complaints made at party congresses about the poor way in which women's organisations were received made little difference to the way in which party committees treated them. In 1928 Artiukhina, then Director of the *Zhenotdel*, reported that, though the party formally regretted that work among women was still weak, the problem was not taken seriously. In some areas discussions of the *Zhenotdel* still, at the end of the 1920s, led to recommendations to abolish it rather than to expressions of commitment to improve its work. Artiukhina also noted that comments against women were openly made, such as 'woman is good for housework, but she is not fit for organisational work'. Artiukhina lamented this situation and also called for a struggle against 'disgraceful attitudes' towards working women that were prevalent in factories. She then itemised various ways in which male factory workers laughed at new female recruits, intimidated them and caused 'unprecedented humiliation'. She cited the case of a woman who had just started work on a machine. A male worker placed a bottle of lime near her, poured water into it and caused an explosion to frighten her (Artiukhina, 1928b, pp. 3–5).

The sentiment that it was too soon to put women forward for work in the soviets, party and social organisations because they were not politically mature enough was frequently expressed (Guliev, 1972, p. 397). Popular attitudes clearly made it hard for many men to cope with women's political activity. Ella Winter reported the following story after her visit to Russia:

> At first many people objected to having women in the Government. A young peasant whose wife had just been made a member of the Central Executive Committee told with tears in his eyes that he would have to get divorced now, though he loved his wife dearly. 'Now that she is a member of a ruling body, how can I scold her? And a husband must have the right to scold his wife!' he cried. (Winter, 1933, p. 108)

It would be too crude to label such feelings as 'anti-women', even though this was their result in practice. Deeply embedded attitudes about the nature of male–female marital relations made the liberation of women a complex emotional task, as well as a political one. This accounts for the passionate outbursts that accompanied liberation and devious manoeuvres which had psychological roots deep below the surface of everyday life. Traditional attitudes were complicated further by hostility to competition from women in the labour force and the fear that men would lose jobs to women. Perhaps it is not surprising that in this context the *Zhenotdel* earned the derogatory nicknames of *Tsentro-Baba* and *Babkomy*, meaning 'Central Old Woman' and 'Old women's committees' respectively (Samoilova, 1921, p. 4).[28] In Azerbaidzhan Klara Zetkin noticed that male communists often joked about the *Zhenotdel* by a play on words. They called it *Zhenotdel-Dzhinotdel*, or Women's Department–Gin Department (Tsetkin, 1926, p. 299).

Conclusion

From a Leninist perspective the existence of the *Zhenotdel* and its delegates' meetings, women's clubs, red tents and other institutional forms brought obvious advantages to women and to the new regime. Women's organisations influenced and mobilised thousands of women, especially in urban areas: some of these women gave loyal support to the regime.

Despite the fact that women's organisations were criticised throughout their existence, they increased in number and extended, albeit unevenly, into different regions. The leaders of the *Zhenotdel* exerted pressure on the government to adopt policies affecting women. Kollontai maintained that it was on the initiative of the *Zhenotdel* that abortion was legalised. She also suggested that it was due to pressure from the *Zhenotdel* that a proposal put forward at the Eighth Congress of Soviets on the rehabilitation of the economy, included women workers. The *Zhenotdel* lobbied successfully too for commissions to be set up to fight prostitution and to protect mothers and children (Kollontai, 1972, p. 165).

Despite these achievements, only a minority of women were reached by women's organisations, and just a fraction of them joined the party. In Leninist terms this meant that most 'politically backward' women remained 'backward'. And although some women did raise their consciousness, the majority of top political jobs remained in male hands. Although advances for women did exist, these then were limited. Moreover, although *Zhenotdel* leaders exerted some influence in the arena of 'high politics', this too was restricted. They were not regularly consulted on all aspects of policy. Even in areas where

Kollontai saw gains for women, such as the legalisation of abortion, the *Zhenotdel* could not ensure that the demand for abortion services was adequately met, as Chapter 1 shows, or see to it that objections to abortion were kept out of women's magazines.

The suspicion of the *Zhenotdel* and hostility to it that pervaded the 1920s probably contributed to its eventual abolition in 1930, even though in the changing economic and political context, it would have been dismantled anyway. Its liquidation coincided with a reorganisation of the party apparatus and other institutions, such as the Jewish section and the national section, also ceased to exist. In 1930 Artiukhina abruptly changed her arguments to fit the fresh party line. She declared that the *Zhenotdel* had to be abolished because 'work among working women and peasants is being raised to a new and higher level'. It was necessary to perform 'a sudden turn' and to 'reconstruct work' so that the party, soviets and trade unions could take over work among women to meet the required pace of liberation. Artiukhina added that there had been a time when a special party apparatus for work among women was needed. But now the *Zhenotdel* had been successful and produced 'a great woman's aktiv'. Precisely because of this achievement, it had made itself redundant. Already 300,000 women worked in the soviets and women made up 13.5 per cent of party members. Thus the time was ripe for 'a great and important step' to reorganise work among women (Artiukhina, 1930b, p. 8). Not long before in April 1928 Artiukhina had lamented that illiteracy still held women back from socialist construction. She had criticised the 'catastrophically weak' movement of working and peasant women into state and cooperative work and pointed out that only 2 per cent of rural women in Belorussia were involved in delegates' meetings (Artiukhina, 1928b, pp. 29–35). In the space of just two years the work of the *Zhenotdel* among women had changed in status from 'weak' to 'so successful that it could cease'.

Breaking the news of the *Zhenotdel*'s demise to readers of *Kommunistka* before Artiukhina, Kaganovich declared that 'the *Zhenotdel* is no longer a progressive centre, but a hindrance'. This was because 'a sufficiently solid group' of women was now on factory committees, in trade unions and on party committees. It was therefore time to treat working women not as women alone, but as workers who were 'equal, grown up and developing' (Kaganovich, 1930, pp. 3–5). The *Zhenotdel* had been set up to reach backward women. Thanks to its work many thousands of women no longer fitted this category. It was therefore politically anachronistic.

Although delegates' meetings persisted into the 1930s and 1940s, their tasks were redefined away from liberating women and were entirely subordinate to economic goals. Plans of work were drawn up for them around the topics of strengthening collectivisation and struggling to fulfil the plan (*Primernyi plan raboty delegatskogo sobraniia kolkhoznits*, 1932). Instruction books for organisers of delegates' meetings were printed on how to publicise the party line and how to work with slogans such as 'the five year plan in four years' (*Programma dlia zhendelegatskikh sobranii*, 1932). Artiukhina joined in official calls for approaching women 'in new ways' and suggested that delegates' meetings should now devote themselves to fulfilling economic plans and fighting the kulaks, or rich peasants, who opposed collectivisation. With class war raging against the kulaks in the countryside and against 'wreckers' of the plan in towns, work among women was devalued since it was not central to the regime's productionist priorities.

Artiukhina's writings, however, differed from official statements in one important respect. She noted that men (both outside and inside the party) still considered women inferior and unfit for education and work. She observed:

> Recently, and with increasing frequency, *delegatki* have been putting this forward: before eliminating their backwardness, before beginning to draw women into work, it is necessary to conduct work among men who do not understand this and who consider women creatures of a lower order. (Artiukhina, 1930a, p.31)

Artiukhina added that:

> It happens that not only non-party men, but communists of low consciousness, look upon women as supplements to themselves and consider that to teach women or to involve them in socialist construction – what for? We must fight against this. We must educate male communists. (Artiukhina, 1930a, p. 31)

'Backward men' needed their consciousness raised. Artiukhina recommended that party meetings discuss the problem of men who refused to listen and men who abandoned, with disapproval, their politically active wives (Artiukhina, 1930a, p. 31). Her plea fell on deaf ears. It is a revealing one, however, since it suggests that although Artiukhina voiced the line that the *Zhenotdel* should disband, she saw immense scope for continued work around the 'woman question', as her earlier writings also indicated. She probably disagreed with party policy on women, but like so many did not dare speak out against it. By 1930 it was no longer safe to disagree with the party line.

The dissolution of the *Zhenotdel* in 1930 was indeed premature. It had started a great deal of painstaking work among women, but contrary to political statements of 1930, the task of liberating them was far from complete. The radical restructuring of the private sphere advocated by Armand, Kollontai and Trotsky had not even begun. The official line that the *Zhenotdel* could be abolished because large numbers of women had been liberated was somewhat hollow. More recent Soviet sources admit the error. As one puts it, 'unfortunately, all these organs were liquidated before they had fulfilled their extremely complicated, exceptional and specific tasks' (Sozaeva, 1973, p. 53).

At best, the closure of the *Zhenotdel* removed an uneasy tension from official ideology. No longer was it necessary to juxtapose the statement that the interests of working women and men were identical with the qualification that special institutions for women were necessary because women were different from men. Even though the formula of 'special but not separate' had justified the existence of women's organisations, it had not curbed fears of bourgeois feminism, nor deterred attacks on work among women. 'Special' had always been suspect.

Notes

1. Elizabeth Waters makes the additional point that after the civil war canteens were not seen as a replacement for private kitchens, but as complements to them. The legislation of private trading in 1921 revived markets and foodstores at a time when the number of canteens was being cut (Waters, 1988).
2. In a letter to Vera Zasulich written in 1881, Marx qualified his general argument that revolution would happen in capitalist systems by admitting the revolutionary potential of the village commune. He commented that 'this community is the fulcrum of Russia's social revival' (Marx, 1975b, p. 320).
3. The most detailed discussion of the *Zhenotdel's* changing priorities and the problems it faced is Carol Eubanks Hayden's PhD dissertation on 'Feminism and Bolshevism: the *Zhenotdel* and the Politics of Women's Emancipation in Russia, 1917–1930' (Hayden, 1979).
4. It also has its roots in policies of the Comintern (Waters, 1988).
5. Soviet political institutions are hierarchically organised, with each level subordinate to the one above. The *guberniia*, or provinces, were divided into *uezdy*, or districts, which were subordinate to them (Pipes, 1974b, p. 5).
6. The ending 'y' is a plural form, similar to 's' in English.
7. The Workers' Opposition was a group which emerged from within the party. It was critical of the new regime for concentrating decision-making power firmly

within the party. It called for greater workers' control and a more active role for trade unions in industry.

8. The *Orgburo*, or Organisational Bureau, was set up in 1919 'to direct all the organizational work of the Party'. It was composed of five members of the Central Committee. The *Secretariat*, formed at the same time, had no clearly defined powers; these evolved in practice. It was decided that in order to achieve coordination of the *Politburo* and *Orgburo*, the Secretary would have a seat on both (Fainsod, 1963, pp. 178–9).

9. 'Low politics' is a concept applied by Seweryn Bialer. It refers to 'the decisions that directly touch the citizen's daily life, the communal matters, and the conditions of the workplace'. Low politics contrasts with 'high politics' which involve 'the principal political issues of society, the abstract ideas and language of politics, the decisions and actions of the societal leadership' (Bialer, 1980, p. 166).

10. The point could be made that given high levels of illiteracy, reading a woman's magazine indicated effort and a degree of political interest.

11. Hayden interprets the attack on feminism within party circles as a reaction to Golubeva and Kollontai. Golubeva had written in *Pravda* that unemployed women were not being reached by women's organisations and that 'special societies' should be set up dedicated to 'full economic, legal and day-to-day emancipation of women'. She argued in favour of the communalisation of daily life. Kollontai, challenged by Klara Zetkin, called for a harnessing of feminist tendencies and suggested that feminism was progressive in a workers' republic. The ideas of Golubeva and Kollontai were condemned at the 12th party Congress in 1923 (Hayden, 1979, pp. 222–30).

12. *Nomenklatura* refers to a list of names matched to specific jobs. Appointments to responsible positions in the USSR are generally decided in advance by party committees. They draw up lists of potential candidates for particular sorts of job. Further details are provided by Bohdan Harasymiw in '*Nomenklatura*: the Soviet Communist Party's Leadership Recruitment System' (Harasymiw, 1969, pp. 493–512).

13. A *subbotnik* is a day of organised and unpaid labour in which groups of citizens work together on particular projects useful to the state. Projects range from planting flowers in public places, to picking up litter or helping to gather in the harvest.

14. There was famine in the Volga region in 1921–1922 (Dobb, 1978, p. 151).

15. Delegates' meetings were used by the party to mobilise women, to involve them in the new political system, and to impart information to the local community about general political questions. Study of organisations such as these enables one to see how the mould of subsequent 'low politics' was formed. Mobilisation 'from above' in the 1970s and 1980s, notwithstanding differences between the Brezhnev and Gorbachev eras, has its roots in the late 1920s (Friedgut, 1979; Bialer, 1980).

16. '*Gorianki*' translates literally as 'hill women'. Dagestan is a highly mountainous republic and those from remote places were hard to draw into political activity.

17. In 1927, even in the best local parties, only 8–10 per cent of all delegates were recruited to the party. Figures for 1928–1929 show that only 2.2 per cent of rural *delegatki* became party members (Hayden, 1979, p. 286; 324).

18. It was arued that although under capitalism women were oppressed, they nevertheless lived in conditions which offered a greater immediate potential for liberation than the pre-capitalist economic formations of some Soviet republics. Central Asia was viewed as more backward than parts of the Caucasus since it lacked the oil industry of Azerbaidzhan. However, small pockets of capitalism did not stop the mullahs in Baku from subjecting the population to the reactionary beliefs of Islam (Chirkov, 1978, p. 46).

19. Central Committee resolutions listed the general tasks of clubs. These lists were compiled from the actual experience of the clubs and did not constitute fresh redefinitions of their brief.

20. The resolution stressed that it was necessary to organise workshops and handicrafts, as well as professional technical schools. This had to be done through the involvement of *Glavprofobr* (*Glavnoe upravlenie professional 'nogo obrazovaniia Narkomprosa RSFSR*), an administrative organ of professional education within *Narkompros* (*Narodnyi Kommissariat prosveshcheniia*), the People's Commissariat of Enlightenment.

21. One report of the period written by an activist in a *uezd* club in Azerbaidzhan noted that 'our relationship with other organisations is very good, with the exception of *Narkompros*, which helps us very little' (*Otdel Rabotnits i Krest'ianok*, 1927, p. 29). There was probably good reason for specifically mentioning *Narkompros* in the Central Committee resolution discussed above in Note 20. Points made in resolutions are frequently reactions to inadequacies in the implementation of policy rather than neutral statements of general goals. Therefore the naming of a particular organisation may be an indication that it has in some respects failed to do what is expected of it. In a subsequent Central Committee resolution of 1929, *Narkompros* was called upon to step up its work in setting up women's schools and liquidation of illiteracy centres for women (*Institut Marksizma–Leninizma*, 1984, vol. 4, pp. 515).

22. Dzheiran Bairamova was born in 1896, became a communist in 1919, and was appointed Head of the Azerbaidzhan *Zhenotdel* (Mamedov, 1973, p. 50).

23. The Club was given an expropriated palace which is today used for wedding ceremonies.

24. The play ends on a note of heavy socialist realism with Sevil' leaving her husband for the factory. As she departs she cries 'the road to freedom for women is only through socialism' (Dzhabarly, 1979, p. 70).

25. One report from the town of Nukhi in Azerbaidzhan suggests that women first discussed the significance of the cultural revolution for themselves and then concluded that the chadra 'stands as an obstacle in our path'. Seventeen of them then took it off (Musaeva, 1964, p. 42).

26. Elizabeth Waters of the History department at Australian National University has commented that conferences were particularly common in the period of war communism. Archival material suggests that meetings persisted right through the 1920s, usually organised in the workplace.

27. The second drive to liquidate the *Zhenotdel* began at the 15th party Congress in 1927. The *Zhenotdel* was criticised for duplicating the work of other departments and for being an institution which did not receive sufficient guidance from the party apparatus. Its critics did not turn the latter charge against the party as seems appropriate, but cited it as a reason for closing the *Zhenotdel*. A commission for rationalisation was set up and some *zhenotdely* were closed down (Hayden, 1979, p. 351).

28. 'Baba' is a derogatory term which emphasises 'un-young', even evil.

3 The Stalin Years: The Woman Question Is Solved

Whereas the years immediately after 1917 were characterised by upheaval, spontaneity and open debate, and were effectively a continuation of the earlier revolutionary situation, the 1930s and 1940s brought a stifling of discussion. By 1930 a clamp squeezed debates into rigid lines. Discussions about topics such as the appropriate path for socialist economic development or the meaning of artistic expression ceased; so did serious efforts to examine the relationship between women's liberation and socialism. There had been some tightening of party lines in the 1920s, particularly after 1924, but in the 1930s ideology was contained to a much greater extent and wedged in the narrow parameters permitted by the regime. Stalinism resulted in a termination of serious discussion of the woman question; at best, isolated critical remarks were made in obscure sources. Stalinism provided a series of hollow phrases about female roles that could be regurgitated whenever appropriate. Some lines on women were the exact opposite of what they had been in the 1920s.

In 1928 the *Zhenotdel* was described as having serious work ahead of it, whereas in 1930 this work was declared a sudden success and over. The 'long and thorny path' to women's liberation was shorter than Armand had anticipated. The woman question was now officially 'solved'. The backwardness of women, which had been emphasised in many political statements of the 1920s, now instantly disappeared. An active 'new woman', who could only be found in the USSR, now appeared:

> The Soviet system has ended exploitation for good and done away with women's lack of rights and their slavery. Woman of the Union of Soviet Socialist Republics – is a new woman, an active participant in the administration of the state and in the running of the economy and cultural

life. 'Such women have never existed and could not have existed before'
[Stalin]. (*Pravda*, 8 March 1937, p. 1)

Thanks to socialist revolution, new legislation and the *Zhenotdel*,
women were now officially liberated, and enjoyed equal opportunities
alongside men in the arts, in science, in the economy and in politics:

> The world-historical importance of the triumph of socialism filled
> women with enthusiasm and mobilised the women of our Soviet land to
> become involved in culture, to master machinery, to develop a know-
> ledge of science, and to be active in the struggle for high labour
> productivity. (*Pravda*, 8 March 1937, p. 1)

Special and distinct political efforts to mobilise women through
women's organisations were anachronistic. The active approach to
changing women's lives once advocated by the leaders of the
Zhenotdel was now defunct, with the exception of some activities in
Muslim areas. Consistent with the 'solved' status of the woman
question, the prominence of the arguments about liberation made by
Armand, Kollontai and Trotsky receded.[1] Women's liberation was no
longer declared essential to the success of socialism. The need to
restructure domestic settings before liberation was possible was not
mentioned either. These arguments were replaced by rosy, gushing,
simplistic and ritualistic slogans which amounted to empty glosses on
women's lives under socialism.

According to official ideology of the 1930s and 1940s, equality of
the sexes was guaranteed through the economic policies of industrialisation and collectivisation. Moreover, as a 'great army of labour' in
industry, agriculture and later in the Great Patriotic War, Soviet
women gave a practical demonstration of their liberation. This
liberation, according to the party line, was accompanied by a
strengthening of the family. Whereas legislation of the 1920s had
emphasised the importance of entering marriage freely and leaving it
without too many restrictions, the 1930s brought attempts to deter
divorce and promote stability in family life. Criticisms of the family
unit also ceased; it became an institution to be revered rather than
analysed. Similarly, childbirth was lavishly praised, a cult of
motherhood fostered and abortion made illegal. Socialism was
applauded for providing the conditions in which women could enjoy
the right to motherhood but not the right to abortion. Under socialism
abortion was unnecessary, unhealthy and rightly banned; under
capitalism abortion was frequently needed by oppressed women, but
wrongly denied.

Economic and political context

In the 1920s Stalin had strengthened his political position in the Soviet leadership and by the end of the decade he was able to redirect Soviet economic development.[2] The market relations of the New Economic Policy were brought to an end in 1928 and thereafter industry was planned 'from above'. Workers had to meet the output targets of centrally drawn up economic plans. Stalin's aim was to build socialism in one country by constructing the economic base that the USSR lacked and which, according to Marx, was a prerequisite of socialism. Priority was given to heavy over light industry.

While workers in the towns were exhorted to produce as much as possible as quickly as possible, peasants in the countryside were encouraged, urged and finally forced to pool their land, animals, buildings, tools and labour. In the early 1930s, land ownership was coercively collectivised in three waves. Resistance from the peasants was fierce and millions of animals were slaughtered by owners who did not wish to share them with other peasants. Kulaks or rich peasants were dispossessed of their land and deported to distant parts of the Union. Many 'middle' peasants were caught up in the confused implementation of 'de-kulakisation' and also packed off on what became known as the 'death trains'. Deportees suffered cold, starvation and death (Lewin, 1968; 1985, pp. 121–41). By 1936, 90 per cent of peasants were living on collective farms.[3]

During these upheavals 'enemies of the people' were said to be lurking in towns and villages. Those who opposed the direction of the changes, as well as thousands of loyal supporters of Stalin, were arrested and interned in labour camps during the crusade against 'left-wing deviationism' and 'right-wing deviationism'. Campaigns against 'enemies of the people' also brought massive purges of party members on fabricated charges, some resulting in orchestrated show trials. Gradually all vocal opposition was eliminated and there was no criticism and debate. Stalin became the great leader beyond criticism – an elevated position in which he was glorified and deified. The most appropriate characterisation of the USSR as 'totalitarian' applies to Stalin's period at the helm (Friedrich and Brzezinski, 1965; Arendt, 1958).

'Stalinism' has been variously construed in the West and there are different interpretations of its character and consequences. Some see its roots firmly in the 1920s and interpret it as an inevitable continuity with Bolshevism; others consider it quite distinct from the 1920s and a qualitatively different phenomenon that could have been averted (Trotsky, 1972; Ellenstein, 1976; Cohen, 1977; Tucker, 1977). There were certainly political features common to the 1920s and 1930s, such as one-party rule, purges and a secret police. However, the party was more authoritarian in the 1930s, the purges more extensive and bloody, the secret police more vigilant, and fear more widespread. Whereas party congresses had been frequent in the 1920s, often one a year in the first half of the decade, there was a 13 year break between the 18th Congress in 1939 and the 19th in 1952 (McAuley, 1977, pp. 116–48; Hough and Fainsod, 1982, pp. 147–91; McCauley, 1983, pp. 42–4). The Central Committee often acted as a rubber stamp for *Politburo* decisions, dictated by Stalin or reached at late night dinner parties in Stalin's dacha.[4] Open debate within the party became less frequent as more political power was concentrated in Stalin's hands. Although there were changes in the years from 1928 to 1953, and different phases of 'Stalinism', certain features of this period made it distinct from the 1920s (Cohen, 1977; Bialer, 1980). Economic changes after 1928 also brought massive upheavals and a reorganisation of industry and of agriculture which led to changes in social structure.

The derivative nature of equality of the sexes

During the years of forced industrialisation, collectivisation and purges, assertions were made about female roles that were removed from reality. On International Women's Day the press regularly proclaimed that in the USSR women not only enjoyed legal equality on paper, but equal rights in practice (*Izvestiia*, 8 March 1933, p. 3). The theoretical arguments of the 1920s about domestic labour, motherhood, marriage and sexuality were smothered. In their place came sweeping assertions which linked equality of the sexes to the heroic events of the October Revolution, the collectivisation of agriculture and the construction of a socialist economy. Equality of the sexes came about, according to the official ideology, as a result of more fundamental changes happening elsewhere in society. It was not a goal which required an autonomous strategy, specific analysis or particular policies aimed at its achievement. The complexities of the woman question were denied and the hurdles in front of women's liberation banished from ideology.

The dominant argument in popular and academic literature of the 1930s and 1940s was that the revolution had guaranteed emancipation and equality. The general theme of the Stalin years was that 'one of the outstanding achievements of the Great October Socialist Revolution is the complete liberation of women' (*Izvestiia*, 8 March 1949). The message was that from the first day of Soviet power woman 'stood shoulder to shoulder with her husband, father and brother in the struggle for a new enlightened life' (*Pravda*, 8 March 1936). Women's liberation was now narrowly conceived as part of the class struggle. Since the triumph of socialism meant that the class struggle had been resolved, it followed that the liberation of working women was assured.

Women activists of the 1920s had shared some of these beliefs. The difference, however, was that although they considered that socialism promised emancipation and self-determination for women, these were not instantly, definitively, or automatically achieved. Armand and Kollontai had therefore concluded that liberation had to be promoted through women's organisations. Attaining equality of the sexes required an investment of time and painstaking effort because it was a multi-faceted task needing structural changes at home, in the workplace and in politics, accompanied by a radical transformation of attitudes. By the late 1920s these transformations had clearly not taken place.

This fact was played down in official ideology. Indeed, because the woman question was officially 'solved', there was no longer a need to discuss the problems of women's lives; they became non-topics. In this context, articles and books about the woman question became rare. 'Work among women' was no longer a regular item on the agenda at party congresses, as it had been in the past. Similarly, resolutions of the Central Committee infrequently mentioned women. There were exceptions to this pattern in Muslim republics, whose Central Committees in the early 1930s continued to devote some time to the position of women in society, but this attention was short-lived (Kuznetsova, 1979). The topic of how best to liberate women was removed from political agendas. Persisting sexual inequalities were not issues of even moderate political salience. Analytic treatment of the woman question was frozen for over 20 years.

The Stalin years were characterised by hollow assertions about the triumph of equality of the sexes and by strident praises for the glories of socialism which had delivered it. Propaganda focused on women's contribution to industrialisation and collectivisation in the 1930s and women's participation in the war effort from 1941 to 1945. The image of women that was projected was one of 'a great strength' for Soviet society and 'a great army of labour' or 'a colossal reserve of labour power'. Women were 'the pride of the Soviet people' (*Izvestiia*, 8 March 1931; *Pravda*, 8 March 1936; 11 March 1936; 8 March 1939). Their collective achievements were put under the ideological spotlight, and not the problems that they faced.

Women as a 'great army of labour'

During the first 12 years of industrialisation, the number of women workers jumped more than fourfold from nearly three million in 1928 to over thirteen million in 1940. During the war years this figure climbed to just under sixteen million, as women replaced men called to the front. By 1945 women comprised 56 per cent of the work-force (TsSu SSSR, 1975a, p. 27; Lapidus, 1978, p. 166). This influx of women into the labour force gave apparent support to the argument that the role of women in the economy, coupled with early Soviet legislation affecting women, demonstrated that equality existed. The demand for labour generated by the Five Year Plans also meant that female unemployment characteristic of NEP was now over. Economic construction needed female labour.

Throughout the first decade of industrialisation women were praised for their active and heroic role in the labour force, rather than for pursuing their own self-determination. This emphasis persisted into the 1940s and early 1950s and continued, less stridently, throughout the 1960s, 1970s and into the 1980s. In the 1930s it was regularly noted, with approval, that 'the number of working women in different branches of industry and transport has greatly increased. The role of women on state farms and collective farms has grown immensely' (Rogov, 1936, p. 17). Towards the end of the 1930s and throughout the 1940s the language became more excitable:

> Millions of women's hands are helping to reconstruct and build anew enterprises, collective farms, state farms, machine tractor stations, railways, and cultural organisations. Working women and peasant women

are striving for new production achievements in the struggle to accelerate the pace of socialist construction and to increase labour productivity in the new ascent of industry and agriculture. (Aralovets, 1947, pp. 4–5)

It was common to congratulate women for entering 'the front line of fighters for the realisation of the great tasks of the new Stalinist five year plan', thereby 'showing themselves to be outstanding examples of self-sacrificing labour' and exhibiting 'a deep understanding of their duty to the state' (Aralovets, 1947, p. 4). According to official ideology, awareness of this duty led women to strive not simply to meet the targets of the economic plans, but to exceed them. Indeed, the press regularly called upon women to work 'much harder' in order to do just this (*Pravda*, 8 March 1941).

Consistent with the official emphasis on production, women workers were exhorted to become *stakhanovki*, or shock workers. This involved overfulfilling output norms and thereby increasing economic productivity. *Stakhanovki* were regularly discussed in women's magazines and individual cases picked out for praise. Beneath their happy photographs, female shock workers described how they had increased their output. *Stakhanovka* Petrova, for example, who worked in a textile factory told readers how:

> I was given a machine. At first I studied how to use it, then they gave me two. Next I transferred to three. On stakhanovite days I moved to work on four, then six ... Our group overfulfilled the plan all the time and moved to six machines, but there are backward groups in our factory. We stakhanovites help them. Our task is to pull the backward workers up to the level of advanced ones. (*Rabotnitsa i Krest'ianka*, no. 16, 1936, p. 8)

Women's participation in the labour force was increasingly discussed in terms of its contribution to output norms rather than its relevance to liberation and self-determination. This was especially the case in 1936 which was declared Stakhanovite Year.

Pictures and illustrations in Soviet books, magazines and newspapers showed smiling women confidently driving tractors and working in factories (*Izvestiia*, 8 March 1930). The front covers of women's magazines such as *Delegatka* which, in the 1920s had frequently been devoted to the political mobilisation of women, now showed enthusiastic women happily gathering the harvest at tremendous speed and performing stakhanovite tasks in the cabbage fields (*Delegatka*, no. 19, June 1931; no. 29, October 1931). Socialist realism was the canon according to which Soviet artists had to work and effectively dictated that life had to be portrayed not as it actually was, but rather as it should be, or was becoming: socialist realism entered visual images of women's roles. Myth became suggested reality, whilst aspects of reality were ignored.

Very positive images of women workers were projected which implied that women had a constructive role to play in social production and that their lives should not be restricted to the domestic sphere. Even if economic goals were fundamental, women's liberation may have been indirectly promoted. But women were mainly portrayed as an economic resource rather than a category of human beings striving for personal fulfilment through creative work and financial independence. There was no accompanying discussion of the agonies and joys of liberation or how to cope with resistance and hostility to new roles for women. These were 'ideological silences'.

Moreover, not all women were encouraged to participate in social production, as might have been expected. The wives of stakhanovite men were a glaring exception to the general mobilisation of women into the economy. These wives were praised for their indirect contribution to economic growth by attentively looking after their husbands. They were congratulated for supporting the admirable efforts of others, but were not especially encouraged to enter the work-force themselves. In pre-Stalinist conditions, Armand and Kollontai had suggested that women should be free to develop their potential as individuals in their own right rather than be subordinate to others. Bebel, Engels and Lenin had similarly believed that participation in social production rather than confinement in the home and economic dependence on another was a necessary aspect of women's liberation. The success of the stakhanovite movement, however, took precedence over the liberation of all women so long as some of these women were able to inspire their husbands to assume stakhanovite status and keep it.

Wives of stakhanovites

Even women who did not work outside the home had a duty to the stakhanovite movement. Although they could not become stakhanovites themselves, they were encouraged to put pressure on their husbands to aspire to this status. If husbands exceeded production targets, wives were told by the party to offer the men every necessary support so that they remained stakhanovites. A conference of the wives of shock workers held in 1936 was convened for precisely this purpose.

In the opening speech the Secretary of the Krai party committee informed the wives that 'Everyone wants to be, and can be, a stakhanovite. The task is to help everyone become one' (*Zhenshchina – bol'shaia sila*, 1936, p. 9). The conference then proceeded with selected wives telling their husbands' stories. The wife of an engineer, for example, talked about her husband's work history, described how he had become a shock worker and then suggested that 'everyday we women must show an interest in how our husbands' work is going'. She stressed that their duty was to know whether their husbands were in the forefront of the stakhanovite movement and to work out 'how to help the shock workers to increase productivity and improve the quality of work' (*Zhenshchina – bol'shaia sila*, 1936, p. 11). Often helping stakhanovite husbands meant reinforcing traditional gender roles in the home. A fitter's wife proudly announced:

> I help my husband in every possible way. I try to be cheerful and do not make him worry about taking care of the home. I assume most of the chores myself. At the same time I try to help my husband by advising him. Everything that I know I pass on to him. I look for the necessary literature for him so that the time he would have spent searching for it, he can spend studying it. (*Zhenshchina – bol'shaia sila*, 1936, p. 14)

Women glorified their roles as traditional wives who made sacrifices for their husbands and effectively lived through them. A reciprocity of support between two independent and affectionate individuals was not arugued for, but a one-way support. This was far removed from Kollontai's calls of the 1920s for women to rid themselves of the restrictions of domestic labour and pursue their own self-development through study and work in social production. It did not contribute to the revolutionary transformation of male–female relations, which Armand, Kollontai and Trotsky had advocated.

The duty of wives of stakhanovites extended beyond their own husbands to men who were not shock workers. These wives approached the wives of other workers and encouraged them to put pressure on their husbands to become stakhanovites. According to one wife: 'We went from flat to flat to the wives of non-stakhanovites, chatted to them and asked what hindered them and what they were not happy with.' She described how the stakhanovites' wives had formed a 'red circle' in their husbands' factory and invited other wives along:

> At the meetings we explained who works well and who badly. Listening to this and not seeing her husband among the best workers, a wife begins to ask him and her neighbours why this is so. Having learned the reasons, she begins to work on her husband. It is necessary that wives come to know the factory, otherwise husbands will explain away their bad work by saying that the bosses suppress initiative. (*Zhenshchina – bol'shaia sila*, 1936, p. 19)

Behaviour in the labour force was everyone's concern, even those outside it; shock workers' wives had an active role to play in boosting economic productivity. This was seen as a laudable pursuit in its own right, and what every politically conscious wife should be doing. This theme in Soviet propaganda in the 1930s was not entirely consistent with the frequently reiterated line that men and women were building socialism side-by-side, performing similar tasks and enjoying equal opportunities.

Equal opportunities for men and women, side-by-side

In the 1920s the dominant themes in official ideology underscored the backwardness of women, whereas writings of the 1930s and 1940s tended to bracket women and men together, emphasising the similar position of the sexes rather than differences between them. A frequent assertion of the 1930s was that opportunities were wide open for women and men alike. Stalin's remarks at the 18th party Congress were a typical whitewash of the period. He proclaimed that 'in every branch of the economy, culture, science and the arts – everywhere stands emancipated woman alongside man, equal with him, performing great tasks, moving socialism forward. Woman in our country has become a great might' (*Pravda*, 8 March 1939). Such comments obscured the concentration of female labour in low-paid light industry and the persistence of the popular belief that some jobs were appropriate for men and others for women. Invariably, women were not standing alongside male workers, but were in different branches of industry and in posts subordinate to men. Although women enjoyed some upward mobility during the war years, they subsequently returned to men the high status jobs they had taken over from them while they were absent at the front. Sexual divisions in the Soviet labour force have already been well documented (Dodge, 1966; Sacks, 1976; Lapidus, 1978; Swafford, 1978; McAuley, 1981). Official ideology of the 1930s and 1940s did not dwell on these. A socialist realist rhetoric displaced accounts of the reality of inequalities in Soviet life.

Equality through collectivisation

The ideological treatment of the position of women in the countryside, following a pattern similar to that of women in industry, stressed that the collectivisation of agriculture brought equality to rural areas. Stalin encapsulated the official line in the formula 'Without collective farms – inequality. With collective farms – equal rights' (*Izvestiia*, 8 March 1933). Stalin also declared that 'only *kolkhoz* life can obliterate inequality and put women on their feet' (*Krest'ianka*, 1936, no. 1). The argument was that, without full-scale collectivisation, fundamental changes in the position of rural female labour were not possible. Collectivisation would provide the conditions 'for the annihilation of inequality' between the sexes (Kazakov, 1931, pp. 3–4).

Although inequality was more readily acknowledged to exist in the countryside than in towns, collectivisation and mechanisation were presented as the remedy. The key to ending female subjugation was to draw as many women as possible into collective farms, to use their labour systematically all year round rather than in concentrated bursts according to season, and to encourage them to raise the level of their skills and use machinery. These changes would result in an increase in female wages and the participation of women in the administration of farms. Women would then be among leaders in the countryside, as well as in the ranks of the led (Kazakov, 1931, pp. 4–10). These thoughts coincided with, and also echoed, a Central Committee resolution of 1931 'Concerning work among *kolkhoz* women' in which it was regretted that progress in mobilising women into farm work had been 'unsatisfactory' and that the level of women's participation in collectivisation was low (*Institut Marksizma–Leninizma*, 1984, vol. 5, pp. 273–5). The central task was therefore to encourage more women to be active in farm work.

There was an ideological emphasis that collectivisation brought wide opportunities for women and that 'woman has now understood that only *kolkhoz* life opens for her a wide road to new things, to full

liberation (*k polnomy raskreposhcheniiu*) from the old oppressed life
of need (Frolov, 1934, p. 17). Moreover, collective labour allegedly
changed attitudes and instilled 'respect for women' (Nukhrat, 1935,
p. 31). Effectively, the woman question in rural areas was entirely
subsumed under the topic of collectivisation. The latter was simply
the guardian of the former and no additional efforts were deemed
necessary to promote liberation. Nadezhda Krupskaia adhered to this
line, maintaining that 'our female *kolkhozniki* feel that they already
stand in earnest before the factual equality of which Il'ich spoke,
which would not be thinkable in any capitalist country'. What this
meant was that what stood in front of rural women was not the
woman question at all, but 'all questions of *kolkhoz* development'
(*Izvestiia*, 8 March 1933). Woman's duty to the state, and to
themselves, was to make collectivisation a success.

Women were encouraged to become stakhanovites in agriculture as
well as in industry. On International Women's Day in 1937 *Pravda*
announced:

> The development of the stakhanovite movement pushed into the
> forefront new heroines in all branches of industry. After the champion
> beet growers, came beet growers who doubled their speed. New heroines
> of the cotton fields and heroine flax growers appeared. And there was a
> remarkable competition of women tractor drivers. (*Pravda*, 8 March
> 1937, p. 1)

Magazines, newspapers, books and pamphlets listed the achievements of female shock workers on farms and published their thoughts
about work. For example, brigade leader Varfolomeva told readers
that driving a tractor was a great social responsibility and that 'I love
the machine very much and try to instil this love for it in the tractor
drivers in my brigade' (*Rabotnitsa i Krest'ianka*, no. 15, 1936, p.
17). Other articles stressed the duty to the collective to reach new
output records. For instance, E. N. Lebedeva was singled out in the
Stalin district of Moscow *oblast* for setting the world record for
harvesting cabbages (Karaseva, 1946, p. 24). It was not uncommon
for editors to send special greetings to stakhanovites on the first pages
of magazines, thereby keeping them in the limelight.[5] One went as
follows:

> We warmly greet the women shock workers of the fields of the Western
> *oblast*. You, the best of the best, an example of the selfless struggle for a
> bumper harvest, a high quality flax and an upgrading of cattle breeding,
> attract thousands of new women collective farmers to the path of

socialist competition and shock work. (Uritskii, 1934; *Krest'ianka v Zapadnoi oblasti*, June 1934, inside cover)

Women's duty to production was uppermost. Increased productivity brought job promotion and guaranteed equality of the sexes. The same editor boldly declared that by 'holding leadership posts on collective farms, you prove correct the words of our great leader Comrade Stalin that women on the farms are a great strength' (Uritskii, 1934). His rhetoric here, however, was tantamount to fiction.

Rural cultural attitudes towards women could not be changed overnight and collectivisation did not propel women into leadership posts. One source indicates that the small number of rural women among leading cadres actually fell in 1930 and 1931 (Nikul'kova, 1932, p. 16). This was hardly a promising start for equality under collectivisation. In one rural district where there were no women among its leaders, it was alleged that men generally kept women out of positions of responsibility by saying 'it is impossible to put her forward, she has children' (Nikul'kova, 1932, p. 16). Female entry rates to the party also fell below expected targets (Nikul'kova, 1932, p. 47). Likewise, their participation in rural soviets was in some districts as low as 4 per cent. This was put down to women's lack of confidence, the exclusionary behaviour of *kulak* class enemies, the male belief that women were only good for cooking and childbirth, and women's lack of time due to a heavy domestic burden (Polianskaia, 1933, pp. 6–9).

Evidence suggests that there was a lack of concern in the countryside for women's liberation amongst party members and representatives in the soviets. One critic argued that work among women was 'quite insufficient' (Nikul'kova, 1932, pp. 30–1). Another charged that 'there is a lack of understanding of the great significance of work among women in several rural soviets and district organisations' (Polianskaia, 1933, p. 30). These voices, however, were tiny manifestations of dissent in a sea of praise for collectivisation and exuberance about what it promised. They went against the dominant ideological grain, according to which the successes of economic and political changes far outweighed their shortcomings.

Women in the Great Patriotic War

The active role of Soviet women during the Great Patriotic War from 1941 to 1945, was also attributed to the prior successes of industrialisation and collectivisation in guaranteeing equality of the sexes. Ideological treatments of women's role in war emphasised, not surprisingly, duty to the state against the enemy. The image of women was one of 'patriots at the front' who fought fascism, nursed the wounded and rejoiced at the triumphs of the Red Army over the enemy (*Pravda*, 8 March 1943, 8 March 1944, 8 March 1945). As in ideological lines on industrialisation and collectivisation, women were coupled with men in their achievements as, for example, in statements such as: 'Soviet woman has proved that she has passed the examination with honour. At the front and in the hinterland, side by side with men, and shoulder to shoulder, equal with them, she helps to forge victory over the enemy' (*Pravda*, 8 March 1942).

Women played a vital role in the war. They assumed responsible positions on the farms in place of absent men, went down mines, provided labour resources for the factories, joined the services, and even commanded male troops (Stishova, 1986). In June 1941 the Presidium of the Supreme Soviet issued a resolution concerning the mobilisation of women and girls into war work and in 1942 the Komsomol directed 8,476 girls into the Red Army and Soviet navy. By December there were three women's battalions. Over 26,000 women also joined the partisans, who were particularly active in Belorussia, conducting dangerous scout work. One source suggests that one-quarter of the partisans were women (Murmantseva, 1979, pp. 126–232).

In keeping with this change in women's work roles, it was announced that 'There are no longer so-called "male" professions. Soviet women have shown that no profession is beyond them' (Karaseva, 1946, p. 6). There was now a more serious ideological challenge to the distinction between 'men's work' and 'women's work' for the highly practical reason that war conditions demanded that women assume jobs traditionally held by men. The attack on the division of occupation according to gender was, therefore, perhaps not particularly surprising. During the war years it was suggested that Soviet superwomen could achieve anything. The proud line became 'Soviet women gave all their strength to the motherland. They endured so many arduous ordeals that no difficulties arising on the path to building peace could frighten them' (Karaseva, 1946, p. 61). All this was only possible 'thanks to the party of Lenin and Stalin' (Karaseva, 1946, p. 40).

Kalinin alleged that the behaviour of women during the war as active and dedicated patriots was explained by the existence of equality:[6]

> Equal rights for women have existed in our country from the first days of the October Revolution. But you have gained the equal rights of women in yet another sphere – in the spontaneous defence of their motherland – with weapons in their hands. You have won the equality of women in a field which up to now they had still not directly entered. (Aralovets, 1947, p. 27)

According to Soviet ideology, revolution, industrialisation and collectivisation had guaranteed women's rights and the role of women during the war was yet another expression of them in practice. Moreover, it was Stalin who was responsible for pursuing the policies that ensured equality. Ideological proclamations contained statements such as:

> The genius of Stalin leads us forward to new strengths of a growing economy and culture, to an unprecedented blossoming in our country, to the full creativity of communism.
>
> Women, together with all the Soviet people, praise our great leader, the creator of our victory, the instigator of our happiness – our own Stalin. (Aralovets, 1947, p. 64)

Writings on women became caught up in Stalin's cult of personality. He was a leader increasingly revered and lauded by women since he was allegedly a champion of their rights and responsible for all positive social changes. But there was nevertheless a revival after the war of the idea that femininity led women to perform 'women's jobs' and masculinity fitted men for some tasks not easily met by women. This argument conveniently matched the re-entry of men into leadership posts and the exit of women from them (Millar, 1971).

Soviet women thank Stalin

The ideological positions on equality at a time of Stalin's cult of personality gave rise to a 'Thank you Stalin' literature. Articles in women's magazines of the 1940s and 1950s were indeed entitled

'Thank you great Stalin'. These often consisted of short biographies of women which illustrated how Stalin's policies had transformed illiterate citizens into purposeful workers with skills and bright futures. A typical paragraph was:

> It now seems to me that my earlier life was some sort of nightmare. Soviet power and the party of Lenin and Stalin gave women economic independence, having raised her dignity to inaccessible heights. Woman is now an equal member of socialist society. You especially feel this when you read the draft of the new constitution, written by our own Stalin. I experience such a feeling of joy when I read these lines. (*Rabotnitsa i Krest'ianka*, no. 14, 1936, p. 14)

This extract refers to the 1936 Constitution which on paper offered Soviet citizens rights and freedoms which the political reality of the 1930s did not remotely allow.

The 'Thank you Stalin' literature contained joyous outbursts to the effect that 'It is wonderful to be alive now.' A letter written by a woman to the newspaper *Kazakhstanskaia Pravda* in 1935 declared 'My happiness is due to the fact that I was born during the years of Great October. Otherwise my life would not have been as beautiful or as happy as it is now' (Astapovich, 1971, p. 258). Such statements were made, it should be remembered, in the context of the terror and bloody purges. Claims of excessive happiness were unhinged from reality, just as were remarks about the progressiveness of the new Constitution. Yet at the same time these heroic glosses on life were very much a part of Soviet political reality because the 'Thank you Stalin' literature played a vital role in propaganda. The theme of the liberation of women was harnessed to the cause of Stalin's personality cult and helped to further the cult.

Forced into a position of thanking Stalin for their liberation, Soviet women could not ask the state to help promote that very same liberation. As equals of men, women were active contributers to the industrial, agricultural and defense priorities of the Soviet state. Since the woman question was solved, they could not draw attention to the officially non-existent difficulties of women's lives. They did not need to be educated and mobilised by women's organisations as they had been in the 1920s. Nevertheless the official line of the 1930s and 1940s was that work among women was still of great significance to the party. It was simply timely for its form and methods to change. The *Zhenotdel* was now criticised for the 'shortcoming' of having taken on all aspects of political work among women, thereby denying a spread of such work through all party departments

(Chirkov, 1978, p. 68). It was also taken to task for narrowly focusing on women's issues. Writings of the 1930s overlooked the *Zhenotdel*'s general brief to promote the domestic and foreign policies of the regime and to rally women to support them.

Party work among women: *Zhensektory*

After the *Zhenotdel* had closed, a *zhensektor*, or women's section, was set up under departments of agitation of party committees at republic, *krai, oblast*, town and district levels. *Zhensektory* were also formed in large enterprises. They were not established, however, in rural areas where a *zhenorganizator*, or women's organiser, was appointed to meet the same goals. The work of the *zhensektor* and *zhenorganizator* concentrated on general political tasks among women, rather than women's issues alone.

The aims of the *zhensektor* were formally defined by the party in 1931. The 'basic content' of the work was firstly 'to ensure the successful implementation of the five year plan for the socialist construction of industry' and secondly 'to build upon the successful achievements of the collectivisation of agriculture' (Chirkov, 1978, p. 69). Their brief extended to mobilising women in elections for the soviets and drawing them into political campaigns. Delegates' meetings and conferences were temporarily retained for these purposes, now under the direction of a *zhensektor*.

The women's sections were even more short-lived than the *Zhenotdel* had been. They were abolished in 1934 on the grounds that in urban industrial areas 'the basic tasks of this work were solved: the majority of women had been drawn into social production and their social backwardness had been overcome' (Chirkov, 1978, p. 71). In keeping with this, institutions such as delegates' meetings, the erstwhile 'schools of communism', now went out of political and ideological fashion. A commentary upon the miniscule number of women in leadership posts on collective farms hastened to point out that 'we are not considering some special work among women' and 'we are now critical of delegates' meetings, the old form of work among women'. Delegates' meetings, it was argued, reached only 'a narrow circle of women' which meant that they were ineffective (Frolov, 1934, p. 18). Moreover, they had sometimes deceived women by over-preoccupation with women's issues at the expense of general political questions. It was now alleged that delegates' meetings of the 1920s had unfortunately been composed of backward women rather than shock workers. These passive women were now attacked for having been unable to take an active part in socialist construction. Delegates' meetings of the 1920s, therefore, had not guaranteed that women would engage in political activity, join work collectives or achieve promotion. These criticisms completely overlooked the point that delegates' meetings after the revolution had targeted politically backward women because they needed help and the regime needed their support. The line of the 1930s was that women were most likely to advance in the workplace if they raised their 'political level', which could be best achieved by political education in the factory or on the farm. It was now argued that female shock workers who devotedly overfulfilled plans should study and win promotion. The task now was to push the most politically aware women further ahead (Frolov, 1934, pp. 17–19).

The position that women had now been liberated posed a stark problem for Muslim areas because it was blatantly obvious that this was not the case for the vast majority. Realities forced a qualification of ideology, without which a serious case of 'ideological dissonance' would have prevailed. It was admitted that the woman question had not been entirely solved in Muslim areas and that therefore the abolition of a special apparatus for work among women was premature. Thus in 1935 women's sections were set up in *oblasts* and *krais* and special instructors were retained in *raions* (Chirkov, 1978, p. 71). Delegates' meetings too continued to function.

But much of the work among Muslim women was geared to fulfilling economic plans rather than promoting women's liberation. From the perspective of the party, the two were now synonymous. One of the main aims of work among women in Uzbekistan, for instance, was to teach them how to raise their labour productivity. After 1934 production conferences of women workers were convened 'aimed at enhancing their activity in the drive to fulfil the plan, and to master production, technology [and] promote socialist attitudes to work' (Aminova, 1977, p. 148). The *zhensektor* then investigated whether or not output quotas were being met in particular factories. A woman's section in Uzbekistan is reported to have monitored production at the Margilan silk mill and concluded that the cultural level and political consciousness of workers had improved (Aminova, 1977, p. 149). The efforts of the *zhensektor* to draw women in production and to fulfil and overfulfil economic plans were complemented by similar activities organised by the Komsomol and trade unions.

The *zhensektor* also spent time encouraging women to join collective farms. In a speech delivered in 1933 to the All-Azerbaidzhan Congress of Young Women, the head of a *zhensektor* declared 'Only the building of collective farms brings peasant women factual liberation (*fakticheskoe raskreposhenie*). And so each female collective farmer must surely remember this' (Kuznetsova, 1979, p. 238). Liberation, according to the organisers of women's sections, came from meeting output quotas and living on collective farms. Of course, examples cited in Soviet literature vary across republics and districts, but their general emphasis is similar. In 1931 in Dagestan, for instance, the party called for an improvement of work among women and suggested that 'special women's collective farms' be set up with responsibility for market gardening, silk worms and poultry (El'darova, 1963, p. 31). Special brigades of older workers were also sent into more remote rural areas to encourage women to enter the labour force and to take courses in knitting and carpet-making.

Conferences were also held with the sole purpose of mobilising the mass of women 'for the fulfilment of the tasks of the five year plan' and helping 'to overcome remaining difficulties'. A conference of *gorianki* held in March 1932 was organised around the goal of plan fulfilment (Gasanova, 1963, pp. 74–5). Similarly, in Azerbaidzhan women were exhorted to participate in the harvesting so that targets could be met. On the initiative of a *zhensektor* in Sal'ianskii okrug, twelve women were sent into the countryside to conduct 'work among women'. This was a euphemism for persuading women to help harvest the cotton crop (Alieva, 1962, p. 91). The activities of delegates' meetings were also geared to the requirements of economic plans. According to one source, at harvest time they must become 'initiators in the struggle for a high cotton crop' and ensure a successful harvest campaign (Rizel', 1932, p. 30).

References to women's sections are rare and always brief in Soviet sources. Many books and articles which discuss the liberation of women in different Soviet republics skip over political work among women in the 1930s and 1940s altogether. At best, they give a summary of statistics which show an impressive increase in the number of women drawn into industry and collective farm life. The serious problems which Muslim women confronted in the 1930s and

1940s (ones which would have been hard for the *zhensektor* and other political institutions to obliterate) were not thoroughly discussed; the few sources that refer to them indicate that there was little interest in tackling them. For example, Babintsev and Turetskii pointed out that crimes against women in Azerbaidzhan in 1934 and 1935 were largely ignored. Murders of Muslim women who were trying to change their lifestyle were not adequately deterred. Muslim customs were hard to change and very large numbers of young girls were still being given away in early marriages (Babintsev and Turetskii, 1936, p. 54). Whilst these were known as realities of Muslim life, likely to continue for some time, they were nevertheless infrequently reported as a 'problem'.

Another difficulty in the more religious parts of the USSR, not confined to Muslim areas, was a reluctance to allow women to join the labour force. Such a 'disgraceful distortion of Soviet democracy' was put down to the failure of citizens to follow Soviet policy, rather than the fault of Soviet policy itself (*Izvestiia*, 8 March 1937). Where religion played a reactionary role and where class war continued, the battle for the liberation of women was described as one aspect of ongoing struggles. Only when the other issues of religion and class had been resolved, would the woman question be resolved. The implication of this ideological line was that the woman question lacked any aspects independent of other problems and also offered no independent input to other questions.

In keeping with this derivative view of women's liberation, and consistent with the assumption that problems in women's lives would automatically be sorted out as soon as other more fundamental problems of class and religion were resolved, attention was no longer paid to the detrimental effects of family life on women. In fact, the implications for oppression and emancipation of how the family was run was no longer directly addressed. Lenin, Armand, Kollontai and Trotsky had argued for an end to domestic labour for women and for some restructuring of traditional roles. Their arguments fell fallow in the 1930s. So did their belief in the importance of easy divorce and an end to the useless mire of divorce proceedings. The message of the 1920s that past restrictions over women should be lifted, now ceased. New restrictions on women and men were introduced. Although divorce had been made easy by laws of 1918 and 1926, disincentives were introduced in legislation of 1936. Abortion had been legalised in 1920, but it was banned in first pregnancies in 1935 and then outlawed altogether in 1936.

The family, divorce, abortion and motherhood

Social policy in the 1930s and 1940s was designed to promote stable nuclear families for several very practical reasons. As we saw in Chapter 1, quick and easy divorce had often worked to the detriment of women. Men frequently abused their duties as fathers, refused to pay alimony and deserted their *de facto* wives. Reproduction took place in a context of insecurity. Thus the state set out to champion domestic security and to wage 'a determined struggle against the criminal attitudes of fathers towards children' (Schlesinger, 1949, pp. 337–8). It was declared that legislation of the 1920s needed amendment 'with the aim of combating light-minded attitudes towards the family and family obligations' (Schlesinger, 1949, p. 278). Divorce was now made difficult and couples had to pay increasingly large amounts for the privilege of being granted one. In 1936 it was decreed that a first divorce would cost 50 roubles and a second one 150 roubles. All subsequent divorces were 300 roubles. Divorced fathers were obliged to pay one-quarter of their wages for the maintenance of one child, one-third for two children and one-half for three or more (Schlesinger, 1949, p. 278). Many women supported this renewed stress on family obligations. Some had suffered during the 1920s, or felt vulnerable; others were in favour of traditional family life and were suspicious about what women's liberation would bring.[7] Many peasants and workers of both sexes, whether party members or not, did not want to see an end to traditional family life. The notion that the family should wither away under socialism enjoyed little support in popular culture. Instead, it was a unit that most young people wanted to forge.

There were other practical reasons for bolstering the family in the 1930s. Massive changes in the running of industry and agriculture brought disruption in daily life and dislocation. Social structure was changing as peasants migrated into towns to swell the industrial labour force. New patterns of life, such as living in dormitories attached to factories and enduring the discipline of production, were difficult for many. Attempts were made to discipline this new workforce by introducing fines for lateness and absenteeism. Infringements of labour discipline were entered into workbooks, without which workers could not be hired. The emotional support provided by families at a time of rapid social change was welcome to many. The privacy of the family unit also offered a 'safe' intimate circle at a time of mass arrests and purges.[8] Terror unleashed by the secret police made the family a haven of protection and security, a retreat from the surrounding chaos.

Stable nuclear families were therefore highly desirable for the state and its citizens for reasons to do with social change, labour discipline, dislocation, the need for emotional support, reaction against the 'liberation' of the 1920s, birth rates and anxiety about war. Arguments about the nature of the family changed; Kollontai's earlier claim that the family was ceasing to be a necessity was condemned, as was her support of state childcare. Concerning the latter, one critic claimed 'This theory of Comrade Kollontai's is undoubtedly harmful, unwittingly vindicating those parents who do not wish to trouble about their children' (Schlesinger, 1949, p. 333). The party literature of the 1930s held that the family grew stronger as socialism progressed. Even those who had agreed with Kollontai in the 1920s subsequently recanted and maintained that 'Assertions that socialism leads to the extinction of the family are profoundly mistaken and harmful. They only help those exponents of the survivals of capitalism' (Schlesinger, 1949, p. 315).

The new socialist family, exhibiting a higher form of comradeship and cooperation than the 'bourgeois marriage trade' of capitalism, would grow ever stronger. This was thanks to the policies of the party of Lenin and Stalin. The hallmark of socialist families was mutual love and friendship (*Rabotnitsa*, no. 30, October 1936, p. 9). Ideology focused on some of the positive characteristics that Engels claimed had existed in proletarian marriages under capitalism, which he thought would develop further under socialism. However, his remarks about the importance of easy divorce and Lenin's view that contraception should be available for women were largely ignored. In a situation where contraceptives were not available, abortion had become a means of contraception. This was not discussed as a problem. It was rarely mentioned when abortion was outlawed in 1936.

The new decree prohibited abortion except 'when the continuation of pregnancy endangers life or threatens serious injury to the health of the pregnant woman and likewise when a serious disease of the parents may be inherited' (Schlesinger, 1949, pp. 270–1). Doctors performing illegal abortions were 'criminally punishable' with one to two years' imprisonment and those without medical training could receive 'not less than three years' imprisonment'. Women undergoing abortion could expect a 'social reprimand', followed by a fine of up to 300 roubles for subsequent offences (*Rabotnitsa*, no. 20–1, July 1936, p. 8).

Ideology was adapted to policy reversals on abortion, divorce and the family by a range of new arguments concocted in *ad hoc* fashion. It was suggested that only the unstable circumstances of 1920 had justified the provision of abortion facilities; 'economic backwardness' in the five years after the Civil War combined with 'the inadequate cultural level of women from the pre-revolutionary epoch' made it hard for women to make full use of the rights accorded to them by the Soviet state. Therefore it was hard at that time for women to perform their duties as citizens and mothers 'without fear of the future' (*Rabotnitsa*, no. 20–1, July 1936, p. 7). In such circumstances abortion was justified; but since these conditions no longer obtained, abortion was not necessary.

An argument characteristic of the 1930s was that the prohibition of abortion carried a very different meaning in different economic systems. Under capitalism, unemployment and exploitation made abortion a necessity since large families were unhappy families. The oppressive bourgeois state denied women the opportunity to abort but in the Soviet state, the situation was 'entirely different'. Abortion was being prohibited only now 'exceptional improvements in well-being' had taken place and 'the prosperity of the working population was increasing in every year, in every month' (Tettenborn, 1936, p. 7). With a growing provision of maternity homes, kindergartens and financial help, socialist mothers had no insecurities to fear, unlike their capitalist counterparts.

Another justification for making abortions illegal was the protection of health. Women's magazines of the 1930s carried articles by doctors who argued that abortions could lead to inflammations, haemorrhage, sterility, blood poisoning and death. One doctor pointed out that abortion was a 'serious operation', dangerous because the doctors operated 'without seeing those parts of the womb which were subject to surgical intervention' which could lead to a puncturing of the uterus. He contrasted ill-effects of abortion with the radiance of pregnancy and good health prompted by childbirth. New mothers 'often blossom anew, feel themselves to be stronger and more cheerful than before pregnancy' (*Rabotnitsa i Krest'ianka*, no. 14, 1936, p. 22). In a similar vein, working women wrote into magazines either telling of the horrors of abortions they had endured or recounting the joys of motherhood. Articles carried titles such as 'The tragedy of my life', 'Abortion brings illness', 'Let children live', 'Every woman must have a child'. 'To be a happy mother' and 'Motherhood – it is a special feeling, it is wonderful!' (*Rabotnitsa*, no. 17, July 1936, pp. 4–6; no. 20–1, July 1936, pp. 12–13; no. 18, July 1936, pp. 12–13).

The dangers of abortion had, of course, been recognised in the 1920s. Abortion had been a heated topic then too, with many opponents, but the political context was such that emancipation outweighed restrictions. By the 1930s, however, a woman's right to choose was entirely dismissed:

> The factors which in the capitalist countries drive women to abortion have here been abolished. Therefore, mass abortions resorted to for egoistic reasons are not to be tolerated. The Soviet state cannot countenance the fact that tens of thousands of women ruin their health and delay the growth of a new generation for socialist society. (Schlesinger, 1949, p. 310)

Motherhood was described as a social responsibility that should not be averted. Artiukhina claimed that the banning of abortion was a most responsible piece of legislation. Armand and Kollontai would have found it hard to agree with Artiukhina's conclusion that the law showed 'that women are receiving even more rights. Those rights which the Great proletarian revolution gave women are being strengthened in every way' (Artiukhina, 1936, p. 3). Such a right had just been abolished, and since this right was established by the revolution. Artiukhina's position lacked logic. She attempted to get around this problem by resorting to the capitalist–socialist distinction. Abortion under socialism was not a right at all. The superior right enjoyed by Soviet women was the right to maternity in good conditions. Other clauses in the new legislation, such as an increase in financial assistance to mothers and a pledge to increase the number of kindergartens all represented in Artiukhina's official view an extension of women's rights under socialism. Artiukhina added that banning abortion under capitalism was cruel since women had to rear children in conditions of great need and unemployment, unable to feed themselves and their children. Under the harsh conditions of capitalism oppressed women would benefit from the right to abortion. By contrast, under socialism where life was better and happier, such a right had no basis since women were not oppressed.

Women's magazines of the 1930s gave the false impression that everyone backed the legislation outlawing abortion. Articles described how women had discussed the draft law in the workplace, responding to it with great enthusiasm and unswerving support. Praise for it was often blended with adoration of Stalin. Workers in a Moscow textile factory, for example, proclaimed 'Two and a half thousand working women greeted this new Stalinist care for women with joy and unanimous approval'. They went on to condemn the harmful effects of abortions (*Rabotnitsa*, no. 16, July 1936, p. 5). A woman from a Moscow biscuit factory suggested that everyone should 'thank the government for their care and love' (*Rabotnitsa*, no. 17, July 1936, p. 4). Another praised the new law for protecting a wife from her husband's insistence that she abort. She wrote:

> I am the first to oppose abortions and those husbands who compel women to abort. Many husbands take advantage of their wife's illiteracy, driving her to have seven to ten abortions. Then they complain that she is ill, forgetting that they themselves instigated the abortion. I thank Soviet power again and our leader Comrade Stalin for caring for us women and our generation. (*Rabotnitsa*, No. 16, July 1926, p. 6)

Dissenting views were rarely printed, but some critics of the law pointed out that young mothers would face various difficulties if they could not terminate a pregnancy. Students, in particular, argued that it would be beneficial for them to delay motherhood, finish their studies and then bring up an offspring in more suitable accommodation than a student hostel. One complained 'if I become pregnant, I shall have to leave the Institute: one cannot live in hostel with children' (Schlesinger, 1949, p. 256). Others pointed out that the prohibition of abortions 'means the compulsory birth of a child to a woman who does not want children' and 'will confront young people with a dilemma: either complete sexual abstinence or the risk of jeopardising their studies and disrupting their lives' (Schlesinger, 1949, p. 257). Counter-arguments condemned women for being selfish and for expecting to put themselves first: with steadily increasing provision of kindergartens and flats, there was no sound basis for deferring motherhood. The state, with Stalin at the helm, had banned abortions out of its love for women's well-being. The state protected women and in return women had a duty to the state to procreate, just as they had a duty to join the labour force and live on collective farms. Abortion was not a private matter.

Supporters of the new legislation failed to mention that Soviet social services were not so plentiful that motherhood was a constant joy: life was hard. There was turmoil, insecurity and famine in the countryside, overcrowding in the towns and poor living conditions (Nove, 1972); Dobb, 1978, pp. 230–68; Lewin, 1985). Neither the 'sound economic basis ' for abortion to which the official ideology referred, nor the conditions for easy motherhood existed.

As part of the new cult of motherhood, women's magazines ran articles on happy families with large numbers of children. The story of the Ivanov family, reported in *Rabotnitsa*, is typical of the period. The Ivanovs had 12 children, the youngest was 7 and the eldest 30. Family members were praised for being happy and industrious and for keeping a clean house. It was noted that 'There was never any great noise in their home nor scandals and scoldings. The Invanovs live in harmony' (*Rabotnitsa*, no. 18, July 1936, pp. 10–11). The general message was that large families were quite normal and brought joy and responsibility rather than hardships and problems. The Ivanovs were a family that everyone should want to emulate! The content of this article was remote from the vision of female self-development and woman's emancipation from domestic chores that had captivated Armand and Kollontai. Admittedly, *Rabotnitsa* praised legislation which offered financial support to mothers, which Armand and Kollontai would also have backed, but articles were in the socialist realist style because they portrayed large families under socialism as problem-free.

The goal of strengthening the family was reiterated in legislation of 1944. Pressure to increase the birth rate was now acute due to heavy wartime losses. Twenty million Soviet people had died in the Great Patriotic War with the result that there was a large preponderance of women in the population. By 1946, women outnumbered men by almost twenty-six million. In order to utilise women's childbearing capacity to the full, the state now encouraged unmarried women to reproduce. Single parents could choose to rear their children with the help of a small state allowance or alternatively place their offspring in a children's home without financial cost to themselves. They also enjoyed the right to remove the child from state care at any time and resume responsibility for the upbringing. With state financial support of the child, the single parent mother could no longer sue for paternity. The loss of this right was enshrined in Article 20 of the Family Law (Schlesinger, 1949, p. 373). Effectively, the state assumed the father's traditional legal responsibilities for offspring born out of wedlock. This dual system of paternal responsibility within marriage and state responsibility outside it, aimed both at bolstering marriage and the family and at encouraging single women to become mothers. Being unable to sue fathers for paternity, single women would not, so it was hoped, cause strain and disruption to established married families (Juviler, 1978, p. 254), To ease childbirth the decree also allowed for women to take 35 calendar days off work before birth and 42 after, an increase from the 63 days already granted to 77. In cases of the birth of twins or difficult births, a woman's leave after birth could be extended to 56 days. Provision was also made for reducing fees by 50 per cent for places in kindergartens and creches, depending upon parental income and the number of children (Schlesinger, 1949, p. 369).

The Family Law of 1944 also tried to promote very large families by the introduction of decorations for motherhood. Women with five children earned a second-class Motherhood Medal and those with six won a first-class Motherhood Medal. First-, second- and third-class awards of Motherhood Glory went to mothers of seven, eight and nine children respectively. Ten children won the jackpot and brought the title of Heroine Mother and a certificate of the Presidium of the Supreme Soviet of the USSR (Schlesinger, 1949, p. 372).

Accompanying these incentives to reproduce, the 1944 law brought disincentives for couples who lived outside wedlock. According to Article 19 of the law, *de facto* marriages were not legally recognised. If couples chose to register them, they could indicate the period of time which they had previously been living together. Once registered, the couple won 'the rights and obligations of husband and wife'. The law also attempted to deter divorce: Article 27 declared that the cost of obtaining a certificate of dissolution of marriage ranged 'from 500 to 2,000 roubles' which 'could be charged to one or to each party' by decision of the court (Schlesinger, 1949, p. 375). Financial disincentives were also attached to remaining childless. Modifying an earlier decree of 1941 'On taxes on bachelors, single and childless citizens of the USSR', the 1944 legislation specified that citizens with no children paid 6 per cent of their income in tax. Citizens with one child paid 1 per cent of their earnings and those with two children paid 0.5 per cent (Schlesinger, 1949, p. 372).

These measures addressed the problems of devastating population loss and a surplus of females. Children were needed to increase the labour force. Stable registered marriages might produce them and financial benefits and motherhood medals would help to encourage larger families. Legal protection for single mothers was also used to encourage more women to bear children. But the stigma of single parenthood was not reduced.

Legislation of 1936 and 1944 affecting marriage, divorce and abortion was enacted in a very different spirit from legislation of 1918, 1920 and 1926. The earlier decrees were concerned to free women from the shackles and restrictions of the past. Women were given freedom to choose whether or not to marry, whether to have a *de facto* or *de jure* union, and whether to divorce. The emphasis of later laws was to encourage women to fulfil their duties to the state. In the 1930s duties dominated rights, although it was argued that by performing duties one was in fact realising newly won rights. Certain features, however, were common to both decades: attempts were also made in the 1920s to protect mothers in *de facto* unions whose husbands had deserted them. The goal of guaranteeing maternity benefits which began soon after the revolution was extended in the 1930s and 1940s. Thus, although the emphasis of the legislation of the 1930s and 1940s differed from that of the 1920s, common strands can nevertheless be identified. The laws of 1926 and 1936 were also debated in the press. The points made by the critics of the 1936 draft law, however, were given less coverage than those of its supporters and ultimately ignored.

In a political climate of conformity to party lines, in which criticism meant personal peril, Kollontai remained relatively silent about the woman question, busying herself with diplomatic work, and preferring to write about the past events of 1917, rather than contemporary developments (Holt, 1977, p. 298). She nevertheless credited the Soviet state with having brought equality to women, even though in domestic, economic and political life, it clearly had not. She also praised women in 1946 for devoting their energy 'to creative labour, to the fulfilment of the monumental tasks set by the five-year plan' (Kollontai, 1984, p. 185). She too had come to use heroic language appropriate to the period. In the 1930s and 1940s she did not develop further her earlier reflections on different aspects of women's liberation. Personal politics, domestic labour and the nature of sexuality were all ideologically taboo.

It was easier for Trotsky in exile to be critical. He argued that the Thermidorian reaction had extended to the family and that the new abortion legislation was underpinned by 'the philosophy of the priest' and enslaved 'with the powers of a gendarme'. He challenged the party's stereotype of the joy of motherhood by arguing that childbirth often meant 'a menace' to woman's position. Trotsky concluded that: 'The Thermidorean legislation is beating a retreat to the bourgeois models, covering its retreat with false speeches about the sacredness of the "new" family. On this question, too, socialist bankruptcy covers itself with hypocritical respectability' (Trotsky, 1970, p. 72). In Trotsky's view, sexual equality did not exist in the USSR and the legislation of 1936 amounted to legislation against women. The rehabilitation of the family was one more indicator for him of the material and cultural bankruptcy of the state for which Stalin and the bureaucracy were to blame (Trotsky, 1970, p. 67).

Conclusion

In the 1930s, debate on the woman question was silenced. Assertions about female roles replaced analysis of them. Women were praised as a 'great force' in industry, agriculture and war. In the home, they were caring mothers, preferably adorned by motherhood medals. Domestic labour, self-determination and sexuality became non-issues, kept off the political agenda and out of ideological tracts. Female shock workers and Heroine Mothers were praised to the hilt. Soviet women were portrayed as great achievers at home and at work, suffering no hardships or obstacles. Prominence was given to the message that women were free and equal with men to perform with smiling enthusiasm their duties to Soviet socialism in production, re-production and defence. In sum, women were an economic and demographic resource to be utilised to the full. It was no accident, as Richard Stites has observed, that the slogan commemorating International Women's Day in 1930 was '100 per cent collectivisation!' (Stites, 1978, p. 344). Women's issues were not high on the list of political priorities, even on 8th March. In the 1940s this analytic silence was perpetuated with images of successful and problem-free Soviet superwomen, ever-ready to contribute to the state and to praise Stalin.

Analytic silence prevailed for several mutually reinforcing reasons. First, prominence was given by Stalin to economic goals and class struggles. These accentuated the 'economistic' and derivative view of women's liberation. Second, women were viewed not as a mass of individuals to be liberated, but as a collective who could usefully contribute to economic growth and participate in fights against class enemies. Literature of the period noted that:

> In working women and peasant women Comrade Stalin sees an enormous reserve, which under the correct policy of the working class is able to become, and must become, 'a real army of the working class, acting against the bourgeoisie'. He said that the decisive task of the working class is 'to mould out of the female labour reserve an army of working women and peasant women, acting side by side with the great army of the proletariat'. (Aralovets, 1947, p. 17)

Third, differences between the sexes were played down; class, not gender, was all determining. Special attention to women's distinct needs was therefore redundant. Fourth, prior to the 1930s, there had already been a de-emphasis in the importance of issues such as domestic labour, for reasons elaborated in the last chapter, and a suspicion of women's organisations. Fifth, the highly authoritarian political system precluded democratic input on issues that some citizens might have found important. Discussions followed cues from above. Finally, rapid social change, upheaval, purges and fear, made reflections on the 'woman question' a luxury when issues of daily survival were pressing.

Notes

1. Stalin viewed Trotsky as a serious political opponent. Stalin engineered Trotsky's expulsion from the party, his exile and his murder in Mexico in 1940. Trotsky's arguments on world revolution clashed with Stalin's on 'socialism in one country'.
2. In the post of General Secretary of the party, Stalin enjoyed power over appointments which he skilfully used to his advantage. He was also able to consolidate his position by making use of the 1921 decree which outlawed factionalism in the party. First he accused Trotsky and the so-called 'left wing' of violating party unity; then he turned the same charge against Bukharin, Rykov and Tomsky on the Right (Deutscher, 1968; Cohen, 1980; Hough and Fainsod, 1982).
3. There was starvation in the countryside too. Peasants sowed less in defiance of collectivisation and famine resulted. Often food was sent to the towns, leaving those in the countryside hungry.
4. Politics was not entirely frozen, however. For a description of administration outside Moscow refer to Merle Fainsod, *Smolensk Under Soviet Rule* (Fainsod, 1958).
5. A wonderful satire on heroine milkmaids and treatment of them by the Soviet press can be found in Vladimir Voinovich's *The Life and Extraordinary Adventures of Private Ivan Chonkin*, which was suppressed in the USSR. The relevant passage reads:

> The first notices about her achievements began appearing in the local and regional press. But Lyushka's real ascent began when a reporter wrote a

sensational article (either it was based on her own words or else he made the whole thing up himself) which reported that Lyushka had broken with the age-old way of milking cows and from now on was going to grab four udders at the same time, two in each hand. That's how it began. Delivering a speech at the Kremlin at a conference of collective farmers, Lyushka assured those present, as well as Comrade Stalin personally, that they were finished with their outmoded technique once and for all. (Voinovich, 1978, p. 144)

Vladimir Voinovich was expelled from the Writers' Union in 1974 for his support of Solzhenitsyn.

6. From 1919 to 1946 M. I. Kalinin held the post of Chairman of the Presidium of the Supreme Soviet.

7. Many citizens did not understand what the Bolsheviks meant by women's liberation. Rumours about its significance for daily life were rife and full of misunderstandings. In the Ukraine a story went around that liberation meant that the young women would be shared by the men and the old women boiled down for soap (Stites, 1978, p. 339).

8. Of course not all families were so safe. Sometimes family members 'informed' on relatives to the secret police.

4 Khrushchev and Women's Political Roles

After the heroic language of the Stalin years which praised women's achievements in industry, agriculture, defence and motherhood, came official recognition that women's successes under socialism were, in fact, more modest. Although women were involved in economic and political life, occasional speeches and articles pointed out that women were largely absent from decision-making responsibilities and positions of leadership. Crude assertions made in the Stalin years about the glorious liberation of women under socialism became more muted and increasingly qualified. Although simplistic claims that women were equal with men persisted, they were not consistent with the observations made in the mid-1950s and 1960s that women's political advancement was held back, in part, by men who hesitated to promote them. Rosy praises of socialism for liberating women also conflicted with the observation that the relatively low level of women's involvement in political activity was partially explained by heavy domestic burdens. Women's organisations again set out to address issues specific to women and to mobilise more women into social production and politics.

The rigidities of Stalin's abortion policy were softened too: in 1955, abortion was once again legalised. This came about not because policy-makers suddenly rediscovered Lenin's support for abortion but because backstreet abortions had become widespread and women's health was suffering. Whereas the ideological justification in 1936 for making abortion illegal alleged that different conditions under capitalism and socialism called for different abortion policies, no such fantastic claims were made in 1955. Little, in fact, was written about the new law. What was said pragmatically drew attention to the hazards for women without access to legal terminations of pregnancy.

The years immediately after Stalin's death brought more reflection about women's political roles, recognition that women's organisations were legitimate under socialism, and a lifting of the ban on abortion, but the woman question still remained officially 'solved'. A tension existed during the Khrushchev era between ideological claims about the successful liberation of women under Soviet socialism and more realistic observations about women's lives.

Political context: De-Stalinisation and democratisation

Stalin died in 1953 and in the power struggle which followed, Nikita Khrushchev emerged as the new Soviet leader.[1] His main aims were to de-Stalinise the Soviet system, revitalise the party and soviets and draw the people back into political activity. He also set out to reform industry and agriculture and decentralise decision-making. However, his administrative reforms which devolved power to the regions earned him opponents at the centre and triggered an abortive attempt to remove him from the leadership in 1957. New plans for administrative reform in 1962 also fuelled opposition to Khrushchev and contributed to the successful attempt to depose him in 1964.[2] Although his successors criticised him for 'hare-brained schemes' and 'adventurism', Khrushchev nevertheless tried hard to convert the USSR's polity from one of arbitrary terror and cult of personality to one of more genuine participation 'from below'.

Khrushchev's drive to mobilise the Soviet people into the administration of their own affairs and his belief that it was vital to 'trust in the masses' and end the 'commandism' of the bureaucracy prompted him to look at who was active in politics and who was not (Breslauer, 1980, p. 55). Since the level of women's political activity was low Khrushchev cast a spotlight on women's political roles. The main focus of his celebrated de-Stalinisation speech at the 20th party Congress of 1956 was on the role of the party, but he did not ignore women in his analysis. He remarked:

> It should not be overlooked that many party and state organs put women forward for leadership posts with timidity. Very few women hold leading posts in the party and soviets, particularly among party committee secretaries, chairpersons of Soviet executive committees, and among directors of industrial enterprises, collective farms, machine tractor stations and state farms. (Khrushchev, 1956, p. 109)

This was a frank statement far removed from the triumphant language of the Stalin years which had portayed women and men as striding forth 'side-by-side'. In 1956 women made up 19.7 per cent of party members and were plainly not always side-by-side with men (Lapidus, 1978, p. 210). The Central Committee of the CPSU had just ten women members out of a total of 244, or 3.9 per cent of the total membership (Lapidus, 1978, p. 219). No woman ever sat on the *Politburo* until 1957 when Ekaterina Furtseva was appointed by Khrushchev, and that was just for three years.[3]

Following Khrushchev's cue, the journal *Partiinaia zhizn'* (Party Life) in April 1956 took up his point about the political neglect of women by party committees and called for discussions about party recruitment in the *oblasts, krais* and republics (Peredovaia, 1956, p. 8). A series of articles on the characteristics of the party also appeared at this time in journals and newspapers. But discussion of the causes of the relative absence of women among party members did not begin until the end of the decade. Female political roles quickly slipped out of discussions. Although Khrushchev introduced the topic of women in politics in 1956, few took it up right away.

This silence may be explained by the far greater interest of party members in the implications of de-Stalinisation than in rectifying an imbalance of the sexes. The nature of Stalinism and whether de-Stalinisation was desirable were the burning political issues of the day, not women's contribution to political activity. Some party members were keen for old wrongs to be righted and for democratisation to proceed. Others were stunned by the revelations of Stalin's so-called crimes against the Soviet people. Those loyal to Stalin resisted change, while others secretly hoped for it but were unsure of what role they should play.

De-Stalinisation was not a smooth process – it moved haltingly and amid opposition. Khrushchev's backing did not guarantee its success; nor could his support for more women in political life make this an instant reality or even a lively topic for debate. However, although the majority of articles on the party in the mid-1950s did not include an analysis of female participation in politics, a minority did. Moreover, greater attention was paid to women's political roles than had been the case for the previous 20 years. More space in *Pravda* and *Izvestiia* on the 8th of March (International Women's Day), for instance, was devoted to women's participation in politics, sometimes extending coverage to the 9th of March as well.

The way in which women's roles were treated in the press was, however, often inconsistent. On the same page a claim could be made that socialist construction had 'brought women liberation, freedom and equal rights' and a request added that 'The Central Committee of the CPSU calls upon Soviet women to participate more actively in politics and society', implying that women did not necessarily exercise their rights to the full (*Pravda*, 8 March 1957, p. 1). Similarly, on International Women's Day in 1955 and 1960 *Komsomol'skaia Pravda* praised the fact that Soviet power had named 'thousands of women' to run collective farms and appointed 'many women' to the posts of party secretary and chairperson of soviet executive committees and yet at the same time suggested that the low level of qualifications held by women should be raised, along with their pay. Behind the praiseworthy contribution of women to Soviet political activity there clearly lay a differential tenure of top jobs according to sex and corresponding disparities in pay (*Komsomol'skaia Pravda*, 8 March 1955, p. 1; 8 March 1958, p. 1; 8 March 1960, p. 1).

A tension existed between old political themes and new attempts to involve women in politics. The woman question had officially been answered and equality of the sexes had allegedly been won, but the facts of women's participation in politics suggested otherwise. This clash was evident in texts containing assertions that socialism had brought 'genuine emancipation' to woman, but which also regretted that combining the roles of mother and worker were difficult due to the organisation of domestic life and the need for more kindergartens (KPSS v. Rezoliutsiiakh, 1972, vol. 8, p. 49). Equality of the sexes had not been fully won, but articles still declared that 'The victory of socialism in the USSR ensured the full and factual equality of women' (Mironova, 1957, p. 1). The heroic language of the past persisted in statements like 'Full equal rights for women in the Soviet Union opened up opportunities for remarkable feats' (*Pravda*, 8 March 1961, p. 1).

Four years after Khrushchev's regret that women were promoted so slowly, *Partiinaia zhizn'* carried a leading article which focused entirely on the successes of Soviet women. It rejoiced that 'Many women of our country occupy leading posts in party, soviet, economic and cultural organisations. At the present time half of all leaders and specialists in the USSR are women' (Peredovaia, 1960, p. 5). Such a glowing overstatement ignored the unsolved problems and future hurdles.

Academic writings also fell into this superficial and sometimes contradictory style, presenting the woman question not as a goal of Soviet socialism, but as a success already achieved. According to Vera Bil'shai, 'The experience of the Communist Party and Soviet state in implementing the factual equality of women and men in social production and in all spheres of state and social activity is of great world historic significance' (Bil'shai, 1959, p. 253). She argued that the new Soviet state had not only granted women equality in law, but 'had done everything' to secure equality in production and administration. Comparing it to solving the national question and the peasant question, she wrote that 'one of the great achievements of Soviet socialist construction is solving the woman question' (Bil'shai, 1959, pp. 3–4).

The solved status of the 'woman question' prevented detailed discussion of a range of problems. Some writings, however, did not claim that all had been accomplished, even if they stressed the appropriateness of the Soviet road. Ekaterina Furtseva, for instance remarked:

> Only with the origin of the revolutionary movement of the proletariat was the woman question put on course in practice, only the working class and its vanguard, a Marxist–Leninist party, indicated the sole correct path for the solution of this question. (Furtseva, 1960, p. 2)

The argument here was slightly different from Bil'shai's. The path was right, but how far down it the Soviet state had travelled was not discussed. The inequalities of capitalism were over, yet the inequalities of socialism had yet to be explored. Furtseva did not go so far as to proclaim the woman question 'unsolved', but she did suggest that equality was not instantly won.

At the end of the 1950s references to the political roles of women reappeared as official documents again stressed the need to democratise politics. At the 21st party Congress in 1959, Khrushchev called for more activity on the part of the masses and for an increased role for the soviets 'on the basis of a further broadening of socialist democracy' (Khrushchev, 1959, p. 117). The June Plenum of the Central Committee of the same year proposed the 'further development of democracy in every way' and the greater involvement of the people in administration (Shitarev, 1961, pp. 10–11). Comrades' courts were set up in workplaces and residential areas, people's volunteer detachments patrolled the streets to uphold 'socialist morality' and the trade unions were encouraged to take more initiative (Mitskevich, 1959, pp. 29–30; Friedgut, 1979).[4] In March 1959, new life was officially given to social organisations when the Central Committee resolved that a 'differentiated approach' to political agitation among the population should be adopted, taking into account 'different characteristics of various groups' (KPSS v. Rezoliutsiiakh, 1971, vol. 7, p. 516). Khrushchev believed that the Soviet population could usefully be subdivided into various groups, such as pensioners, women and young poeople, and that these groups had distinctive characteristics and different needs. As a result, the *zhensovety*, or women's councils, were revived and extended to deal with issues which specifically concerned women.[5] In 1961, at the 22nd party Congress, Khrushchev reiterated his commitment to the 'creative initiative of the masses' and this was included in the new party programme approved at the same congress (Khrushchev, 1962, p. 128).

Khrushchev's plea at the 20th party Congress to pay more attention to female political roles was more seriously heeded after 1959 than before, and gained some momentum from 1961 to 1964. Articles now castigated the party for not having done sufficient educational work among women. A *raikom* party secretary suggested that 'in the recent past' this had been 'one of the weakest parts of our district party's activity' and 'to a considerable degree hindered the growth of the political and labour activity of female workers and *kolkhoz* women' (Saltykov, 1960, p. 50). A secretary of the Ivanov *obkom* declared that 'party organisations in our *oblast* are trying to widen the boundaries of propaganda and political work among women, to make it specific, many-sided and flexible' (Zakhovaeva, 1961, p. 20). A Central Committee resolution of January 1960 called for more propaganda work among women geared firstly to drawing the remaining housewives both into work and into political activity and secondly to combating 'feudal attitudes' towards women (KPSS v. Rezoliutsiiakh, 1972, vol. 8, p. 49).

Once attention was given to the low level of women's political activity, reasons other than party negligence were found. Women's heavy domestic burden which included childcare, preparing meals, cleaning the flat, washing clothes 'and many small, unnoticed, but absolutely necessary tasks' were cited as factors (Nashi besedy, 1962, p. 60). These combined could take up to four or more hours a day, making it harder for women than men to attend political meetings, listen to talks and participate in the collective (Zakhovaeva, 1961,

p. 20). Thus domestic chores and childcare prevented women 'from fully developing their talents and abilities' (Kriakvin, 1960, p. 53). The reason behind women's reluctance to join social organisations or enter the labour force 'depends not only on their consciousness, but upon those conditions in which they find themselves' (Drozdetskaia, 1961, p. 27). At last it was recognised that the popular expectation that women should perform housework was one factor which held women back from participating in political work; another was the inadequate supply of kindergartens. Despite the increasing number of childcare facilities 'many women do not have the opportunity to work or actively participate in social organisations because they have nowhere to leave their children' (Unanian, 1960, p. 49; Zakhovaeva, 1961, p. 19).

More critical remarks about several aspects of women's lives were made at congresses of women. The 8th Congress of Women of Dagestan deplored poor working conditions for women such as the lack of air ventilators in some factories. The hardships of working in an atmosphere of steam were given a public airing. Speeches also regretted the lack of women in positions of authority and made the point that even the leaders of entirely female work brigades were usually men; this situation was 'not normal' and reflected 'incorrect attitudes toward woman and disbelief in her strength and abilities' (Zdorovets, 1961, pp. 58–64). The Muslim practice of removing young girls from the education system at a very young age, often resulting in schools having male pupils only was also criticised (Zdorovets, 1961, p. 67).

Although Khrushchev initially prompted discussions of women's political roles, these soon extended to women's domestic predicament and attitudes towards women. Women's low profile in political activity was traced back to heavy domestic obligations. Extensive analyses of the domestic division of labour were not yet conducted, but the link between women's roles was re-established after 30 years of neglect. The Khrushchev years, therefore, opened up the possibility of delving further into inequalities.

From democracy to recognition of inequalities

The lives of women were not as ecstatic as socialist realism of the Stalin years had frequently implied. It was recognised at the 22nd party Congress of 1961 that:

Remnants of inequality in the position of women in everyday life must be completely eliminated. Conditions must be created for the harmonious combination of motherhood with a more active participation of women in the labour force, society, science and the arts. Women must be given lighter work, which is at the same time adequately paid. (Materialy XXII s"ezda KPSS, 1961, p. 393)

Longer maternity leave and more household appliances were also called for and attention was directed at the need for more public dining rooms. The woman question was not yet declared unsolved, but the hardships of the double burden were implicitly defined as problems.

In 1965, just three months after Khrushchev's loss of office, the First Secretary of Turkmenistan argued in *Partiinaia zhizn'* that:

Profound revolutionary changes have come about in the position of women and their psychology. However far from all has been done to allow women to use their rights and knowledge to the full or to display more completely their talent. There are many unanswered problems. Vestiges of the past and traditional views still hold women's development back and retard their political and economic activity. (Ov-ezov, 1965, p. 9)

Unanswered problems were edging onto the agenda. A month later *Partiinaia zhizn'* drew attention to Lenin's distinction between formal and factual equality, saying that attaining factual equality, that is economic and social equality as distinct from legal equality, was 'a protracted struggle, connected with changes in technology, changing daily life, the general struggle of the working class and successes of socialist construction' (Murav'eva, 1965, p. 8). Equality, then, took time to come about and was linked to several variables, including the nature of socialist construction. The implication was that equality of the sexes was not an instant reality after revolution. The article went on to regret that the proportion of female managers in industry had fallen from 7 per cent in 1956 to 6 per cent in 1964 (Murav'eva, 1965, p. 10). Without explicitly saying so, factual equality was clearly wanting. But the 'woman question' was still proclaimed 'solved' and praised as a Leninist achievement (Murv'eva, 1965, p. 8). Nevertheless, the political literature of the Khrushchev years haltingly moved towards a deeper examination of women's lives and attempts were made both to discuss women's issues and to mobilise women into politics by the *zhensovety*.

Women's organisations and the differentiated approach to politics

The *zhensovety* were one part of the 'differentiated approach' to politics advocated by Khrushchev. Women's organisations were now justified on the grounds that they targeted one group within the population, just as other organisations dealt with particular groups, such as youth and pensioners. The *raison d'être* was no longer based on the argument that women were more backward than men and needed special help to overcome this backwardness. The differentiated approach catered to various groups within society, of which women were one. The argument ran:

> It is nothing new that education and organisational work among different groups of workers has to be conducted in different ways. It must be taken into account that each group has its characteristics and needs. To pursue work according to the calculation of some 'average' person is to ignore people's requirements, and consequently to weaken our influence on them. (Kazantseva, 1958, p. 44)

This neatly by-passed the need to dwell on fears of bourgeois feminism and separatism because attention to the needs of various groups did not divide the working class and was a sensible way of dealing with different categories of people. Indeed, each group could be further subdivided: youth was composed of boys and girls; and women could be broken down into workers, *kolkhozniki*, housewives and girls. Thus the work of different *zhensovety* varied depending upon the 'category of woman' with which they were dealing (Saltykov, 1960, p. 52). Women were not a homogeneous mass, but a varied group, even though the problems faced by women could be contrasted with those of men. The ideological soul-searching about the legitimacy of women's organisations under socialism typical of the 1920s was largely absent.

It was now accepted that one of the weakest areas of party work had been the political education of women, which had 'to a considerable degree hindered the growth of the political and labour activity of working women and *kolkhoz* workers' (Saltykov, 1960, p. 50). This shortcoming could be quickly and easily tackled by women working with women.

Zhensovety: *Organisation, goals and activities*

The *zhensovety* were set up at the *oblast, krai* and *raion* levels of administration and were established in factories, offices and farms. No detailed instructions were issued about how the women's councils should be organised, which gave them some flexibility. As a rule, however, the *oblast* women's councils had 30–50 members and the district level gathered 15–20 members. *Zhensovety* in factories and on farms attracted smaller groups of 5 to 17. The larger *zhensovety* tended to have a chairperson, deputy chair and secretary (Stoiakina, 1962, p. 6).

There was no uniform pattern of work throughout the USSR; some *zhensovety* worked closely with the party and others with the soviets. The *zhensovet* of the Ashkhabad sewing factory in Turkmenia, for example, worked 'under the leadership of the party organisation' whereas in the Altai *krai* 'the executive committees of the local soviets constantly direct the work of the women's councils' (Brazhnikova, 1961, p. 4; Miatieva, 1973, p. 5). Those directed by the party worked, in theory, according to defined quarterly and monthly plans, which the party helped to draw up and approved at meetings of its *buro*. The role of the party was to 'extend help to the *zhensovet* and control its work'. The chairpersons of women's councils had to attend meetings with the party organisation four times a year to report on their progress (Gurova and Krivenko, 1960, p. 25). Similarly, where the soviets supervised the *zhensovety*, Soviet executive committees held regular meetings and seminars at which they 'discussed immediate tasks and exchanged work experience'. The aim of the soviet was 'to support in every way and strengthen the women's councils'. As well as these regular gatherings between the *zhensovety* and the party and soviets, the chairpersons of the *zhensovety* were sometimes invited to attend party meetings and sessions of the town and district soviets, depending upon whether they came under the oversight of the party or soviets (Brazhnikova, 1961, p. 4; Dugarzhapova, 1965, p. 53). The aim of this invitation was to give the *zhensovety* opportunities to keep abreast of local events and issues of the day (Miatieva, 1973, pp. 12–13).

In some factories the *zhensovet* worked more closely with the trade union than with the party or soviets. In fact, the work of the *zhensovety* often overlapped with the activities of the trade unions. The trade unions had their own permanent commissions for work among women with sections similar to those of the *zhensovety*

(Drozdetskaia, 1961, p. 24). Trade unions also set up special clubs for women which ran lectures on 'Scientific atheism', 'Young housewives' and 'Parents' day off'. They organised sewing circles, drama groups and choral evenings (Zakhovaeva, 1961, p. 21). Increased trade union activity was another element of Khrushchev's policy to reinvigorate political life and promote democratisation. The women's conferences and congresses of the late 1950s, had the similar objective of mobilising women and focusing on problems affecting their lives (Zdorovets, 1961).

The official goals of the *zhensovety* of the late 1950s and 1960s were variously described, often in very general terms, but occasionally in narrow and specific terms. According to one source they 'strive to ensure that every woman consciously participates in the great creative work of the people' and that Marxist–Leninist ideas reach every institution (Alkhazova, 1964, p. 23). Another suggested that their aim was to encourage women into political activity and, if they were still housewives, into the work-force. The *zhensovety* also set out to challenge religious prejudices and petty bourgeois narrow-mindedness (Stoiakina, 1962, p. 8). A third stressed that 'in order better to satisfy the needs of workers the *zhensovet* attempts to understand more fully the conditions of life of each working woman and their interests and desires'. The *zhensovety* allegedly addressed fresh questions every day and 'continually widen the circle of their activities, drawing all women into active participation in production, helping party and trade union organisations, better managing questions connected with educating the new person as a builder of communist society' (Nemirova, 1962, p. 50). The *zhensovety*, according to this description, were aimed at furthering the under-standing of the problems and interests of women as a group, and simultaneously helping the CPSU to construct 'new women'. The implication here is that the needs of women which were selected for attention were those which coincided with party priorities about the aspects of women's lives needing change to match socialist aspir-ations. If women had been allowed to define their own objectives, different goals could have pulled in different directions and perhaps clashed with official priorities. The *zhensovety*'s lack of autonomy from the party meant that activities followed directions specified by the party (Browning, 1987). Though the *zhensovety* developed the 'abilities and activities' of women, it was also clear that this was done by helping the party 'to create a reserve of female cadres for drawing into positions of leadership' and 'to educate them in the spirit of high ideas, the friendship of peoples and proletarian internationalism' (Rakhimova, 1967, p. 60). Certain politically approved abilities were to be developed. More specific goals were that they ensured that labour laws were properly implemented and pressed for more public dining rooms (Zakhovaeva, 1961, p. 20).

Just as the work of the women's clubs of the 1920s was divided into sections, so too were the activities of the *zhensovety*. Typical sections included mass-political work, production, daily life, culture, work among children, healthcare and the organisation of public services (Unanian, 1960, p. 50; Brazhnikova, 1961, p. 4; Stoiakina, 1962, p. 7). Common in less urban parts of the union were sections which concentrated on sanitation and hygiene. Less frequent were sections such as tree-planting (Dugarzhapova, 1965, p. 53). Some *zhensovety* are reported as having as few as three sections, others as many as nine. From five to twenty activists directed the work of each section (Brazhnikova, 1961, p. 4; Browning, 1987, p. 81).

The activities of each of the *zhensovet*'s sections reflected official party priorities for work among women. The aims of the section for mass-political work, for instance, were to educate women politically and to mobilise them into production and political activity. The chairperson of one women's council in a factory declared that from the first days of its work the council 'saw its main task as bringing all women without exception into active participation in production and social life'. Women were encouraged to become economically productive and particular attention was given to the political education of women. Over 200 women from the factory floor were encouraged to study the documents of the 22nd party Congress and to think about general questions of economics and party life (Nemirova, 1962, p. 49). Most *zhensovety* also held regular meetings at which various issues, defined 'from above', were examined including 'the role of women in the struggle for peace' and 'preparation for 8 March' (Gurova and Krivenko, 1960, p. 24).

Production sections encouraged female workers to raise the level of their qualifications and attend night school (Brazhnikova, 1961, p. 5). Inevitably, different production sections gave attention to different sorts of issues. One section in a factory in Dagestan asked why women earned less than men, despite being equals. Its members went on to discuss why many professions were seen as 'men's work' and what made it so hard for them to become 'women's work'. They debated the significance of lower qualification levels and then encouraged women to be trained as lathe operators, crane-drivers, painters, metal workers, varnishers and polishers (Alkhazova, 1964, pp. 5–6; Gasanbekova, 1979, p. 99). More in line with official aims, other *zhensovety* encouraged women to become shock workers and to participate in socialist competitions (Alkhazova, 1964, pp. 17–20). Production sections also aided industry and agriculture at times of difficulty. For instance, the collective farm 'Banner of October' in the Kliuchevskii district of the Altai suffered heavy rains during the harvest of 1960. Since the farm lacked enough workers for intensive harvesting after the weather improved, the *zhensovet* mobilised over 60 housewives to help with the harvest (Brazhnikova, 1961, pp. 4–5).

The section for daily life (*byt*) aimed to ease the hardships of working days. This involved the chairperson of the *zhensovet* liaising with factory directors; sometimes section members pressed administrators to guarantee cleaner and more comfortable working conditions (Mishova, 1960, p. 85; Alkhazova, 1964, pp. 20–1). This 'complicated and painstaking' work 'necessitated great attention and sensitivity towards people' (Alkhazova, 1964, p. 21). The section for daily life also responded to requests from workers for help in getting their flats repaired or their children placed in kindergartens. Although the section's work was not directly concerned with output *per se*, its emphasis on the improvement of working conditions was viewed as assisting efficient and productive work.

Cultural sections embraced a wide range of activities, often overlapping with political sections. They organised lectures and discussion groups on international affairs, law, politics, society, morality and aesthetics. Meetings were also held to discuss articles in the press. The work of cultural sections in some factories occasionally overlapped with health sections by arranging talks and discussions on medical matters. Some cultural sections organised evenings around more general themes, such as 'what is good taste?' Others set up artistic groups among housewives whose members knitted sweaters, wove carpets and produced embroidery. They sometimes held exhibitions of what they had produced (Brazhnikova, 1961, pp. 7–8). In Komi one cultural section organised evenings in factories called 'My dear mother'. Mothers of all ages and professions were invited to meet each other and to describe their work, children, social duties, the technological progress in their factories and their difficulties and achievements (Mishova, 1960, p. 84). Thus cultural sections generally drew women together in various social settings for relaxation and discussion.

Sections for work with children were also involved with an assortment of social activities. In the Komi republic, for instance, these sections became involved in the administration of the House of Pioneers, the House of Culture and a cinema frequented by young people.[6] Members of the section claimed that their presence had a positive influence on the children and deterred rude and cheeky behaviour. Members of the section also patrolled the streets at night and stopped young children to ask what they were doing and why their parents allowed them out alone. Visits to parents who were thought to be neglecting their offspring followed. Activities were also organised for children out of school hours, such as a party to commemorate the 90th anniversary of the birth of Lenin (Mishova, 1960, p. 84).

In other republics, members of the section for children helped teachers to lead excursions, organise sporting events and arrange summer camps (Alkhazova, 1964, p. 21). They prepared the children to perform dances at 'parents' days' which were occasions when parents visited schools and asked questions about progress and health (Brazhnikova, 1961, pp. 8–9). Sometimes their attention extended to juveniles who had been low achievers at school and were now drifting without jobs. The women activists tried to encourage the teenagers to find paid employment (Mishova, 1960, p. 84).

The section for work among children also aimed to help parents in difficulty and to set up services to ease the lives of working mothers. They compiled lists of families with large numbers of children and also single parent families; they visited them to see what help they needed (Brazhnikova, 1961, p. 8). Setting up creches was another common activity, for which members of the *zhensovet* often made curtains, table cloths and sheets (Brazhnikova, 1961, p. 8).

The aim of health sections was, more specifically, to promote health education. This often led to a 'health university' being organised in the workplace at which medical workers read lectures on different aspects of women's health. As many as 200 women might attend these (Alkhazova, 1964, p. 22). More detailed information on this and other sections is thin in the majority of available primary sources.

Meetings of members of similar sections took place across administrative levels. Particular sections at the *oblast* level liaised with their counterparts at the district level; an *oblast* production section would have contacts with district production sections. Meetings organised at the *oblast* level also drew together chairpersons of district *zhensovety* and leaders of their sections. Similarly, leaders of *zhensovety* in factories came together for meetings at the district level. Generally, activists from one level were hosted by the higher administrative level for discussions (Stoiakina, 1962, p. 7)

How successful were the Zhensovety?

The level of access to women by them was moderately good in some areas but the *zhensovety* were certainly not evenly spread throughout republics and were, in fact, absent from some towns and republics. According to Genia Browning, Soviet sources suggest that there were no *zhensovety* in Estonia, Georgia and Armenia (Browning, 1987, p. 139). Unfortunately, official statistics of their numbers throughout republics have not been systematically compiled and occasional references give only an impression of their extent. For example, by the end of the 1960s, there were over 1,000 *zhensovety* in Dagestan, where there was a female population of over half-a-million (Gasenbekova, 1979, p. 105; TsSU SSSR, 1975a, p. 15). However, due to the mountainous nature of that republic and the remoteness of many small settlements, urban rather than rural women were more likely to have been involved in them.

How successful were the *zhensovety* in encouraging women to join the party? Table 4.1 shows that in 1956 women comprised 19.7 per cent of party members. This fell to 19.5 per cent in 1961 – hardly evidence to support a successful political mobilisation of women. By

Table 4.1 Female membership of the CPSU, 1937–1966

Year	Number of women members	Percentage of total membership
1937	293,059	14.8
1939	333,821	14.5
1946	1,033,115	18.7
1950	1,312,418	20.7
1952	1,276,560	19.0
1956	1,414,456	19.7
1961	1,809,688	19.5
1966	2,548,901	20.6

Source: Lapidus, 1978, p. 210

Table 4.2 Female membership of the Communist Party
of Turkmenistan, 1938–1967

Year	Number of women members	Percentage of total membership
1938	829	12.0
1941	2,595	13.6
1944	5,018	29.1
1946	5,802	24.7
1950	6,272	18.7
1956	7,253	19.3
1960	8,437	18.7
1962	9,426	18.7
1967	11,379	18.2

Source: Lapidus, 1978, p. 213

1966 the figure had crept up to just 20.6 per cent (Lapidus, 1978, p. 210). Some Muslim republics showed consistently falling female percentages, which was not a uniform pattern across republics (Mickiewicz, 1977). From 29.1 per cent of party members in Turkmenistan in 1944, women decreased to 18.7 per cent in 1950, falling to 18.2 per cent in 1967. Similarly in Tadzhikistan, the female percentage of party members was reduced from 30.3 per cent in 1944 to 18.0 per cent in 1950, maintaining the same percentage in 1967 (Lapidus, 1978, p. 213). These declining percentages should be treated with caution since, as Tables 4.1 and 4.2 indicate, they do not necessarily mean accompanying falls in the total number of women. Indeed, throughout these years the number of women in the party grew, with the exception of a small fall in 1952. The reason for the declining female percentage lies in much higher entry rates of men into the party. Even though women were encouraged to join the party, they did so at a much slower rate than men, causing their overall percentage to decline.

An important and unanswerable question remains: would even fewer women have joined the party had the *zhensovety* not existed at all? One cannot derive from Soviet sources the number of women who joined the party due to the efforts of the women's councils.[7] Thus, evaluation of the political impact of the *zhensovety* is hazardous; nor can one determine whether the activities of the *zhensovety* led to more women being placed on *nomenklatura* lists. Certainly, women were less likely than men to be put forward for top jobs. Although the details of *nomenklatura* lists are not published, one Soviet dissertation unearthed from archives the fact that by 1967 just 21 women were on *nomenklatura* list of the Kasumkenskii *raion* in Dagestan out of a total of 214 names (Gasanbekova, 1979, p. 113). One can conclude that in some parts of the USSR, the *zhensovety* and their sections involved women in various political, social and cultural activities but the extent to which they promoted party membership and the career prospects of women is uncertain.

Just as the party was criticised in the 1920s for not always taking the *Zhenotdel* seriously enough and for dismissing the importance of the women's clubs and delegates' meetings, so the charge has been made that 'not all party organisations paid the necessary attention to the activities of the women's councils'. This applied, for example, to the 'Red October' state farm in the Sergokalinskii district of Dagestan which was also criticised for its 'weak leadership' and for tolerating the practice of withdrawing young girls from schooling. Similar shortcomings in party work in other parts of Dagestan have been cited in *obkom* party archives (Gasanbekova, 1979, pp. 103–5). Speeches delivered at the 8th Congress of women of Dagestan held after the 21st party Congress of 1959 also drew attention to 'considerable difficulties', 'serious shortcomings' and 'unsolved problems' connected with work among women (Zdorovets, 1961, p. 39). The Congress criticised party leaders and directors of enterprises for not paying serious attention to the provision of kindergartens and called upon the *zhensovety* to be 'more persistent' and helpful in addressing questions of daily life (Zdorovets, 1961, p. 60).

Women's issues may not all have been given prominence or loudly debated, but they began to edge into higher visibility due to the work of the *zhensovety* and the convening of women's congresses. Khrushchev's differentiated approach to political activity gave work among women a legitimacy that it had been denied under Stalin. Notwithstanding the *zhensovety's* rather modest results in boosting female entry into the CPSU, their efforts in this direction helped to keep women's political roles on the political agenda. Despite the *zhensovety's* uneven and limited access to women, some women were nevertheless drawn into aspects of collective life and given the opportunity to discuss women's issues. One issue of vital importance for women's self-determination that quietly reappeared was the availability of abortion. It was not given as much coverage as women's public political roles, but its implications for women's lives and personal politics were more far-reaching.

Abortion policy

Abortion was first legalised in 1920, amid some controversy, made illegal in 1936 and legalised again in 1955. In Chapter 3 reference was made to numerous articles in the press and women's magazines applauding the 1936 ban on abortion. By contrast, legalisation in 1955 was given very little coverage by the media. Whereas readers of women's magazines in 1935 and 1936 were well-informed about the new abortion policy, this was not the case in 1955 and 1956. *Rabotnitsa*, for instance, continued in the 1950s to praise motherhood and neglected to discuss the significance of woman's renewed right to abortion. There was no public debate surrounding the new legislation. It was briefly reported in the press alongside other fresh legislation with terse comment (*Izvestiia*, 23 November 1955, p. 2).

This relative silence was because Soviet leaders did not wish large numbers of women to resort to abortion instead of childbirth. The promotion of motherhood remained an important priority; a widespread information campaign about the availability of abortion would go against official pro-natalism. Abortion was being legalised not so much as a right for women but as a corrective against resorting to illegal abortions. Several articles in the press during 1955 made it clear that illegal abortions were now widespread and causing serious medical complications for women. The absence of contraception in the USSR forced women to seek abortions as a means of birth control. This was never admitted in the 1950s and it was not until 1966 that the press gave sparse coverage to the promotion of the Soviet intra-uterine device, extolling its virtues over birth control pills (Pod"iachikh, 1966, p. 4). In the 1950s remarks were restricted to the hazards of illegal abortions without tackling the sensitive topic of contraception. The message projected by the press was that by making abortion legal the state was yet again protecting women from threats to their good health. This time the threat came from abortions performed in unsanitary conditions.

Brief articles in Soviet newspapers reported the details of specific cases. One ran as follows:

> Dr. S. Khrebtovich secretly performed an abortion on Citizen P. under unsanitary conditions. As a result, she had to be taken to the hospital in an extremely critical condition and undergo an emergency operation. Citizen P. became an invalid.
>
> The Mogilev Province Court sentenced Khrebtovich to three years' imprisonment.

The Belorussian Supreme Court upheld the sentence. (*Current Digest to the Soviet Press*, vol. VII, no. 1, 1955, p. 28)

Another case reported in Turkmenia revealed that one Mariia Vasilenko had been performing illegal abortions for a number of years. Apparently:

> Vasilenko had no medical training and performed them under unsanitary conditions, sometimes even in an intoxicated condition. In February 1955, she performed an abortion on Citizeness Z. The woman was admitted to a hospital in a serious condition and died shortly afterward. (*Current Digest to the Soviet Press*, vol. VII, no. 22, 1955, p. 20)

Vasilenko was sentenced to eight years' imprisonment. These articles were printed in 1955, after 20 years of silence about abortion, in the months before abortion was legalised and prepared opinion for a change in policy. As soon as the law had changed such articles ceased to appear.

When *Izvestiia* reported the new law it noted that the legalisation of abortion helped to avert 'the harm caused to the health of women by abortions performed outside medical establishments' (*Izvestiia*, 30 November 1955, p. 2). The practical reasons for the legislation did not prevent ideological statements. *Izvestiia* introduced the decree 'On Revoking the Ban on Abortions' in the following manner:

> The decree points out that the measures taken by the Soviet state to encourage motherhood and protect children, together with the unceasing growth in the awareness and cultural level of women actively participating in all spheres of the country's national economic, cultural and social life, make it possible to dispense at the present time with the prohibition of abortion carried out according to the law, and states that the prevention of abortion can be ensured by extending further the state measures for the encouragement of motherhood and measures of an educational and explanatory nature. (*Current Digest to the Soviet Press*, vol. VII, no. 48, 1955, p. 25)

The promotion of motherhood remained an explicit and central theme of Soviet social policy and the legislation of abortion was not supposed to detract from this.

Ideology played down the problem of women's insistence on abortion in the absence of contraception and claimed that the 'awareness and cultural level of women' meant that Soviet women would realise their duties to the socialist state to reproduce. However, if abortion was legalised in 1955 on the strength of women's high cultural level which led them to recognise the overriding duty of motherhood, then abortion in 1936 should logically have been banned due to women's low cultural level and inability to recognise the importance of motherhood. But in the 1930s, as pointed out in Chapter 3, the official line was that the low cultural level of women in the 1920s combined with unstable circumstances had justified legal abortions. By implication, women's cultural level had been raised by the 1930s. Surely then, the banning of abortions according to this line of reasoning had been unreasonable. Moreover, now in the 1950s, high cultural level was a justification for the legalisation of abortion whereas in the 1920s low cultural level had been one pressing reason. These inconsistencies could, of course, be explained away by the classic flexibility of 'different and changing conditions' justifying different policies and lines.

The same held for arguments about the protection of women's health. In 1936 abortions were banned on the grounds that they were harmful to women's health. In 1955 they were legalised not because they were considered less harmful than in the 1930s but because illegal abortions were even more detrimental to women's lives. A large number of women were resorting to illegal abortions, despite their allegedly higher cultural level, and the state was, effectively, forced to respond to this pressure.

A third justification for the law was that it would 'give women the possibility of deciding the question of motherhood for themselves' (*Izvestiia*, 23 November 1955, p. 2). This was more in line with the views of Armand, Kollontai and Lenin on abortion. But it was contrary to the argument of the 1930s that 'mass abortions resorted to for egoistic reasons are not to be tolerated' (Schlesinger, 1949, p. 310). Thus, women in the 1950s were given a right to choose that in the 1930s had been denied. Abortion was not officially described as a right in the way that maternity leave and pensions were, but its status moved in this direction since women were again allowed the opportunity to reflect upon whether or not they wanted one. Although the conditions of legal abortions were so degrading, humiliating and painful that the abortion clinics became known as 'slaughterhouses', they were at least available (Golubeva, 1980, p. 55).

The little written in the Soviet press about the legalisation of abortion in 1955, suggests that the demand from society for illegal abortion was the main reason behind a volte-face in policy. Pressure on hospital facilities to cope with the unfortunate results of illegal abortions must have indicated the scope of the problem. Social pressure and illegal demand were the practical stimulants for abortion facilities, not fidelity to early Marxist texts.

Conclusion

Khrushchev did not examine the theoretical status of the woman question and it remained officially solved. His concern to democratise the Soviet system, however, led him to focus on women's political roles and to ask why women were not as politically active as men. This question inevitably raised issues concerning domestic roles and queries about the availability of kindergartens and household appliances. Khrushchev's aims of de-Stalinising the USSR and drawing the Soviet people into politics through involvement in social organisations also led to the re-establishment of women's organisations. His advocacy of the differentiated approach to politics gave a legitimacy to women's organisations and helped to remove the stigma of the 1920s that they served to divide the working class and were incubators of bourgeois feminism.

The female roles selected for scrutiny, how they were treated, and the sequence in which they were considered, were affected by broader policy priorities. Although Khrushchev did not reopen the woman question at the level of theory, he put women's issues back on the political agenda and opened up the possibility of delving further into inequalities between the sexes. Discussions of aspects of women's lives were more public than they had been in the 1940s, although the woman question was still not tackled head-on. The direction from 1956 to 1964 can be viewed as building up to the possibility of reopening the woman question, but the Khrushchev years were a time when theoretical developments lagged behind practicalities.

Notes

1. For details of the power struggle after Stalin's death, refer to Jerry Hough and Merle Fainsod, *How the Soviet Union is Governed*, Roy Medvedev, *Khrushchev* and Mary McAuley, *Politics and the Soviet Union* (Hough and Fainsod, 1982, pp. 194–210; Medvedev, 1982, pp. 56–71; and McAuley, 1977, pp. 168–75). Another useful introduction to the policies of the Khrushchev years is provided by Martin McCauley (ed.) *Khrushchev and Khrushchevism* (McCauley, 1987).
2. Khrushchev won opponents among the Soviet leadership for several reasons. His administrative reforms of the party and state caused confusion and chaos and were

resented by those at the 'centre' who lost political status to those in the regions. He was also unpopular among the general population for raising prices. Harvest failures reflected badly on his agricultural policies. Foreign policy blunders, such as the Cuban missile crisis, fuelled criticisms of his 'adventurism' and 'hare-brained' schemes (Medvedev, 1982, pp. 165–235).

3. Ekaterina Furtseva held her post on the *Politburo* from 1957 to 1960 when she was relieved of it upon becoming Minister of Culture. She remained Minister of Culture until her death in 1974 (Mandel, 1975, pp. 287–90).

4. The extent to which the comrades' courts and people's volunteer detachments involved women is unclear.

5. According to Genia Browning, some *zhensovety* were set up as early as 1958 (Browning, 1987, p. 63). Browning's book *Women and Politics in the USSR: Consciousness Raising and Soviet Women's Groups* is the only published work in the West which offers a comprehensive analysis of the *zhensovety* (Browning, 1987). Her PhD thesis provides more detailed discussion (Browning, 1985a).

6. Most Soviet youngsters under 14 years of age are members of the Young Pioneers. After 14 they become members of the Komsomol, or Young Communist League, which can usefully be seen as the youth group of the CPSU.

7. Genia Browning points out that the Soviet academic Ol'ga Tallya has claimed, without adequate evidence, that the work of the *zhensovety* resulted in increased party membership (Browning, 1987, pp. 91–2).

5 The Brezhnev Years: The Woman Question Has Not Been Solved After All

The main contribution of the Brezhnev years (1964–1982) to the woman question was the declaration that it was 'unsolved'. This removed, at last, the strait-jacket of its earlier 'solved' status which since 1930 prevented any serious analysis of gender roles. Once reopened, the woman question provoked intense, broad discussion and one of 'growing heat' (Lapidus, 1978, p. 287). The vitality of the debate contrasted sharply with the absence of serious thinking during the Stalin years.

The reopening of the question followed logically from Khrushchev's concern about the lack of women in politics and from the growing awareness in the late 1950s that 'problems' existed in women's lives, particularly in combining participation in the workforce and in political life with domestic labour. The official claim that the woman question had already been solved, however, prevented thorough scrutiny in the 1950s of these problems. Developments in Marxist–Leninist doctrine under Brezhnev made possible the switch from a 'solved' woman question to an 'unsolved' one. Serious economic and demographic problems of the 1960s and 1970s were pressures which made this switch compelling. Policy makers needed more detailed analyses of women's lives before they could recommend ways of improving economic growth rates or account for falling birth rates. The reinvigoration of Soviet sociology under Brezhnev facilitated these enquiries. Thus a combination of factors fuelled the most lively reflections about female roles for over 30 years.

Developments in Marxism–Leninism: Developed socialism and its non-antagonistic contradictions

Sociological investigations into 'problems' faced by women became ideologically legitimate in the 1960s and 1970s due to the recognition of 'non-antagonistic contradictions' under 'developed socialism'. In the late 1960s Brezhnev announced that the USSR had become a 'developed socialist' or 'mature socialist' society. Soviet theorists elaborated that 'developed socialism' was a particular 'stage' of socialist development on the road to communism (Evans, 1977). They claimed that the fundamentals of socialism had been built in the 1930s. In other words a stage had been reached 'characterised by substantially greater socialisation of production, a further increase in output, and an increased complexity of the national economic structure' (Mochalov, 1980, p. 40). The developed socialism of the 1960s was assisted by a scientific–technological revolution. It suffered, however, from 'non-antagonistic contradictions', or unsolved problems. Developed socialism was a long and complicated stage in which remaining problems were addressed and the prerequisites of communism finally established.

Khrushchev's rash proclamation made in 1961 that the Soviet Union would achieve communism by the 1980s was abandoned. Soviet political textbooks informed readers that socialist society 'cannot occur without some contradictions, without numerous difficulties, some of them extremely serious, that have to be overcome' (Konstantinov, 1974, p. 589). Non-antagonistic contradictions referred to problems which could be solved without radically transforming the economic base of society, unlike the central antagonistic contradiction between capital and labour under capitalism which demanded a socialist mode of production for its resolution. But non-antagonistic contradictions could not be solved spontaneously; they had to be worked on. Before this could happen, they had to be recognised and understood. Out of their identification and analysis would come policy proposals to overcome them.

The notions of 'developed socialism' and 'non-antagonistic contradiction' made room for difficulties in Soviet society and generated theoretical space for the reopening of the woman question. Iankova, Gruzdeva and many others could now point out that the woman question was 'unsolved' and be guaranteed ideological protection. Slotting the woman question into the logic of developed socialism,

Nagiev could safely argue that 'the attainment of factual equality, as distinct from obtaining political rights, is a protracted, complicated and many-sided process' (Nagiev, 1971, p. 7). Like all protracted and complicated processes, attaining equality of the sexes demanded grappling with and resolving non-antagonistic contradictions. Their persistence was responsible for 'vestiges of the past' and their resolution was the key to solving the woman question. The main non-antagonistic contradiction affecting the lives of women was identified as the tension between performing roles in production and reproduction.

Developed socialism and the woman question

The new line under Brezhnev was that while the Soviet state had made great strides towards promoting equality, 'it would be incorrect to think that all questions were solved, that difficulties needing to be overcome did not exist, and that new problems would not arise' (Tatarinova, 1979, p. 7). The nature of the woman question at any given time was linked to the development of socialism. Just as socialism itself progressed through stages, so too did the woman question. As Gruzdeva wrote, 'Solving the woman question passes through different stages at different levels of the development of socialism' (Gruzdeva, 1979a, p. 1). Although socialist revolution had brought about legal equality of the sexes, it could not bring about all aspects of equality. Attaining equality was a long and complex process, like the building of socialism.

Quoting Lenin, theorists now proclaimed that while legal changes had constituted a 'most decisive revolution', the attainment of 'complete liberation' (*polnoe osvobozhdenie*) meant going 'considerably further' (Gruzdeva, 1979b, p. 182). While solving the woman question was only possible under socialism, writers warned that 'it does not come easily'. So whereas the liberation of women had been declared a great achievement of socialism as early as the 1930s, by the late 1960s the definition of this 'achievement' had considerably narrowed. The 'social task' of 'great historic significance' that had been solved was legal equality of the sexes. The woman question in its entirety had not been answered after all, but just one aspect of it.

In the new theoretical context of 'developed socialism', the distinction between equal rights (*ravnopravie*) and equality (*ravenstvo*) was increasingly stressed. *Ravnopravie* amounted to formal equality (*formal'noe ravenstvo*) before the law. *Ravnopravie* as *formal'noe ravenstvo* was therefore legal equality (*iuridicheskoe ravenstvo* or *pravovoe ravenstvo*). But *ravenstvo* itself was much broader embracing 'political, economic and everyday life'. *Ravenstvo* was synonymous with equality in practice and viewed as factual equality, referred to as *fakticheskoe ravenstvo* or sometimes as factual social equality, or *fakticheskoe sotsial'noe ravenstvo* (Brova, 1968, p. 4). Where formal equality entailed legislation, factual equality demanded changes in behaviour and attitudes.

Factual equality was not won after the revolution because 'vestiges of inequality' (*ostatki neravenstvo*) or 'remnants of factual inequality' (*ostatki fakticheskogo neravenstvo*) remained (Lysakova, 1966, p. 3; Iankova, 1975, p. 44). Drawing women into social production and liberating them from housework were part of a subsequent 'complex process' connected with profound socio-economic transformations such as socialist industrialisation and cultural revolution. Priorities generated by socio-economic changes at different levels of socialist and communist construction delimited what the female role in social production would be. Women's activity in the economy was conceived as relative to changing economic imperatives. Under developed socialism, at a time of scientific–technological revolution, 'the central problem of female labour becomes increasing its effectiveness' in keeping with the general priority of raising productivity (Gruzdeva, 1979b, p. 184). Thus, the relevance of the woman question could alter according to the economic and political priorities of any given period and itself moved through different stages. The task for social scientists in the late 1960s and 1970s was to identify these stages and distinguish between the inequalities considered inevitable and unavoidable at a given stage from those which were not.

Political and economic context

Brezhnev was preoccupied with problems of falling economic productivity, declining birth rates and labour shortages. The high economic growth rates of the Stalin years had fallen considerably and the rigidities of Stalinist central planning had resulted in a stagnating economy unresponsive to consumer needs (Goldman, 1983). Moreover, there were labour shortages, exacerbated by declining family size in Russia, Belorussia, the Ukraine and Baltic republics. As a vital 51 per cent of the labour force, women were needed in the economy, but were expected to rear children as well. For the requirements of the Soviet economy to be met, an answer had to be provided to the question of how women could combine their roles in production and reproduction without neglecting either role, simultaneously increase their efficiency in the work-force and also bear more children. How women could fulfil the roles of worker and mother with high productivity in each was of increasing importance to the Soviet state. Economic and demographic problems of the 1960s and 1970s required, therefore, detailed investigations into how women organised their lives.

Concern about female roles was expressed at party congresses. While the 23rd Congress over which Brezhnev first presided as General Secretary in 1966 paid little attention to issues directly affecting women, the 24th Congress of 1971 made the official party position clear:

> In the past five year plan a series of important measures were taken on Party initiative with the aim of improving the working conditions of women and simultaneously easing their domestic work.... It is well known, comrades, that in the forthcoming five year plan several further steps in this direction are envisaged.
>
> The goal of party policy is for Soviet woman to have new opportunities regarding childrearing, participation in society, recreation and study. (*Materialy XXIV s"ezda* KPSS, 1972, p. 75)

In the same spirit, the 25th party Congress of 1976 announced that 'the party considers it its duty continually to protect women, to improve their position as workers, mothers, childrearers and housewives' (*Materialy XXV s"ezda* KPSS, 1976, p. 85). A vigorous debate ensued in which sociologists, economists, demographers, lawyers and journalists suggested how women could best combine production with reproduction.

The reinvigoration of the Soviet social sciences encouraged this debate. In 1967 a Central Committee resolution 'On measures for further developing the social sciences and heightening their role in communist construction' called upon social scientists to contribute to building communist society through analysing social problems (Hahn, 1977, p. 36). To aid this contribution official backing was now given to 'concrete social research' or empirical enquiry, so long as it was guided by general sociology, or historical materialism. The Institute of Concrete Social Research was opened in 1968 in Moscow, later renamed the Institute for Sociological Research. Sociology was no longer branded 'bourgeois' or dismissed as a non-discipline (Weinberg, 1974; Shlapentokh, 1987). The CPSU at last gave its blessing to sociological research, both empirical and theoretical, as an input to policy-making, thus legitimising sociological enquiries into women's lives.

Economic problems and female roles

Soviet economists were generally agreed that falling economic growth rates under developed socialism required analysis and called for a more rational use of labour resources. Some argued that a means to promote a more efficient use of labour was to be found in the female labour force since women constituted half of the total number of workers and generally held less skilled jobs than men (Iuk, 1968; Kozachenko, 1969; Shishkan, 1969, 1976; Panova, 1970; Eremina, 1972; Samokhina, 1972; Kotliar and Turchaninova, 1975; Sonin, 1978; Tatarinova, 1979). Improvements in economic performance depended therefore on improvements in the 'quality' of female labour (Eremina, 1972, p. 3). However, economists approached the problem of the 'quality' of female labour with different emphases. Samokhina, for instance, suggested that the fortunes of the economy were linked to female roles in it whereas Shishkan maintained that the liquidation of all socio-economic inequalities of the sexes was directly connected to solving problems of the rational use of labour resources. Thus, in Shishkan's view the fate of the woman question hung on economic solutions and was dependent upon answering questions of economic rationality (Shishkan, 1969, p. 8).

In the 1960s and 1970s, the findings of economic research repeatedly showed that female labour had characteristics which distinguished it from male labour. Numerous findings substantiated Kozachenko's conclusion that a social division of labour existed between men and women. Kozachenko's data on collective farms in Moldavia indicated that men worked in either skilled mechanised jobs or in administrative posts, while women performed unskilled manual tasks (Kozachenko, 1969, p. 6). It was generally the case that women did different work from men and received lower pay. Empirical social science also showed that inequalities persisted in housework and childrearing; consequently women enjoyed less free time than men.[2] In turn, women had fewer opportunities to increase their qualifications at night-school or through correspondence courses. It was stressed that this sexual division of labour was not caused by discrimination against women, but by different levels of training and by low levels of mechanisation (Panova, 1970, p. 1).

Shishkan argued that women's skills should be increased by harnessing the results of the scientific–technological revolution. Mechanisation of the jobs women performed and a retraining of female labour would result in a reduction in the number of women in manual work and a narrowing of the existing division between 'male' and 'female' spheres (Shishkan, 1969, p. 14). Furthermore, labour would be more productive and rationally organised; women would benefit and so would the economy. The ideological claim made was such improvements were possible because socialism had destroyed the foundations of the contradiction between male and female labour inherent in capitalism (Lukashuk, 1976, p. 7). Socialist planning could rectify any remaining non-antagonistic contradictions.

But mechanisation alone, Gruzdeva argued, would not necessarily increase women's qualification level or end inequalities in pay. Non-antagonistic contradictions in skills and earnings would not be resolved by actions in the workplace alone; changes in domestic roles also were necessary. This was because woman's role as worker was not shaped solely by the level of mechanisation. The second shift of work, in particular motherhood, conflicted with a role in the workforce; there was a non-antagonistic contradiction between the roles of mother and worker. Moreover, the tension between them was made more acute by queuing for food, cooking, cleaning, washing and ironing (Gruzdeva, 1979b, p. 192). Nevertheless, under socialism state action could soften the contradiction of the female 'double burden' or 'double shift': firstly, the socialist state could protect the health of working women; secondly, it could improve social services; and thirdly, it could offer women the opportunity to work part-time.

There was general agreement that the female organism should be protected from harmful working conditions, such as dust, chemicals, noise and wide fluctuations in temperature. It was regretted that poor working conditions persisted under socialism, which harmed women's health (Panova, 1970, p. 16). Various recommendations were put forward to combat this, including special commissions for examining women's working conditions, a department of women's work to be attached to local soviets to monitor labour conditions, and a year off work after childbirth rather than an immediate return to the workplace. In 1976 the newly named State Committee on Labour and Social Questions, previously known as the USSR State Committee on Questions of Labour and Wages, broadened its scope to devote greater attention to problems faced by working women. In addition, Commissions for Questions Concerning the Work and Daily Life of Women and For the Protection of Mothers and Children were set up in both the Supreme Soviet and in the legislatures of each union republic. Similarly, trade union commissions began to inspect women's working conditions and to offer recommendations for improvement (Moses, 1978b, pp. 46–8; Volkova *et al.*, 1979, 1984).

It was also considered important to make more provision of public dining rooms, kindergartens, creches, social services and household appliances. Public catering would reduce woman's time spent shopping, preparing food and washing up, more up-to-date appliances, such as washing machines, would ease housework; an increase in the quantity and quality of kindergartens would reduce the demands of childcare. More services were particularly needed in rural areas where they were markedly lacking; a non-antagonistic contradiction existed between town and country, with the former far-outstripping the latter in services. Another non-antagonistic contradiction prevailed between small- and medium-sized towns on the one hand and large towns on the other. More jobs were available in large towns due to an unequal distribution of industry across territory. Very often small- and medium-sized towns lacked the employment opportunities for women that large towns offered. In those small towns where opportunities did exist, kindergarten provision was frequently deficient. This made it hard for mothers to be workers (Panova, 1970, p. 11).

The vast majority of Soviet women continued to endure second domestic shifts.[3] The main solution to this exhausting workload was thought to be an increase in state services. Yet some sociologists, frequently women, mentioned the need for the 'creation of collective relations in the family' and the desirability of changes in the structure of family domestic tasks. Iankova quickly qualified this thesis by arguing that a sharing of the domestic shift was temporary – the long-term goal of socialism was 'the liquidation of these functions'. In the meantime, it was desirable for housework to be shared, but it did not follow that domestic duties should be divided 'in equal parts between men and women' (Iankova, 1975, p. 50). This was not viewed as an issue directly connected to attaining 'factual equality' since ultimately it was state provision rather than adjustment of personal relations, which would ease housework. Avoiding extensive discussion of the domestic division of labour and the nature of men's contribution to domestic work, Iankova and others bypassed questions of the nature of male–female relations in the home and their relevance to equality. Discourse around the theme of the 'personal is political' was precluded.

Shishkan and others argued that 'One of the ways of solving problems of the effective use of female labour is to grant women the opportunity to work a part-time day, or a part of the working week (Shishkan, 1969, p. 17; 1976, pp. 163–80). Shishkan considered the rationalisation of female labour had to take both domestic and non-domestic roles into account. Shishkan maintained that the advantages of part-time labour would both secure greater harmony between the roles of the workplace and home and result in higher output by women in their jobs. She cited evidence suggesting that the productivity of those working part-time is higher than that of those in full-time jobs and argued that some workers would prefer part-time jobs. Results of a questionnaire indicated that 12 per cent of women and 5 per cent of men approached expressed the wish to work part-time (Shishkan, 1969, p. 17). A survey conducted by Panova in a Lithuanian enterprise employing mainly women revealed that 19.6 per cent of women wanted part-time work, 80.7 per cent of whom were under 40. They gave childcare, poor health and the desire to study as the main reasons (Panova, 1970, pp. 17–18). No doubt more would be in favour of it, added Shishkan, if a drop in pay did not come with a reduction in hours worked outside the home.

Despite her support for part-time labour, Shishkan believed that it 'has only subsidiary significance for solving questions of female labour'. Mechanising production and increasing the levels of technical skills were of paramount importance since 'The solution of these problems will provide the opportunity not only to raise the effectiveness of female labour, but also bring about factual social equality of the sexes' (Shishkan, 1969, p. 19). Attaining factual equality was thus explicitly tied to mechanisation and an increase in skills. The economic determinism of Marxism proved to be highly durable.

The controversial aspect of Shishkan's thesis was the desirability of part-time labour for women. Panova claimed that equality of the sexes did not necessarily mean equal time in the workforce for men and women if this meant a heavier overall burden for women (Panova, 1970, p. 18). Another economist interviewed in Moscow argued that she would like to see all women with children up to 4 years of age enjoy shorter working hours without a reduction in pay. As she put it:

> That would fulfil what Lenin wanted. Equality does not mean equality of work demands. Equality means to achieve according to abilities. Women have two main roles – one in the economy and one as mother. Therefore, to be equal means women should have less time at work, and in the long run her work hours would be the same as a man's. (Buckley, 1986a, pp. 55–6)

Others skipped any such notion of equality and argued like one Soviet lawyer that 'part-time labour is not a step backwards. If a woman worked one hour less, her role in the family would be performed much better' (Buckley, 1986a, p. 94). Another lawyer contested this position with the following argument:

> A shortening of the working day would make it impossible for women to hold leadership positions. These jobs would be given to men. Part-time labour would mean a regression in the development of the individual. Women need to attain a certain qualification level. They should not be ashamed in front of men. Women should want to be on a par with men. They should not want less. (Buckley, 1986a, p. 87)

In a similar vein, one sociologist interviewed acknowledged:

> Experts have different opinions about part-time labour. It is not a bad thing, but only for some women, not for many. It is mainly for those with small children. Part-time labour has its complications. In some jobs it is difficult to arrange. It depends on the qualification level of women, and in some fields it is not possible. It is not the most pressing problem we have to solve because we have a high demand for workers which is increasing. Women, therefore, cannot just choose to do part-time work.... Part-time labour does lead to a lowering of the position of women in the labour force. If I worked part-time, I would feel that people would judge me as doing half a job and I would feel bad. (Buckley, 1986a, pp. 22–3)

Disagreement not only took place between specialists, but was also openly acknowledged in interviews and in printed material.

The CPSU, however, made its position on part-time labour clear at the 25th party Congress in 1976 by declaring its commitment to 'create greater opportunities for women with children to work a part-day or part-week and also to work at home (*Materialy XXV s"ezda*, 1976, p. 217). The debate about the desirability of part-time work had raged in the 1960s and continued throughout the 1970s. This official policy appeared after discussion had been going on for ten years among social scientists. Arguments about the implications of part-time labour did not cease immediately after the party line was declared. Debate was sufficiently heated to have created a strong momentum. Similarly lively disagreements took place over the seriousness of the decline in the birth rate and its implications for women's reproductive life. The two issues of part-time labour and desirable family size stand out in the 1970s as being especially controversial.

Demographic problems and female roles

Falling birth rates became an issue since projections suggested that labour shortages, which already existed by the 1970s, would be aggravated in the future. Before the 1960s the supply of workers generally exceeded demand by as many as 200–300 thousand. By 1970, however, there was a shortage of 1.7 million industrial workers relative to plan requirements (Feshbach and Rapawy, 1973, p. 487). To the regret of many demographers one-child families were increasingly popular, as Table 5.1 shows.

Urbanisation, industrialisation and population losses all contributed to falling birth rates and smaller families.[4] The number of births per 1,000 population had fallen from 44.0 in 1926 to 26.7 in 1950, as Table 5.2 shows. This decline continued, albeit more gently, to reach 24.9 births per 1,000 population in 1960 and 17.4 in 1970. Although the population was still increasing in size, the rate of increase had fallen considerably. Soviet estimates projected further falls up to the year 2000.

The Soviet demographer Viktor Perevedentsev pointed out in the

Table 5.1 Percentage distribution of Soviet children according to order of birth

Year	First child	Second child	Third child	Fourth child	Fifth (and later) child
1965	34.4	27.4	14.0	8.7	15.5
1975	45.3	28.5	9.0	5.0	11.4

Source: Perevedentsev, 1977, p. 12

Table 5.2 Natural increases in the Soviet population, 1926–1978, with projections to 2000, as estimated in the 1970s (per 1,000 population)

Year	Births	Deaths	Natural increase
1926	44.0	20.3	23.7
1940	31.2	18.0	13.2
1950	26.7	9.7	17.0
1960	24.9	7.1	17.8
1970	17.4	8.2	9.2
1978	18.3	9.8	8.5
1990	17.3	9.8	7.5
2000	16.0	10.2	5.2

Sources: Perevedentsev, 1979, p. 6; Feshbach and Rapawy, 1976, p. 112

1970s that the population was ageing. The economy needed a young work-force, not an elderly population requiring extensive social services and pensions. According to Perevedentsev, in the late 1920s the net reproduction rate (the replacement rate of women of a mother's generation by their daughters) was 1.7, but it subsequently fell to 1.3 in the 1950s and 1.1 at the end of the 1960s. Only in Transcaucasia, Kazakhstan and Soviet Central Asia was this index in the 1970s over 2.0. In areas containing three-quarters of the population, the net reproduction rate was less than 1.0 (Perevedentsev, 1975, p. 120). Disparities in net reproduction rates in different parts of the Soviet Union reflected different attitudes to family size. In Azerbaidzhan, for instance, 54 per cent of rural families had four or more children, compared with 8.1 per cent of rural families in the Russian republic and a tiny 4 per cent in Estonia. Slavic and Baltic women, in particular, were choosing to have smaller families and were more active in the labour force, whilst in Muslim areas relatively large families remained the norm.

A breakdown of the data according to ethnic group rather than republic, as in Table 5.3, shows that the rate of population increase for Russians, Baltic peoples, Ukrainians and Belorussians between 1959 and 1970 fell below the average annual rate of population growth for these years of 1.3 per cent. By contrast, the rates of increase among Muslim groups, such as Uzbeks, Tadzhiks and Azerbaidzhanis, were nearly three times this national level. These trends caused concern in Moscow for political, economic and military reasons.[5]

Table 5.3 Average annual rates of increase of
principal ethnic groups, 1959–1970 (%)

Estonian	0.2	Armenian	2.3
Latvian	0.2	Kazakh	3.5
Ukrainian	0.8	Azerbaidzhani	3.7
Russian	1.1	Kirgiz	3.7
Belorussian	1.2	Tadzhik	3.9
Lithuanian	1.2	Turkmenian	3.9
Georgian	1.7	Uzbek	3.9
Moldavian	1.8		

Source: Leedy, 1973, p. 450

Demographers, in particular, viewed the situation with concern. As one interviewed in Moscow said:

> The drop in the birth rate is a very grave problem. It is very interesting. There is no similar example in history. There has always been a high birth rate. Today European Russia has a low birth rate. No change is likely in the future. Moscow seems to be twenty years ahead of the rest of the country demographically. There will be a demographic catastrophe if all areas go the way Moscow has gone. We need to increase the prestige of woman, wife and mother. We could give women work to do at home. We can do this through the party using political measures. (Buckley, 1986a, p. 76)

Another demographer concurred:

> The fall in the birth rate is a serious problem. There is a need for a demographic policy. I would like women to give up work after childbirth. I would like to stimulate the birth rate. We do not want de-population. Each woman must have 2.8 children to prevent de-population. (Buckley, 1986a, p. 76)

However, not all social scientists reached the same conclusions as these male demographers. A female economist, for instance, acknowledged that:

> It is a serious problem and a complicated one to solve. We can give women a shorter working day. Again we need the conditions for a combination of roles. If a woman does not want three children, then there is no need to have them. (Buckley, 1986a, p. 59)

Another economist hesitated to encourage families to produce children they did not really want by arguing:

> Most people say that the birth rate needs to increase. But there is also the question of the quality of the child's upbringing. We need to raise that

quality. Furthermore, we cannot influence the individual desires of families. It is their business how many children they have. (Buckley, 1986a, p. 51)

Among those social scientists who took declining birth rates seriously, not all saw the problem as deserving attention at the expense of other priorities. However as the 1970s progressed, greater importance was attached by social scientists to the demographic structure of the population and stronger measures were put forward to influence it. Newspaper articles also tried to encourage women to marry young, anticipating that more children would result than from later marriages. One even re-interpreted the writings of Engels in an attempt to give this suggestion ideological legitimacy: 'Engels warned that a drawn-out courtship is in nine cases out of ten a schooling for conjugal infidelity, whereas a short courtship lends stability to the marriage' (Baltianskii, 1971, p. 3).[6] Another article suggested that 'passion' between the sexes was an important ingredient in long-term unions. Although Kollontai was cited as the inspiration for this thought, adherence to the overall spirit of her writings on male–female relations was lacking (*Komsomol'skaia Pravda*, 14 April 1976). Demographers and others subordinated the professional advancement of women to an increase in the prestige of marriage and motherhood. They gave precedence to childrearing over woman's role in economic production and political life.

Those who argued against the points made by demographers stressed the importance of women's professional roles, not just to the economy, but to the personal development of women themselves. One economist expressed his objections this way:

> There is an emotional reaction to the fall in the birth rate. It is like crying wolf. But we do need to balance the growth rate between republics. No catastrophe exists. I disagree with Urlanis[7] who wants women to have three children and a break after each one. Women cannot be strong on all fronts at once. It would mean that there would be no time for professional women to be professional. There is no need to panic about the birth rate. (Buckley, 1986a, p. 46)

A sociologist similarly emphasised that motherhood is just one aspect of a woman's life and therefore 'To give oneself wholeheartedly to children is not enough. Children demand attention and this demands time. If you cannot give time, you should not have children' (Buckley, 1986a, p. 23). The resistance to an official natalist policy was couched around the themes of women's professional and personal development, the quality of childcare and personal choice.

In debates about the desirability of part-time labour and the gravity of the decline in the birth rate, there was general agreement that women workers constituted a 'special category' of labour due to their roles in production and reproduction. But there was no debate at all about the relevance of feminism to women's lives, nor any suggestion that feminism might be anything other than bourgeois. The rather rigid orthodoxy was that women were a separate group of workers from men and a specific category of social labour due to the 'inalienable and irreplaceable' functions of motherhood. Moreover, female 'psychophysiological characteristics' rendered women not only different from men in physiology, but in character too (Zagrebel'nyi, 1977, p. 1; Kotliar and Turchaninova, 1975, p. 6). Women were portrayed as emotional, gentle, delicate, thoughtful, kind, sensitive and understanding (Iankova, 1978, p. 125). These character traits, which stem from biological and psychological differences between the sexes, meant that women devoted more time than men to the upbringing of children because they were better suited to nurturing roles. Furthermore, 'psychophysiological differences' challenged the need for a rigid sharing of roles in society or in the home. The existence of these important differences led theorists to conclude that communism would not eliminate the division of labour between the sexes (Nagiev, 1971, p. 21; Alibekova, 1972, p. 23).

This strand of Soviet ideology underlined woman's potential as warm childrearer and sensitive educator, but played down other aspects of her many-sided potential. Also by implication, the biological inability of men to give birth denied them the kindness and understanding typical of women and made them less suited to certain domestic roles. This was not explicitly stated in Soviet ideology, merely implied. The male role as childrearer was a non-topic in the 1960s and 1970s.

Traditional gender role stereotypes were reinforced by these arguments, and questions as to whether nature, nurture or an interaction of both, resulted in different characteristics was not posed.[8] Indeed, comments on socialisation maintained that 'natural' differences between the sexes should be reinforced; femininity and masculinity should be cultivated, not denied. It was not suggested that casting woman as the main childrearer, cook, shopper, washer and cleaner might result in gender inequalities. Such a suggestion was regarded as typical of bourgeois feminism.

Against bourgeois feminism

The growth of Western research in the 1960s and 1970s into the position of women in the USSR provoked an attack on Western feminism and a renewed stress on the argument made in the 1920s that the woman question should not be separated from other problems and/did not need an independent women's movement. Iankova, in particular, maintained that 'the problem of woman's social equality is impossible to solve if not connected to general tasks of social liberation' (Iankova, 1975, p. 42). Many Western feminists would agree but they would still argue in favour of examining different aspects of the woman question more thoroughly and against always defining women's issues as relative to other problems.

Ignoring the different perspectives within Western feminism, Iankova challenged the alleged position of American feminists that equality of the sexes means that women should be identical with men. If men and women were alike, objected Iankova, important gender role differences would be ruled out; but these should be preserved.[9] The 'anti-family tendencies' supposedly typical of Western feminists were also condemned since they were in the interests neither of society nor of women (Iankova, 1975, p. 48). The family was the nucleus of socialist society in which individual and social interests coincided and an institution which grows stronger as socialism progresses. Where Marx and Engels left the nature of the future family an open question, the Soviet state from 1930 until the present has been committed to stable nuclear families. Against Kollontai's statement that 'the family is ceasing to be a necessity', many Soviet sociologists subscribe to the view that 'Kollontai stood like most Marxists on all points, except on the future of the family. History has proved her wrong on this. New forms of the family do not last' (Buckley, 1986a, p. 12). According to official Soviet ideology of the 1970s, the transformation of the family was a complicated process, but at every stage of its development, the family reflected the material and cultural level of society.

Women's political roles

Just as society determined family structure, so society shaped opportunities for political participation. Under Brezhnev, women's political roles were less salient than their economic and domestic lives due to the priority given to production and reproduction; the primacy given by Khrushchev to political roles ceased. Nevertheless, ideology did not ignore women and politics. In the 1970s it became popular to argue that political equality was one element of factual equality and that the extent of women's participation in politics 'depends on the level of development of the social organism in general', on the character of economic relations and the level of consciousness of the working people (Main, 1974, p. 13). However, women's political activity under developed socialism suffered from the non-antagonistic contradiction between what is 'possible' and what 'is'. Equality of political participation was indeed 'possible', but reality or what 'is' lagged behind (Main, 1974, pp. 3–4).

Writers who drew attention to different levels of political activity according to sex tended to fall back on labelling them as unsolved problems, or vestiges of the past, and blaming weak services, the double burden and lack of free time (Rakhimova, 1967, p. 60; Dirzhinskaite, 1975, p. 28; Mollaeva, 1978, p. 62). An expanding literature in the Soviet discipline of 'scientific atheism' also focused on the religious roots of women's reluctance to engage in politics (Vagabov, 1975; Ashirov, 1978; Bairamsakhatov, 1979). Authors generally concluded that a concerted effort was needed to encourage more women to become involved in political activity and thereby render what 'is ' commensurate with the 'possible' and 'necessary'. Such an effort was to be directed by the party, trade unions and social organisations, in particular the *zhensovety*.

The *zhensovety* or women's councils continued, at least, a formal existence throughout the Brezhnev years. The little written about them echoed points made under Khrushchev. They were praised for encouraging women to participate in social activities and for improving their qualifications. Their central aims were said to be to raise women's political consciousness and cultural level and to persuade women to develop their abilities (Dirzhinskaite, 1975, p. 28; Browning, 1987). Evidence suggests, however, that more challenging questions about gender roles and political consciousness were posed by the *zhensovety* during the Khrushchev years, rather than in the Brezhnev era (Saltykov, 1960; Zakhovaeva, 1961, pp. 18–19; Alkhazova, 1964, pp. 4–27).

As under Khrushchev, the *zhensovety* were billed as 'helpers' of the CPSU by creating a 'reserve of female cadres for promotion to leadership positions' (Rakhimova, 1967, p. 60). But the promotion of women was not a hallmark of the Brezhnev era. No woman sat on the *Politburo* throughout the entire 18 years of Brezhnev's leadership. By 1976, 14 women out of a total of 426 members made up just 3.3 per cent of the Central Committee, a slight decrease from their 3.8 per cent in 1971 (15 out of 397) and 4.2 per cent in 1966 (15 out of 360). At the last party Congress over which Brezhnev presided in 1981, the number of women rose to 19, but since the size of the Central Committee increased to 470, the percentage of female members fell to 4.0 per cent. [10] Women were similarly absent from top jobs in the middle levels of the party hierarchy. No woman attained the powerful post of *oblast*, or regional, first secretary; women comprised 4 per cent of urban and district party secretaries and only at the local level were they prominent, where one-third of first secretaries of primary party organisations were women. More impressive at first sight, the number of women in the CPSU increased from 2.5 million in 1966 to 3.9 million in 1977 and to 4.6 million in 1981. But these increases amounted to only small proportional rises from 20.6 per cent of all party members in 1966 to 24.7 per cent in 1977 and to 26.5 per cent in 1981 (*Partiinaia zhizn'*, no. 14, July 1981, pp. 13–26; Browning, 1987, pp. 25–7). There is what Jerry Hough accurately describes as a 'gross over-representation' of males in the CPSU (Hough, 1976, p. 120).

By focusing on easily visible reasons for women's low participation in politics and slow promotion to top administrative jobs, such as the double burden, social scientists failed to raise the possibility of structures of inequality in the Soviet system. They did not explore mechanisms of excluding women from important political posts such as the informal networks of Soviet city administration which served to screen women out through what Stephen Sternheimer calls their 'male bias' (Sternheimer, 1983, pp. 149–50). *Inter alia* men were more likely to drink vodka with male colleagues and to conduct informal business without women. The relationship between the exclusion of women from such networks on the one hand and hiring, promotion and *nomenklatura* on the other, was not even hinted at by social scientists as a possibility. Ideological 'gatekeepers' prevented discussion of discrimination against women in the compilation of *nomenklatura* lists and Soviet social scientists therefore did not examine why the female presence was higher in local party politics, but fell off sharply at higher levels. Social scientists did not even draw attention to these variations. The question of why there was not a female *obkom* first secretary was not posed because it was ideologically out of bounds. The question of the relevance to political mobilisation of skills practised in the *zhensovety*, such as sewing, was not raised either (Browning, 1985b, p. 221). The notion that high politics was 'dirty' and demanding 'very hard work' continued to be the rationalisation given by Soviet social scientists in interviews for why politics was a male preserve. The rationalisation itself suggests the existence of mechanisms of exclusion.

In these years, Soviet social scientists did not investigate many questions about female roles. Among these were: the significance of top political leaders and administrators being concentrated among one sex; the many different forms of discrimination against women that existed under socialism; the reason why jobs performed by men tended to be paid more than jobs done by women; physical violence against women; the significance of a lack of contraception and a high abortion rate. Ideological and political constraints precluded these channels of inquiry which were pursued only in the underground *samizdat* literature, and even there they received minimal treatment (Women in Eastern Europe Group, 1980). Nevertheless, debate about female roles was much wider between 1965 and 1981 than had been the case for almost 40 years. Moreover, policy-makers became more sensitive to the need to address inequalities in practice. However, preoccupation in the late 1970s and early 1980s with declining birth rates and the importance of motherhood led to concentration on woman's role as mother and childrearer.

The early 1980s: Demographic policy and the woman question

While many of the arguments of the 1960s and 1970s were reiterated in the early 1980s during Brezhnev's final years and the brief leaderships of Iuri Andropov and Konstantin Chernenko, treatment of the 'woman question' shifted.[11] It differed from the past in that it was linked directly to 'the problems of encouraging a growth in the birth rate and rearing the future generations (Rzhanitsina, 1983, p. 73). The explicit linkage of the woman question to the 'population problem' was consistent with the message of the 26th party Congress of 1981 which declared:

In accordance with the instructions of the 25th party Congress the Central Committee has given serious attention to the drawing up and implementation of an effective *demographic policy*, aggravated in recent years by the population problem. The main way to solve it is through greater concern for the family, newlyweds and above all women. [applause] It is surely clear to everyone how at times it is not easy to combine the duties of motherhood with active participation in production and society. (*Materialy XXVI s"ezda*, 1981, p. 54)

Declaring strong support for a natalist policy, the Congress noted that despite all the measures already taken to ease the female double burden, 'a noticeable turning point has not yet come about. Wider and more effective measures are needed' (*Materialy XXVI s"ezda*, 1981, p. 55). Support was reaffirmed for more kindergartens, part-time labour for women and up to a year off work after childbirth. More explicitly than under Khrushchev official policy was committed to boosting the birth rate and more wholeheartedly than hitherto to alleviating the double burden.

In keeping with the official connection between the woman question and the population problem, demographers' contributions to discussions began to carry greater legitimacy and weight. After the 26th party Congress, Perevedentsev argued forcefully that unless the birth rate rose considerably in the 1990s, there could be a serious strain on labour resources during the second decade of the twenty-first century when the particularly large cohort born in the 1950s reached retirement age. Perevedentsev argued that 'it is important to act now' in order to prevent negative population trends from intensifying and, if possible, 'to optimise the process of population reproduction' (Perevedentsev, 1982, pp. 80–8). This could be done, he suggested, through a special programme for supporting marriage and family relations. Similar arguments were being put forward at conferences on demography and were voiced with increasing regularity in Soviet academic journals and newspapers.

Demography as a subject seemed to increase in status: by the early 1980s its standing was higher than it had ever been in the USSR and was certainly not as precarious as it had been from the 1930s to the 1950s (Desfosses, 1976, pp. 244–56). Most issues of the journal *Sotsiologicheskie Issledovaniia* (Sociological Research), carried a section on demography and a stream of books with titles such as *Demograficheskaia Politika v SSSR* (Demographic policy in the USSR) and *Demograficheskie Problemy i Sem'ia* (Demographic problems and the family) began appearing in greater numbers in the late 1970s and early 1980s (Vishnevskii, 1977; Riabushkin, 1978; Shuvalov, 1978; Riabushkin and Galetskaia, 1983; Valentei, 1983a). The number of titles on women and work typical of the late 1960s and early 1970s, declined as those on demography increased.

A more popular literature also appeared giving advice on marriage, contraception and sex. One manual published in 1981 carried a chapter entitled 'Soon a child in the family' which propagandised:

> Pregnancy and birth are necessary for the female organism. It is well known that after childbirth woman blossoms for a second time, and starts to live a full life. Women who have many children usually look younger than their age and younger than those without children. (Khodakov, 1981, p. 99)

The special programme for supporting the institution of marriage favoured by Perevedentsev had clearly commenced.

The ideology of demographic policy was somewhat vague. According to Dmitri Valentei:

> The handling of demographic policy is legitimately regarded as an organic part of socio-economic policy at the stage of developed socialism: changes in population reflect the course of social progress and, at the same time, exercise a major influence on the economy and the growth of productive forces. (Valentei, 1983b, p. 44)

'Demographic control' was viewed as an 'organic part of the complex problem of socio-economic management' (Valentei, 1983b, p. 13). The way to accomplish 'communist population development', according to Timon Riabushkin, was to adopt a 'systems approach' to deal with the 'complex' and 'contradictory' demographic situation. Major demographic problems, he argued, could not be solved through 'individual measures', but only by 'coping with the whole gamut of socio-economic problems' (Riabushkin, 1983, p. 44).

The precise relationships between elements of the 'whole gamut' was hard to specify. Riabushkin insisted that the current level of knowledge in the USSR 'does not yet allow us to determine the precise extent of the interaction between demographic and socio-economic processes'. In particular, it was not easy 'to assess the impact of individual social or economic factors on a particular change in the population'. Once again the reason behind these difficulties lay in the 'unusually complex processes of social life'. At best, Riabushkin suggested, one could state that socio-economic relations played a determining role in both socio-economic processes and demographic changes, these latter being 'two independently developing components of the historical process' (Riabushkin, 1983, p. 44). One of the tasks of the 1980s was to enquire into the relationship between these components.

The central problem under developed socialism was identified as the declining birth rate. But this, Valentei stressed, was nothing to do with socialism *per se*. Rather:

> There are several objective factors why there are fewer children in the family. However, it is hardly a permanent process natural to socialism. Rather the present trend toward a declining birth rate stems from the specific contradictions of the moment, a certain period in Soviet society's economic development, when the best possible balance between all fields of material production and the non-productive sphere has not yet been secured. (Valentei, 1983b, p. 15)

The lag in the development of the 'non-productive sphere' was seen as all important. Insufficient kindergarten facilities, inadequate pre-school education, not enough new flats and shortcomings in the service sphere deterred working women from having more than one child. Some, like Valentei, depicted these lags as non-antagonistic contradictions. Riabushkin characterised them as 'difficulties' associated with 'a number of objective circumstances' which were not 'serious contradictions' (Riabushkin, 1983, p. 48).

In addition to these objective reasons for small families are subjective ones. Riabushkin regretted that the position of women in the family 'does not always correspond to their social status' (Riabushkin, 1983, p. 48). While respected by co-workers in the labour force, women were 'overburdened' at home. Whereas during the period 1965–1981 there was little discussion about changing male domestic roles, writers of the early 1980s rather gingerly edged the issue onto the agenda.

The early 1980s: Male roles and domestic labour

Brezhnev, speaking to the Trade Union Congress in March 1977, thanked women for their 'self-sacrificing work' and said 'To speak plainly: we men are indebted to them [applause]. We have still done far from everything to ease the double burden' (*Pravda*, 22 March 1977, p. 1). Whilst Iankova had hesitated to develop this theme in the 1970s, Novikova, Sidorova and Turchaninova in the 1980s came out clearly in favour of husbands and children actively participating in housework. They maintained that many trade unions 'are striving to overcome the tenacious tradition of shifting all the housework onto the shoulders of women and are propagandising the structure of families where men and children actively participate in housework' (Novikova *et al.* 1984, p. 162). Rzhanitsina warned that the unfair distribution of household responsibilities led to female discontent in marriage. If men assumed more active domestic roles, the female double burden would be alleviated, marriage might be more stable, divorce less likely and more children a possibility.

But like Iankova before her, Rzhanitsina hesitated to prescribe the boundaries of the male role in domestic labour and qualified her support for changing male roles:

> Of course we are not embarking on an itemised distribution of absolutely every household responsibility and chores between husband and wife and other members of the family, but are speaking about a rational distribution of work and the creation of the best possible situation for each member of the family. (Rzhanitsina, 1983, p. 168)

More labour-saving household appliances, she felt, would create opportunities for 'restructuring' the traditional distribution of household chores allowing men to 'help out' with the arduous tasks. Where restructuring domestic labour meant no more than a helping hand for Rzhanitsina, it meant much more for Novikova, Sidorova and Turchaninova and became an issue for propaganda.

Linking the male domestic role to the decline in the birth rate gave it the status of a legitimate problem. It was not raised due to a concern with sexual equality *per se*, as it was in the 1920s. Nevertheless, interviews conducted in the Soviet Union in 1979, 1980 and 1984 with female sociologists made clear that its relevance to equality was on their minds, even if they did not usually express it in this way on paper. However, going further than others, Gruzdeva and Chertikhina devoted a whole section of a book published in 1983 to 'Children, Husbands, Free Time' (Gruzdeva and Chertikhina, 1983, pp. 182–208). They documented how men spent more time than women watching television; walking in the park; meeting friends; reading books, newspapers and journals; going to dances, the cinema, theatre, concerts and museums; studying; and pursuing hobbies such as photography, painting, sport, hunting and fishing. While teenage women spent more time reading than men, as soon as they married, and even before children were born, their reading time fell substantially. Married men, by contrast, read more. Interestingly the great drop for women did not take place after children were born, when only a small reduction occurred, but before. Gruzdeva and Chertik-hina did not develop their findings into a coherent critique of traditional gender roles and attitudes, but they ended their book with a gentle appeal to men:

> Women readers will undoubtedly be overjoyed at the great attention the state has devoted to them in the process of socialist and communist transformation. Male readers will more than once have noted the relevance of themselves to the creation for women of the most propitious circumstances for the successful combination of a chosen profession with the roles of mother and housewife. Men who have read this book should recall that 'The height of culture is defined by relations towards woman' [Gor'kii]. (Gruzdeva and Chertikhina, 1983, pp. 220–1)

The Gor'kii quotation echoed the views of Fourier and Marx on the nature of human relations discussed in Chapter 1.

More pointed comments about male behaviour towards women were made by a writer from Czechoslovakia whose work was translated into Russian in 1982. Frantishek Khorvat criticised the lack of a male domestic shift, condemned the attitudes that go with it and reprimanded young bridegrooms who shortly after their weddings:

> start to demand from their wives those privileges that their fathers enjoyed. They do not think about the fact that their wives work, just as they do. These young men do not understand that it is no longer possible to live as in 'their home', that today it is not possible to live with old ideas about the family and love. (Khorvat, 1982, p. 89)

The re-education of men was recommended as the key to the ending of traditional male attitudes. Khorvat stated:

> Without doubt, contemporary fathers can consciously correct the mistakes of their education. A great deal here depends on their wives, who to a considerable extent can educate and re-educate husbands. However, this depends upon the consciousness of the women themselves. (Khorvat, 1982, p. 89)

While Khorvat's work left many questions unbroached, such as what constitutes the 'consciousness of women' and what the 're-education' of males actually entailed, it moved in the direction of a much broader analysis of female–male relations than had been seen in the USSR since Kollontai's preliminary tracts of the 1920s.

Equality, problem solving and social integration

The woman question was declared relevant to a host of other issues because of theoretical elaborations on what 'developed socialism' entailed. Soviet theoretical writings now represented developed socialist society as one in which there are 'ever greater opportunities for the solution to problems' because greater 'scientific control' of socio-economic processes was possible than in previous stages of social development (Valentei, 1983b, p. 11; Novikova et al., 1984, p. 8). The analysis of social phenomena, which involved exposure of society's shortcomings and a search for ways to overcome them was a necessary precondition of this control. It was acknowledged that thorough enquiry into the position of women in society had only recently been undertaken because solutions were just not possible in the past (Novikova et al., 1984, p. 5). This was consistent with Marx's observation that mankind only sets itself those problems which it can solve. Novikova, Sidorova and Turchaninova argued that 'Before, mainly for economic reasons, it was not possible to solve many problems at once, therefore at each stage of socialist construction priority was given to the most urgent' (Novikova et al., 1984, p. 154). Under developed socialism problems could be solved, but sensitivity to their complexity and awareness of their relationships to other problems was necessary. 'Complexity' was the key word. While the existence of several such 'complexities' was noted in the 1960s and 1970s, specification of the intricacies of processes of social change was the task of the 1980s.

The complexity of solving the woman question was now connected in principle to processes of social integration, attaining social homo-geneity, achieving equality, developing democracy, promoting collective agreement and pursuing communist morality. Furthermore, these processes were all seen as interrelated because the stage of developed socialism, later declared 'a whole historical epoch' by Chernenko, heralded 'the turning of the socialist system into a totality' (Kosolapov et al., 1983, p. 40; Bakinskii Rabochii, 5 April 1985, p. 2). As an organic whole, developed socialism faced inter-related tasks of broadening scope.

Promoting equality was thus just one of its tasks. Moreover, the process of attaining complete social equality according to sex (*polnoe sotsial'noe ravenstvo zhenshchin i myzhchin*) was now cast as part of two distinct, albeit related, general processes of constructing a socially homogeneous society and a classless one (Novikova *et al.*, 1984, p 4). Social homogeneity referred to complete abolition of the old division of labour. Processes which in the past made the working class and collective farm peasantry different from each other were now said to be on the wane. The general trend of developed socialism was social integration, which led to 'the increasingly greater assertion of social equality' (Kosalapov, 1983, p. 133).

The process of social integration was associated with a growth in the role of non-class or inter-class distinctions in everyday life. Harking back to a theme popularised by Khrushchev, differences between social groups such as women, pensioners, young workers, young farmers, students and pupils were emphasised together with the desirability of a differentiated approach to cope with their various needs (Neliubin, 1983, p. 69). Theorists insisted that these non-class distinctions did not clash with social integration since they were not divisive in the manner of class antagonisms.

A 'differentiated approach' to suit the distinct needs of different social groups would be catered for by the development of democracy, the increased role of trade unions and development of forms of collective agreement (*kollektivnye dogovory*) (Novikova *et al.*, 1984, pp. 153–249). In recognising women as a distinct social group, trade union commissions could analyse the difficulties they faced and offer policy recommendations to the CPSU to alleviate them. Participation in policy-making was, in theory at least, broadened through collective agreement. At the 17th Trade Union Congress in 1982, Brezhnev reasserted the relevance of trade unions to the development of democracy, and also scolded them, along with three ministries, for not paying sufficient attention to issues affecting women (*Materialy XVII s"ezda professional'nykh soiuzov*, 1982, p. 55).

Just as the role of the trade unions was one aspect of developing democracy, so too was an increase in female participation in leadership roles. It was now argued that although socialism created the conditions for female participation in leadership roles, 'due to a number of reasons women do not always take full advantage of these opportunities' (Novikova *et al.*, 1984, p. 155). Yet again a differentiated approach to political mobilisation allegedly eased access to management posts and triggered broader processes such as 'the growth of creative activity' and 'the many-sided harmonious development of the identity (*lichnost'*) of women' (Novikova *et al.*, 1984, p. 159). More spare time for women was seen as conducive to *lichnost'*, which in turn was made possible by more kindergartens, more new flats, part-time labour, skilled labour and male participation in domestic work. In addition, an expansion of skilled work was part of the general goal of ending all manual, unskilled and heavy labour, as proclaimed at the 26th party Congress and the 17th Trade Union Congress.

One dimension of this process of transforming labour was the definitive freeing of women (*okonchatel'noe osvobozhdenie*) from heavy physical work, night-shifts and work in dangerous conditions. This would not only contribute to the resolution of the non-antagonistic contradiction between mental and manual labour, but would also reduce the social division of labour according to sex, diminish disparities in skill and wages, promote the rational organisation of labour, ease the double burden, create more free time and render motherhood more attractive. In short, 'wide and effective measures' for facilitating a combination of female roles were characteristic of the organic totality of developed socialist society.

Conclusion

In the late 1960s and 1970s, a lively debate took place about female roles, although this liveliness faded in the early 1980s as demographic questions became more urgent. Aspects of women's lives, never addressed by Stalin and only broached by Khrushchev, were examined in some depth. The 'unsolved' status of the woman question under developed socialism made it possible for sociologists, economists, demographers, lawyers and journalists to examine women's roles in the home, at work and, to a lesser extent, in political life. A steady spate of books and articles on the woman question considered the relationships between these roles and made suggestions about how they could be modified. Different views were expressed and competing recommendations made as the latitude for discussion broadened and the number of non-topics correspondingly shrank. Some of the exchanges between social scientists of differing opinions were heated and exciting.

The various arguments about how best to ease the female double burden were triggered by economic worries about productivity and labour supply rather than by official interest in women's liberation. Scrutiny of the supply of kindergartens, creches and public dining rooms was prompted, not out of a concern to establish whether the preconditions of female self-determination were present, but by an interest in encouraging reproduction. Discussion of male roles edged gently onto the agenda not out of a burning desire within the male political leadership to analyse men's contribution to housework, but from anxiety about the heavy load which fell to women and which contributed to smaller family size and, possibly, to an increasing divorce rate. The official boundaries of debate about female roles had been widened, not through the conviction held by Armand and Kollontai that socialism could thrive only if women were successfully liberated, but for immediate practical problems of economic growth and labour resources.

The intensity and momentum of debate can also be attributed, in part, to the belief of some female sociologists that modifications in gender roles were overdue and that the conditions of motherhood should be made more pleasant. Once reopened, the woman question generated a range of arguments relating to women's liberation, going beyond the practical questions from which this reopening derived its legitimacy. The arguments made about female roles were different from those of the 1920s because of the different context in which they were made; they were certainly less radical. Social scientists in the 1970s and early 1980s were not inspired in the way that Kollontai had been in the 1920s to reflect upon the significance of socialist revolution for women's liberation, domestic labour, relations with men, sex life and motherhood. Notwithstanding the politically imposed limits to debate, a new freshness and dynamism now characterised discussions of female roles.

Notes

1. After Khrushchev was removed from his posts of First Secretary of the party and Chairman of the Council of Ministers, a collective leadership of Leonid Brezhnev, Alexei Kosygin and Nikolai Podgorny assumed, respectively, the positions of First Secretary (renamed General Secretary in 1966), Chairman of the Council of Ministers, and President. Upon the 'retirement' of Podgorny in 1977 for reasons of 'ill health' Brezhnev further consolidated his already growing power by taking on the office of President of the Supreme Soviet as well. Kosygin resigned in 1980 and died two months later, making Brezhnev the only survivor of the collective team.

2. Soviet sociological studies of the 1970s showed that women on average spend 10–12 hours a week preparing meals, 6 hours shopping and another 6 doing the laundry. The corresponding figures for men are 1.5–2.0 hours, 3 hours and 20–30 minutes (Pankratova and Iankova, 1978, p. 26). Soviet working women thus

Table 5.4 The Soviet population according to sex (millions)

Year	Women	Men	Preponderance of women
1897	62.9	62.0	+ 0.9
1926	75.9	71.0	+ 4.9
1939	88.0	81.6	+ 7.4
1946	100.9	75.0	+25.9
1959	114.8	94.0	+20.8
1969	129.4	110.1	+19.3
1979	140.0	122.4	+17.6

Sources: Dodge, 1966, p. 252; TsSU SSSR, 1978, p.8; TsSU SSSR, 1979, p. 4

endured a 13–15 hour day. The resulting pressures and stresses were vividly described in a short story by Natal'ia Baranskaia entitled 'A week like any other' which was published in *Novyi Mir* (Baranskaia, 1969).

3. Soviet sources show that by the end of the 1960s, 80 per cent of women of working age were employed outside the home and 7.5 per cent were studying (Pankratova and Iankova, 1978, p. 27).

4. Population losses during the Second World War created a large imbalance between the sexes. By 1946 there were 25.9 million more Soviet women than Soviet men. This deficit of males contributed to a greater mobilisation of women into the paid work-force than might otherwise have been the case. It also affected social life and many women were unable to find male partners, particularly in the older age groups. The huge number of male fatalities still left its imprint on Soviet society in the 1970s. In 1974 there were only 863 males for every 1,000 females (Perevedentsev, 1979, p. 77).

There had, in fact, been a predominance of women in the population since the early years of Soviet power. The casualties of the First World War, the Revolution and the Civil War affected the sex ratio such that in 1926 there were 71 million males to almost 76 million females. As Table 5.4 shows, this preponderance was aggravated by the losses caused by collectivisation and the purges. The close timing of these events, topped by 20 million deaths during the Second World War, had a cumulative effect on the structure of the Soviet population.

5. The proportional increase of Muslims in the USSR is viewed by some in Moscow as an increase in potentially less loyal Soviet citizens who are ethnically inferior. Believers in Russian national chauvinism do not wish to see a weakening of Slavic numerical dominance. There are also concerns about the implications of a changing ethnic composition for political stability and security. Some fear that growing numbers of Muslims may make more political demands on Moscow. Others focus on the changing composition of the Soviet army. By the end of this century one in three of the 18-year-olds joining the Soviet army is likely to be from a Muslim background. Finally, population growth is not taking place in the areas where it is most needed for economic reasons. Labour shortages under Brezhnev existed in areas of low population growth, whereas in Muslim areas there were more workers than jobs.

6. In a very different context, Engels wrote:

While women are more and more deprived of the sexual freedom of group marriage, the men are not. Actually, for men, group marriage exists to this day ... Among women, prostitution degrades only those unfortunates who fall into its clutches; and even these are not degraded to the degree it is generally believed. On the other hand it degrades the character of the entire male world. Thus, in nine cases out of ten, a long engagement is practically a preparatory school for conjugal infidelity. (Engels, 1968, p. 502)

7. Boris Urlanis was a Soviet demographer who died in the early 1980s. He was a fervent advocate of the three-child family.

8. For details of the treatment of these issues by Soviet psychologists and pedagogues, refer to Lynne Attwood, *The New Soviet Man and Woman – Sex Role Socialisation in the Soviet Union* (Attwood, 1988).

9. Iankova seems unaware of the numerous strands of Western feminism and its complexities. In particular, she cannot have read recent works which give importance to the very 'differences' between the sexes that she herself applauds.

10. For biographical details of the women named to the Central Committee of the CPSU in 1981 refer to Genia Browning, *Women and Politics in the USSR* (Browning, 1987, pp. 29–34).

11. Brezhnev died in November 1982 at the age of 76. Iuri Andropov succeeded him for just 15 months until his death in February 1984. An elderly and ailing Konstantin Chernenko then became General Secretary until he too died in March 1985.

6 Gorbachev: The Woman Question on the Move Again

Mikhail Gorbachev became General Secretary of the CPSU in March 1985 after the death of Konstantin Chernenko. By 1987 a burst of Soviet writings on female roles indicated that the woman question was on the move; lively and acrimonious debates about women's lives were again likely. Although some issues affecting women were opened up under Brezhnev, discussions have become more extensive under Gorbachev. Aspects of the woman question addressed in 1987 and 1988 were not even mentioned as recently as 1984. Analyses of previously taboo subjects are invariably prefaced with comment to the effect that hitherto there has been insufficient research into the problem. Gorbachev's policy of *perestroika* has made this possible.

Gorbachev had several initial policy priorities for women: firstly, general support for the combination of motherhood with participation in the work-force; secondly, increasing opportunities for part-time work; thirdly, promoting more women to senior posts; and fourthly, the revival of women's councils. None of these was new in the Soviet state. The first priority had been stressed under Brezhnev, with the second and third coming on to the agenda during his period of office, although with lower salience. The fourth was a revamped aspiration of the Khrushchev years. The hallmark of Gorbachev's policies on women in his early years was increased commitment to past policies. A second stage in the development of policy commenced in 1987–1988, when a qualitative change in the nature of debate about female roles can be noticed due to the growing strength of *glasnost'*. Discussions, however, are not unbounded. Some topics are more ideologically acceptable than others and are analysed in greater depth. Women's participation in the labour force and the shortcomings of working conditions fall into this category due to their relevance to economic productivity. By contrast, why contraceptives have been so poorly developed in the USSR, why prostitution exists under socialism, and why abortion is carried out in stressful conditions, are questions which, at the time of writing in 1988, have not been seriously debated. Contraception, prostitution and abortion have all been mentioned in the Soviet press, however, which in itself is significant given the stern ideological silence about them for most of the history of the Soviet state (*Sovetskaia Rossiia*, 12 March 1987, p. 4; 19 March 1987, p. 4; *Komsomol'skaia Pravda*, 19 September 1987, p. 2).[1]

Probing into the obvious failures of Soviet socialism is also uncharted terrain; many are hesitant to be too critical too soon, being so well-socialised into regurgitating in public arenas its alleged successes and adept at following cues 'from above'. Social scientists and journalists also had to be careful in Gorbachev's first years as General Secretary; had he overstepped the mark and lost power because his political position had not been sufficiently consolidated, as outspoken critics of failures in policy they might be vulnerable.

The context of *perestroika*

Gorbachev introduced two terms, *perestroika* and *glasnost'* which became inseparable from his name, and famous the world over.[2] The concept of *perestroika* means 'reconstruction' or 'restructuring'. According to Gorbachev, it refers to 'radical', 'revolutionary' and 'serious' changes in Soviet economics, politics and society, which are interrelated. *Perestroika* is 'not a single act of one moment', but a complicated and uneven process (*Bakinskii Rabochii*, 1 October 1986). In theory at least, *perestroika* demands initiative, efficiency and a new psychology to overcome the inertia and sluggishness of Soviet production and administration (Gorbachev, 1987).

In industry and agriculture *perestroika* requires 'cost accounting' (*khozraschet*), self-financing, a greater latitude in decision-making for managers and a renewal of equipment in order to increase productivity. Labour discipline and campaigns against alcoholism are part of the drive for higher productivity and efficiency. By tying wage levels to output, an attempt is being made to foster responsibility in the workplace. By 1988 the success of *khozraschet* was limited.[3] More independent economic cooperatives have also been permitted, working outside the state planning system; by October 1987 there were 8,000 cooperatives employing 88,000 people (*Pravda*, 25 November 1987). By March 1988 a further 14,000 had been set up.

In politics, *perestroika* implies further democratisation, ranging from greater involvement of the people in the administration of their own affairs, such as electing their own rectors in institutes or directors in factories, to an as yet undefined political accountability of party leaders. In 1987, the practice of multi-candidate elections to the soviets began in some constituencies. Vesting more authority in the soviets was officially defined as central to the reform of the political system at the 19th All-Union Conference of the CPSU. The role of social organisations is also reviving and expanding, which includes the reinvigoration of the *zhensovety*, or women's councils.

Reconstructing society requires the development of a 'new psychology', the practice of 'criticism and self-criticism' and the pursuit of 'new ways' from milkmaids and construction workers to ministers and party leaders. Everyone is being encouraged to speak out against the shortcomings of society, such as theft of socialist property and fabrication of output statistics, so that weaknesses can be identified and problems subsequently tackled. These new practices are based on the concept of *glasnost'* which can be translated as 'publicity' or 'openness'. A resolution of the 19th All-Union Conference of the CPSU declared *glasnost'* to be 'a developing process', indispensable for the democratising of socialism (Resolutions of the 19th All-Union Conference of the CPSU, 1988, p. 152).

Although *glasnost'* is related to *perestroika* and being practised as a means to this broader end, *glasnost'* has implications for the imparting of information, honesty in reporting and more general cultural changes. For example, plays by Bulgakov now showing in Moscow at the Sovremennik and Taganka theatres were previously banned. The portrayal of Trotsky and Bukharin on stage was not permitted until the play *Brestskii Mir*, or the Brest peace, was put on in 1987 at the Vakhtangov theatre on the Arbat. Similarly, lectures delivered on Thursday evenings at the Historical Archival Institute in Moscow explore harshly silenced topics of the past such as Stalin's role as leader and what it was like to work on the editorial board of the journal *Novyi Mir* in the 1960s and 1970s. Although there are limits to *glasnost'*, it has nevertheless served to lift many past restrictions and prompt wider debates about various aspects of culture, history and daily life. Themes which were in the past taboo, such as the existence of drug addiction and the high number of abortions undergone by women due to the lack of contraception, are now more acceptable. It would be inconsistent for the woman question to be unaffected by the current changes.

Perestroika, *glasnost'* and the woman question

Perestroika and *glasnost'* have widened the boundaries of discussion about problems in women's lives to include the low quality of care in maternity hospitals, high infant mortality rates, sexual and psychological problems within marriage, difficulties faced by single-parent families, the lack of contraceptives, the existence of prostitution, the murder of Muslim women by their fathers for disobeying them and the continued Muslim practice of abducting teenage girls. Whereas these were non-topics, in the past, they are now 'ideologically legitimate' issues. Other topics, which in the past received cursory treatment, such as the domestic division of labour, harsh working conditions and the absence of women from top jobs, are being more thoroughly examined. If current trends continue, *perestroika* could give rise to an extensive and serious discussion of women's lives and gender roles.

However, greater freedom of debate under Gorbachev may not move policy and debate in a feminist direction just because many women's issues have long been suppressed. Fresh interpretations of the woman question will not automatically coincide with the earlier views of Kollontai and Armand. Some apparently 'feminist' ideas have surfaced, but conservative opinions about women's place in the home have also been expressed. In 1987 Gorbachev stated that one element of *perestroika* entailed debating how woman's 'truly female destiny' could be 'fully' returned to her since socialist development had not left her sufficient time for housework, childrearing and family life (Gorbachev, 1987, p. 117). Placing the woman question higher on the political agenda does not, therefore, guarantee feminist policy recommendations. *Glasnost'* allows the expression of a range of views, including highly traditional ones. Moreover, *glasnost'* has not yet undermined some of the central claims of Soviet ideology, even if it implicitly challenges them.

The proposition that stable nuclear families develop under socialism has gone unchallenged, despite an increasing number of articles on divorce, problems within marriage and single parenthood.[4] An 'ideological dissonance' exists between the claim that stable nuclear families will triumph and the recognition that this is not, in fact, happening. Notions of 'femininity' and 'masculinity', discussed in Chapter 5, also remain firmly intact. Yet the line that women are 'gentle and caring' and men 'strong and determined' is not entirely consistent with the call made at the All-Union Conference of Women in January 1987 for the 'reconstruction' of men (*Izvestiia*, 1 February 1987). The need to alter men's behaviour and attitudes is evident in some articles on domestic labour but it is absent from those which suggest that women should devote more time to maternity.

So the woman question under Gorbachev is rather open-ended; traditional lines on the need to strengthen the family co-exist alongside fresh pressures for more frank discussion of problems faced by women.[5] This has resulted in a mixed literature. Traditional arguments about strengthening the family ignore issues of female self-determination and equality of the sexes by proposing *inter alia* that *perestroika* should develop the means to prevent couples from divorcing (Kozlov, 1987, p. 122; Tupitsin, 1987; Zhvinklenie, 1987).[6] The link between the woman question and demographic policy is often made explicit and is consistent with the demographic priorities of the later Brezhnev years, reaffirmed by Gorbachev at the 27th party Congress. More critical arguments draw attention to sexual inequalities in the structure of family life and suggest that difficulties in women's lives prevent them from developing their full potential as citizens (Bozhkov and Golofast, 1986; Dzhunus"aev, 1985).[7]

There are also new arguments which have no precedent in the Soviet past and which jar with Marxism. In the late 1980s some economists are contending that female labour should be 're-structured' out of the work-force and return to the home.[8] Contemporary economic goals demand automation, cost-effectiveness and efficiency, which may ultimately lead to unemployment. The economic and demographic needs of the Soviet state could possibly be met if women rather than men left the work-force and devoted themselves to their families, thus cushioning the impact of unemployment.

This scenario is a difficult one for Soviet ideology since Engels, Marx and Lenin all saw participation in social production as the key to woman's emancipation. Engels, Lenin, Kollontai and Trotsky condemned the narrow confines of domestic life. Through productive labour woman could realise her ability to develop into a creative social being. Woman's duty to socialism has always been participation in production, politics and reproduction. Since 1917 ideology stressed that the Soviet state offered men and women equal opportunities in education and the work-force, unlike the inequalities of capitalism. Some contemporary economists, however, closer in spirit to the thinking of the New Right in Western liberal democracies than to the socialist tradition, are advocating the advantages of different and effectively unequal patterns of life. The development of the many-sided potential of individuals that Marx dreamt of in the *German Ideology* is here supplanted by the one-sided development of women through motherhood. This argument is highly provocative and likely to be condemned by some – Zoia Pukhova, Chairperson of the Soviet Women's Committee and successor to Valentina Tereshkova, was moved to speak out against it at the 19th All-Union Party Conference in June 1988.[9] Her intervention suggested that a support for the exit of some women from the work-force exists among policymakers and their advisers. With the possibility of unemployment, the belief that women rather than men should lose jobs is also likely to resurface in popular culture. Historically this has been the pattern under both capitalism and socialism (Bobroff, 1974; Rosenburg, 1985).

The CPSU, however, is unlikely radically to change the official line on the link between employment and women's liberation. It sits at the core of Marxist ideology, and puts a limit on modifications in line. Nevertheless, a flexible policy on female employment can accommodate the Marxist heritage as well as support for a withdrawal of some women from the work-force. Party policy in the late 1980s is characterised by this flexibility. It encourages women to bear and rear children, if they so wish, but also backs women who seek promotion through work. Women who choose to combine work and motherhood are officially supported as well. Party policy currently supports different categories of women in different life choices.

The development of party policy on women

Soon after Gorbachev became General Secretary, it became clear that female roles were remaining on the political agenda. The draft party programme which was released in 1985 made commitments to women as political actors and mothers. It stated the intention to appoint to leading posts the more politically mature and competent individuals, including women. It pledged further improvement in the position of women with children and reiterated the promise of past party congresses to create favourable conditions for the successful combination of motherhood with work in social production. Practical steps proposed were a longer break from employment after childbirth and more flexibility in employment patterns, including part-time labour for women. A commitment was made to improving the network of sanatoria and rest homes for family relaxation.

The draft party programme also acknowledged 'the great significance for the state' of improving family care: the nuclear family was increasingly important in the healthcare and education of the younger generation, in promoting the social and economic progress of society and in improving the birth rate (*Bakinskii Rabochii*, 26 October 1985). The draft programme stressed that the basic characteristics of individuals are formed, and their attitudes towards work and morality developed, in the family. These themes were echoed in Gorbachev's Political Report of the Central Committee, presented in February 1986 to the 27th party Congress. He observed that 'the formation of a new family is not a simple matter. It is a complicated process' (*Materialy XXVII s"ezda KPSS*, p. 15). Gorbachev lamented the existence of unhappy families and regretted, despite some improvement, the high divorce rate. In his view, poor family life negatively affects the education of children, the moral condition of husband and wife and their participation in economic, social and political activity. Gorbachev also argued that young people need preparation for family life and young families need protection. Priority should be given to the creation of work conditions and service provisions which enable women successfully to combine motherhood with active participation in the work-force. These themes are taken up in the 12th Five Year Plan for the years 1986 to 1990 in which a further growth of part-time labour for women, a shortening of the working week and the development of home-work for women is envisaged. Mothers are now entitled to a year and a half's maternity leave after the birth of a child and more kindergartens are to be built.

Concerning women's political roles, Gorbachev announced at the 27th party Congress that 'women are being moved into leadership posts more actively. They have become more numerous in the composition of the organs of the party and the soviets' (*Bakinskii Rabochii*, 26 February 1986). This was confirmed in 1986 in individual cases, such as by the appointment of Alexandra Biriukova to the Secretariat of the Central Committee of the CPSU and by the promotion of Svetlana Kasumova to both the *Politburo* and Secretariat of the Communist party of Azerbaidzhan (*Bakinskii Rabochii*, 2 February 1986). However, widespread changes in the political status of women have yet to occur. Despite approval at the 27th party Congress of an increase in female membership of the Central Committee from 19 to 22, this is just 4.6 per cent of the total membership of 475. At the 27th party Congress, Gorbachev also recommended that the *zhensovety*, or women's councils, be revived in the workplace and in residential areas and come under the unified structure of the Soviet Women's Committee. The *zhensovety*, he argued, could help to solve a wide range of social questions.

The plenary meeting of the Central Committee of January 1987 (delayed more than once due to disagreement over economic policy) was the occasion of even more radical statements. Gorbachev made an extremely bold call for reform and attacked opposition to change (*Pravda*, 28 January 1987; 29 January 1987; 30 January 1987). Before and after the plenum, conferences and congresses were organised on a large scale to discuss what *perestroika* meant for citizens and for the different groups to which they belonged. In January 1987 Trade Union Congresses took place in the Soviet republics, followed in February by a huge All-Union Congress in Moscow to discuss what the unions could do to implement changes and what *perestroika* meant for union members (*Bakinskii Rabochii*, 27 January 1987; 25 February 1987). In March, congresses of Komsomol members were called in the republics, to be followed by an All-Union Congress in Moscow, to debate how young people could give their support to *perestroika* (*Bakinskii Rabochii*, 10 March 1987). Journalists and social scientists also held meetings to reflect upon the relevance of *perestroika* to their jobs (*Bakinskii Rabochii*, 13 February 1987). Women were among the numerous groups in the USSR, at different levels of the system, which met to discuss how *perestroika* and *glasnost'* could direct their lives.

At the end of January 1987, an All-Union Conference of Women took place in Moscow. The Conference raised many issues with a frankness that would not have been possible three years earlier. This conference marked a watershed since some of the participants attempted to reinvigorate and redefine the boundaries of the debate. Traditional arguments were repeated alongside calls for change but, in general, speeches critical of the status quo and demanding action predominated. Some remarks moved in a 'feminist' direction, although those who made them may hesitate to accept this label.

In June 1988 Gorbachev broke the routine of Soviet politics by convening the 19th All-Union Conference of the CPSU, specifically to discuss the progress of *perestroika* and the hurdles it faced. In his Report to the Conference, Gorbachev described the woman question as 'yet another question of state importance'. After noting that 'It has often been asserted that this question has been resolved in this country once and for all', Gorbachev drew attention to several problems which indicated that it had not been solved. His general message was that 'there are still daily cares largely preventing women from enjoying their rights fully'. By implication, women were less than equal citizens with men. Going one step further, Gorbachev regretted that 'this situation could exist for years' because 'women's opinions were not duly reckoned with' and added that 'Women are not duly represented in governing bodies. And the women's movement as a whole, which gained momentum after the October Revolution, has gradually come to a standstill or has become formal' (Gorbachev, 1988, pp. 71–2).

Unlike Stalin, Khrushchev and Brezhnev, Gorbachev argued that women were not listened to, and that this had been the case for years. The 'solved' status of the woman question had been a myth. Moreover, he recognised the importance of women's activities in the 1920s and, by implication, gave legitimacy to some of the concerns of Kollontai and Armand. He also criticised the fact that the women's movement had reached a 'standstill' or had at best a 'formal' existence. His very positive use of the term 'women's movement' was an advance for a Soviet leader. Gorbachev concluded that:

> We must work to change the situation essentially, so that the door should be open wide for them to governing bodies at all levels, and that questions directly concerning women's interests would not be solved without their participation and without their decisive judgement. (Gorbachev, 1988, p. 72)

Gorbachev gave more emphasis to the need to expand women's contribution to decision-making and top jobs; this was reiterated at the Conference by Pukhova (*Izvestiia*, 2 July 1988, p. 10). Three months later, in September 1988, Alexandra Biriukova was appointed a candidate (non-voting) members of the Politburo, making her the most powerful Soviet woman for 28 years (*Pravda* 1 October 1988,

p. 1). If political 'gatekeepers' are more ready to appoint women to positions of higher authority, this will be reflected in the composition of the Central Committee named at the 28th party Congress, due to convene in 1991. Realists, however, doubt that widespread changes in patterns of promotion will occur quickly. Like Larisa Kuznetsova they may conclude that although 'it's high time we saw women among the country's leaders', in fact 'We are elbowing women out of leading positions, assigning them to the roles merely of political extras' (Kuznetsova, 1988). One gauge of the CPSU's commitment to women in reality rather than in rhetoric will be the pace of female appointments to top jobs.

The 1987 All-Union Conference of Women

Since Gorbachev took office, female roles have been included on the agenda at the 27th party Congress in 1986 and the special 19th All-Union Conference of the CPSU in 1988. They received far more discussion at the All-Union Conference of Women which convened in Moscow in January 1987. The purpose of the Conference was to serve *perestroika*, but in so doing questions were inevitably raised about changes in women's lives. As long as *perestroika* directed attention to the failings of Soviet socialism, women were likely to benefit. As one delegate put it, 'Who suffers most in society from the negative aspects of our life? Women. And because of this we shall indeed be the main strength of perestroika – we have a vital interest in it' (*Bakinskii Rabochii*, 31 January 1987). Pukhova repeated this point in 1988 at the 19th All-Union Conference of the CPSU, arguing that success in solving the problems of women's lives depended on the success of *perestroika*, and, the success of *perestroika* depended upon women's contribution to it (*Izvestiia*, 2 July 1988, p. 10).

Perestroika and *glasnost'* allowed long-suppressed aspects of the woman question to surface at the Women's Conference. Among the topics which received increased critical treatment were: promotion, manual labour, socialisation, working conditions, domestic labour, alcoholism, the oppression of Muslim women, the media treatment of women's lives, infant mortality rates, healthcare and research into the position of women in society. Many of these were addressed by Valentina Tereshkova, the astronaut and outgoing chair of the Soviet Women's Committee. These topics are given more detailed coverage below since how they were approached by the Conference may foretell some of the arguments Soviet women will make about their lives into the 1990s. Zoia Pukhova has already reiterated several of the conclusions reached in the Conference at the 19th party Conference.

Women in the work-force: promotion, manual labour, socialisation and working conditions

A commonplace of Soviet ideology for many years has been that equality of opportunity exists in the USSR and that women, like men, can win promotion: the Soviet tendency has been to avoid comparisons between male and female achievements and instead emphasise the successes of both sexes. Such claims are usually followed by statistics which highlight the many thousands of women with prominent positions. At the All-Union Women's Conference, Tereshkova pointedly commented that 'for every 12 engineers and other important specialists, only 1 is a woman. Even in those branches of industry where women are in the overwhelming majority, they hold few directorships' (*Izvestiia*, 1 February 1987). Pukhova made a similar point at the 19th All-Union Party Conference:

How can we explain the fact that out of the number of men with higher and secondary special education, sociological research shows that every second one, or 48 per cent, hold leadership positions at all levels, but among women the figure is just 7 per cent. (*Izvestiia*, 2 July 1988, p. 10)

She also noted that 'Women make up 7 per cent of party secretaries of *obkoms* and *kraikoms*, even though 29 per cent of party members are women' (*Izvestiia*, 2 July 1988, p. 10). The upward mobility of women within the party lagged behind men. By citing comparative statistics, Tereshkova and Pukhova have thereby shown the precise extent to which equality of result had not obtained. Although Khrushchev and Gorbachev both raised questions at authoritative party gatherings about the dearth of women in positions of leadership, Pukhova now indicated the precise extent of the difference in upward mobility of men and women.

Taking the argument further, Tereshkova suggested that, for too long, those in positions of responsibility had not been particularly interested in promoting equality of opportunity between the sexes; this disinterest was especially evident in the work place. One of the main concerns expressed both at the Women's Conference by Tereshkova and at the 19th party Conference by Pukhova was that women continue to perform heavy manual work and are not sufficiently encouraged to move into better-paying mechanised jobs. This had been an issue under Brezhnev, but in the Gorbachev era it is receiving more prominence. Tereshkova repeated the well-known statistic that in rural areas as much as 98 per cent of unmechanised agricultural work is done by women and some of it very heavy – sacks of animal feed weighing 50–60 kilos were being carried by women. Tereshkova regretted that an earlier recommendation from the Council of Ministers that women be encouraged to do mechanised work was not being implemented. She blamed some leaders for inertia and lack of interest in the health of women workers. She deplored that, even in the textile industry where there is a high concentration of women, the needs of women were not being taken into account. With 30 years experience in the textile industry, Pukhova added her authority by denouncing, at the 19th All-Union Party Conference, the unacceptable noise and dust levels in textile factories and arduous night-shifts.[10] Women textile workers, she told the Conference, working under these stressful conditions, had pulse rates of 90 beats per minute and pay levels which illustrated 'factual inequality' (*fakticheskoe neravenstvo*).[11]

The conventional ideological prediction was that as socialism progressed, equality of the sexes would occur. Equality would result from more fundamental economic changes. At the Women's Conference Tereshkova implied that equality of the sexes in the workplace was not automatic, and that special measures were needed to promote it: Pukhova informed delegates in 1988 that inequalities between the sexes obviously existed. More radically, both suggested that individuals in positions of authority under socialism were blocking the alleged inevitable advance of equality.

Tereshkova also suggested that women were not moving into mechanised work because machines and equipment, such as tractors and machinery in factories, were designed for men, not women: 'It is paradoxical, but a fact: institutions and organisations responsible for the production of new technology gear themselves only to the average working man' (*Izvestiia*, 1 February 1987). Tereshkova recommended that Gosplan, the state planning committee, should set up a special section to examine the professional and social problems of female employment, implying that male labour was currently favoured over female. This was a sharp contrast with the heroic literature of the Stalin years in which male and female workers always advanced 'shoulder to shoulder' and 'together'. Although Tereshkova did not employ the concept 'sex discrimination', much of her speech referred to aspects of it.[12]

The professional and social problems of female employment extend beyond the design of machinery to include the education of children and socialisation into attitudes about work. In this respect, Tereshkova cautioned that 'it is important to instil from school days an interest in technology in girls, not only in boys' (*Izvestiia*, 1 February 1987). Soviet writings have often drawn attention to different capabilities and skills of the sexes. Men have been praised for their strength and women for their ability at performing dexterous work; boys in towns have been channelled into woodwork and girls into needlework and cookery. Tereshkova's comments questioned the division into men's skills and women's skills and indicated that, for some, differential treatment of the sexes in schools and in the workplace is becoming an issue; so is the sexual division of labour at home.

Women at home: Domestic labour, male alcoholism and vestiges of the past

The hardships of the double burden had been thoroughly explored in the 1970s. Developing the conclusions drawn then, the Women's Conference declared firmly in favour of men and women sharing domestic labour and childcare: 'We strive to achieve the situation in which husband and wife carry out household chores equally and take responsibility for childrearing' (*Izvestiia*, 1 February 1987). This implicitly challenges the claim that women rather than men are better suited to domestic labour and nurturing roles.

Pukhova continued the attack against the image of women as creatures of the home at the 19th All-Union Party Conference. She pointed out that despite the uniqueness of motherhood and the importance of a mother's responsibilities, fathers had responsibilities too. 'It has become customary to link home, family and childcare solely with women', but Pukhova concluded that 'It is necessary to increase the prestige of fatherhood'. She did not elaborate what this would entail, but nonetheless she introduced male roles to the agenda (*Izvestiia*, 2 July 1988, p. 10). Pukhova also noted that due to the double burden women were far too tired. This had led some to suggest that women had lost their looks and should be allowed to stay in the home. 'Is this conclusion just?', she asked, because it amounted to depriving women the opportunity of attaining factual equality (*fakticheskoe ravenstvo*) and denying them a chance to develop their creative abilities. Moreover, 80 per cent of Soviet women would not voluntarily leave the labour force, even if their families did not need their wages.

Another aspect of men's lives of concern to women is alcoholism. Male alcoholism has been more openly discussed in the 1980s due to the anti-alcohol campaign which began under Andropov in 1982 and because of continuing official concern about the relationship between drunkenness and absenteeism from work, economic productivity, divorce statistics and family size. The implications of male alcoholism for domestic life were raised at the Women's Conference, returning to themes addressed by the *zhensovety* in the 1960s (Browning, 1987, pp. 99–100). The Secretary of the Presidium of the Supreme Soviet of the Tatar Autonomous Republic and Chair of that republic's *zhensovet*, D. S. Davletshina, asked: 'What is most important for us today? It is necessary to pull out of the bog of the indifference and drunkenness of many of our men, to protect our young from this misfortune' (*Izvestiia*, 2 February 1987). A theme long-cloaked in official silence, the effect of alcohol on the way in which men treat women was also referred to. If this theme is developed, it could extend into discussions of male violence towards women and gender politics.

Remarks at the conference closest to the notion that the personal is political concerned the specific problems of family life in the Soviet Muslim republics. A Secretary of the Central Committee of Tadzhikistan, G. B. Bobosadykova, drew attention to the persistence of unregistered marriages, the marriage of under-age girls, payment of *kalym* or bride-price, and the restriction of women's activities outside the home by their husbands. Much of this was attributed to 'indifference and compromise with vestiges of the past'. Bobosadykova emphasised the need to step up 'atheistic propaganda and education' and recommended that the *zhensovety* become involved in this (*Izvestiia*, 2 February 1987).[13] Other aspects of women's private lives also received attention, such as marital discord and the loneliness of urban women. L. A. Chursina, an actress, argued that the cinema should devote more energy to 'the tragedy of female loneliness and to adverse family relations, especially in cities' (*Izvestiia*, 2 February 1987). She said that although the cinema had dealt successfully with some aspects of women's lives, it had not captured the bitterness of social problems that everyone knew existed, but which were not adequately acknowledged. Chursina then called upon the *zhensovety* to liaise with women working in the theatre, cinema and circus.

Infant mortality rates

Another anxiety of women's personal lives is the death of newborn children. Recently released Soviet statistics on infant mortality show that whereas in 1970 in rural areas, 26.2 Soviet children per 1,000 births had died before reaching the age of 1, by 1985 this figure had increased to 32.0 deaths in the first year of life per 1,000 births. Urban infant mortality rates also remained relatively high, with just minor improvement from 23.4 deaths up to 1 year of age per 1,000 births in 1970, falling to 21.7 in 1985 (*Vestnik Statistiki*, no. 12, 1986, p. 71).[14] In the past, infant mortality rates were not published and the topic was not discussed.

Tereshkova tabled the view that 'At our conference we cannot pass over such a mother's worry as infant mortality. To talk of this painful, but necessary.... The death of children up to 1 year of age is higher here than in capitalist countries' (*Izvestiia*, 1 February 1987). A speaker from Uzbekistan also regretted that the infant mortality rate was particularly high in her republic (*Izvestiia*, 2 February 1987). Tereshkova went on to itemise the 'many reasons for this'. They included: 'the weak material technical base' of some medical institutions, the 'low level of qualifications of many doctors', shortages of junior and middle level staff and insufficient attention of the Ministry of Health of the USSR and its local organs (*Izvestiia*, 1 February 1987). Tamilla Rzaeva, a delegate from Azerbaidzhan, also pointed to the inadequacies of the health service. Left out of her speech printed in *Izvestiia*, but included in the longer version released in *Bakinskii Rabochii*, the daily party paper of the Soviet republic of Azerbaidzhan, she remarked 'the high level of chemicals in the countryside worries us, which affects the birth and health of children'. She added that 'this problem is connected, as are others, with the protection of the surrounding areas, which in our opinion scholars should examine more' (*Bakinskii Rabochii*, 1 February 1987). These statements showed that, as in the West, there is a link between some ecological and some women's concerns.

Women and political action

The conference illustrated that Soviet women in the 1980s are worried about a range of problems which span healthcare, working conditions, education and domestic life. What political action can they take? Some delegates recommended that the appropriate ministries should investigate the problems that come under their control. Tereshkova asserted that women themselves had a vital role to play. Regarding problems in the health service, she commented that 'We should not forget that 68 per cent of our qualified doctors are women. This means that we should be asking ourselves! The women's councils in the hospitals, clinics and maternity homes have a lot to do so that women who work in them take greater responsibility in fulfilling their social duty' (*Izvestiia*, 1 February 1987). The official reason for the revival of the *zhensovety* was to exert political pressure to bring about desired changes: whether they can do this is an open question. They are viewed as 'helpers of the party' by encouraging women to join more actively in socio-political life and have the officially approved tasks of defence of the rights and interests of women, cultivation of the creative abilities of women and promotion of legislation to protect mothers and children at work and at play (*Bakinskii Rabochii*, 31 January 1987).

Identifying problems is an essential first step, but tackling these problems is ultimately beyond the powers of the *zhensovety* and women's conferences. However, if Soviet women begin to use the *zhensovety* to pinpoint, define and discuss problems, and if they convene more conferences to pool information and ideas, then issues will receive some input from the constituency most affected by them. Involving more powerful political actors in the work of the *zhensovety* could be one way of promoting an awareness of women's views. The presence at the All-Union Women's Conference of the First Deputy Minister of Health, O. P. Shchepin, was highly appropriate. Although signalling the achievements of Soviet medicine, Shchepin's speech admitted its 'negative side' and listed unsolved problems affecting women that the relevant ministries had failed to tackle (*Izvestiia*, 2 February 1987). The key question, however, is to what extent the ministries have the commitment, resources and ability to rectify problems once the *zhensovety* and women's conferences have drawn attention to them.

Although one of the reasons for convening the Women's Conference was to spur the *zhensovety* into action, the speeches did not discuss at length how the women's councils could best fulfil their political brief. Participants concentrated on problem areas, rather than on the organisation of the *zhensovety*. The main focus of the conference fell on the immediate and concrete problems of daily life, rather than political strategies to tackle them. Nevertheless, the boundaries of discourse widened considerably through the highly critical remarks made about the condition of women. Reflections even touched on the nature of the relationship between the fate of the woman question and the general course of socialism.

Theorising about the woman question

For over 50 years Soviet ideologists have not admitted that theorising about the woman question is poorly developed in the USSR. The general contention is that Soviet writings take a scientifically correct approach to the woman question, based on Marxism–Leninism. Even though ideological positions on female roles have shifted somewhat in emphasis as the content of policy has changed, the nature of the approach to them under socialism has never been queried. Questioning the depth of Soviet research and theorising, and calling for more rigorous work, Tereshkova maintained:

> We should pay attention to the fact that we do not have profound, fundamental and theoretical research into the position of women in socialist society which would creatively develop the woman question on the basis of Marxist–Leninist theory. It is essential that we take a stand against all anti-scientific phenomena and reactionary views of the role of women in society. We feel the urgent need for deep historical research, for serious philosophical generalisations, based on economic and social prognoses. (*Izvestiia*, 1 February 1987)

It is tempting to read into this paragraph a new attempt at the integration of feminism and Marxism. This is probably not what Tereshkova intended because, as Chapters 1 and 5 have already shown, feminism as a body of thought has long been criticised in the USSR on three grounds: firstly, it divides the working class and thereby mistakenly separates women from men, when in fact their needs are similar; secondly, it is a form of bourgeois self-indulgence; and thirdly, it wrongly assumes that equality means that men and women should be identical, when on physiological and psychological grounds they cannot be. Western feminism and also the works of Western feminists on the position of women in the USSR have in recent years come in for opprobrium (Kondakova, 1981; Mikhailiuk, 1981). But Tereshkova's appeal for more sophisticated research into the position of women in the USSR has a place, notwithstanding official Soviet reservations about Western feminists and harassment of dissident feminist groups which sprang up in 1979 (Holt, 1985; Buckley, 1986b). Research into female roles by Soviet social scientists grew substantially in the 1970s, but theorising about their implications for socialism, and vice versa, was not seriously pursued. Tereshkova's remarks indicated awareness of a theoretical gap and amounted to a plea to scholars to take the topic more seriously.

Numerous issues affecting women were revived or raised for the first time at the Women's Conference, many of which had suffered years of silence. It provided a setting for a fresh, if hesitant, airing of issues, and a forum for criticism of aspects of Soviet life considered detrimental to women's self-development. Speeches suggested that conservative assumptions about gender roles continue to pervade many topics, but occasionally they are questioned. The pace of change may seem frustratingly slow, but the re-definition of the woman question has to confront many obstacles in a male-dominated and highly traditional system. The repetition by Pukhova at the 19th All-Union Conference of the CPSU of many of the points made at the Women's Conference means that they are gaining ground.

Articles appearing in late 1988 confirm this and also indicate subsequent conceptual developments. Since Gorbachev's enlightened remarks on the woman question at the 19th Party Conference, some Soviet women have spoken out in public arenas about the implications of living in a male-dominated society. Ol'ga Voronina, a philosopher, published an article in *Sovetskaia Zhenshchina* (Soviet Woman) entitled 'Men have created the world for themselves'. Voronina asked how men dared to be so distant from their children and to perform just one-third of the amount of housework done by working women. Quoting Lenin, she pointed out that the 'real emancipation of women' and 'genuine communism' begin only when a mass struggle against the pettiness of housework takes place. She boldly concluded that the 'spiritual progress' of the USSR depends in part 'upon the overcoming of patriarchal attitudes of men towards women, and upon the development of a new system of social relations between the sexes, based on the principles of equality and partnership' (Voronina, 1988, p. 15). The charge that Soviet society outside its Muslim areas is patriarchal has not, since 1930, been permitted in print, except in dissident materials. Voronina is not the only woman to suggest that patriarchy is a problem.

In a similar spirit, Larisa Kuznetsova recently posed several challenging questions about 'our flourishing patriarchy'. Why, she asked, did only five women delegates out of a total of 1,258, deliver speeches at the 19th party Conference? Why did only one of these five give women's issues 'political dimensions'? Why are Soviet contraceptives 'roughly on a par with personal computers: rock bottom?' Why is the 'hell' and 'futile killing' of resulting abortions naïvely not seen as a 'political issue'? Why do women have to switch from 'biological specimens', rather than human beings, in 'the world's cruellest abortion system', to 'ladies' in decision-making arenas, where women cannot raise their voices, just their hands? And why does the USSR lack a serious women's movement? Kuznetsova, like Voronina, concludes that 'we need to abandon patriarchal habits' (Kuznetsova, 1988, p. 15).

Kuznetsova's questions need thorough answers and deeper analyses of society than Soviet social science has hitherto produced. But that they are being posed at all, and with such verve, is a radical departure from the past. They will, of course, have their opponents, who are likely to include supporters of the first beauty contest ever to be held in the USSR in 1988 which was reported to be 'highly favoured by the majority of the male population' (*Sputnik*, December 1988, p. 32). But protected by *glasnost'*, Kuznetsova's questions could develop an exciting momentum of debate. Some may hope that the *zhensovety* will spur them forward.

Women's organisations in the 1980s: Revival of the *zhensovety*

Chapter 2 discussed how the existence of the *Zhenotdel* in the 1920s was precarious for both theoretical and practical reasons, despite the energy of its early leaders. Chapter 4 traced the revival of women's organisations in the 1950s and 1960s after Khrushchev called for the establishment of *zhensovety*. Although the *zhensovety* persisted in some areas during the Brezhnev years, there was less attention to them in Soviet writings, as the last chapter indicated. In 1988, as mentioned above, Gorbachev criticised the women's movement since the 1920s as, at best, 'formal', suggesting that the *zhensovety* under Brezhnev were moribund. By implication, the USSR has not seen very lively women's organisations for just over half a century. Whether the *zhensovety* of the late 1980s and 1990s will match the dynamism of the *Zhenotdel* in their leadership and the scale of their activities seems unlikely. Nevertheless, Gorbachev, Biriukova and Pukhova are calling upon women to defend their own interests.

By April 1988 there were reported to be 236,000 women's councils involving 2.3 million female activists (*Sovetskaia Zhenshchina*, no. 4, 1988, p. 18). Few articles and books have yet appeared on them in the USSR; occasional pieces in newspapers and academic journals have been published. Often they reveal no more than the fact that a *zhensovet* exists in a particular factory (*Pravda*, 6 December 1987). More thorough commentaries are found in the magazines *Rabotnitsa* (Working Woman), *Krest'ianka* (Peasant Woman) and *Sovetskaia Zhenshchina* (Soviet Woman), which now devote regular columns to the work of the *zhensovety*.[15]

Three zhensovety *in Moscow: goals and practices*

What, then, do the *zhensovety* do in practice and in theory? Three women's councils that I visited in December 1987, located in a textile factory, a boot and shoe factory and a university, were all set up in late 1986, soon after Gorbachev's recommendation at the 27th party Congress that the *zhensovety* be revived and following the announcement in the Soviet press that a *Politburo* meeting of October 1986 had discussed proposals to set them up (*Pravda*, 24 October 1986, p. 1). Women in the textile factory were particularly enthusiastic and open about their endeavours and appeared to have a clear idea of their future agenda. Similarly, the women's council in the university had a broad plan of activities, if more diffuse. By contrast, the one woman whom I met from the *zhensovet* in the boot and shoe factory had only a vague notion of its work as a distinct organisation. Indeed, she found it hard to distinguish the concerns of the *zhensovet* from those of the trade union.

Membership of these three women's councils was 26, 11 and 30 respectively. Articles in Soviet women's magazines also suggest that the size of membership varies (*Rabotnitsa*, no. 1, 1987, p. 13). The 26 members of the *zhensovet* in the textile factory included women workers from the factory floor and women in administrative positions; they represented different departments, sections and shifts within the factory, which had a work-force of 2,400. Party and non-party members alike sat on the women's council. They met once a month and sometimes delegated business to a smaller Presidium of 11 members. Covering three work shifts, they regretted that sometimes it was hard to find a time to meet convenient to everyone. Like many other women's councils described in *Rabotnitsa* and *Krest'ianka*, they divided the responsibilities of the *zhensovet* into four sections: production; daily life (*byt*) and social problems; children; and culture. However, by far the most attention is devoted to social problems and *byt*.

The women in the textile factory described the main goal of their *zhensovet* as addressing the needs of women workers. In order to discover these, the *zhensovet* sent out a questionnaire. As one woman put it, 'we wanted to find out what women workers were happy with, what they disliked and what they wanted'. The overwhelming majority of responses called for a service in the workplace that would enable workers to place orders for food to save time queuing after work. Some women workers also asked for a shop to be opened in the factory where they could buy fruit and vegetables. Others requested a shoe repair service in the workplace and a hairdresser. Members of the *zhensovet* see a large part of their job as trying to organise the services requested in the responses to the questionnaire. Women's journals indicate that this technique of sending out questionnaires is common to many *zhensovety* (*Rabotnitsa*, no. 1, 1987, pp. 12–13).

Another aspect of the work of the *zhensovet* defined by its members as important, concerns family life. As one woman put it, 'today we have the terrible problem of divorce. Our aim is to keep the family together.' By talking to couples under strain or by referring them to psychological counselling services in the factory, the *zhensovet* hopes to save marriages whenever possible. This is consistent with the goals of Soviet demographic policy. The same woman continued that 'there is also the problem of old age. We arrange to take milk and bread to old people who worked here who have no children to look after them. We have put together a list of addresses and telephone numbers of people who need help.' Members of the *zhensovet* see themselves as community helpers, fostering a sense of caring for the workers of their factory and their families.

Issues concerning production, children and culture were only touched upon in this interview and seemed to pale in significance for *zhensovet* members in comparison with problems of daily life, or *byt*. The aims of the *zhensovet* in these areas, mentioned only in passing, were to improve working conditions, expand the health unit (which already includes basic medical and dental care, psychological counselling, an exercise room and facilities for massage in a hot tub), to extend the five kindergartens and two nurseries attached to the factory and to improve living conditions in the factory hostel. From the women's press it seems that other *zhensovety* place higher priority on problems connected with production and children. For example, *zhensovety* in rural areas have been discussing the problems of manual labour for women (*Krest'ianka*, no. 4, 1987, p. 2). Women's councils in the Tatar Autonomous Republic have paid more attention to their children's education; they have been agitating for the adoption in schools of a 'system of aesthetic education' which includes music, art and craft work. Apparently, educationalists had promised them this curriculum, but it has not been introduced (*Krest'ianka*, no. 6, 1987, p. 4). Elsewhere, where kindergarten provision is weak, mothers in the *zhensovety* are pushing for an expansion of childcare facilities (*Krest'ianka*, no. 2, 1987, p. 9).

All of the activities being pursued by the *zhensovet* in the textile factory are consistent with Gorbachev's policies outlined at the 27th party Congress. An attempt is being made to ease the female double burden by bringing shopping to the workplace; efforts are devoted to deterring divorce and maintaining family unity; help is given to the elderly; attention is directed at improving housing, childcare facilities and health. All this is being done in close collaboration with the party, or as one member of the *zhensovet* put it 'under the leadership of the *partkom*, or party committee'. Another added 'the existence of the *zhensovet* means more work for the *partkom*. This is because the *zhensovet* is subordinate to it.' This fits the general institutional pattern in the USSR in which the CPSU exerts its 'leading and guiding' role over policy and social organisations. It also allays any fears of bourgeois feminism emerging. Working so closely with the *partkom*, or with the trade union as is the case in the boot and shoe factory visited, the activities of the *zhensovety* merely supplement those of other organisations within the workplace. The *zhensovety* do not constitute an independent force to shake up institutional arrangements, but are merely a minor addition to them. The emphasis of their work differs from that of other bodies but their activities are theoretically on the same course.

Despite the new streamlining of the *zhensovety* under the Soviet Women's Committee, this appears to have no practical significance in the eyes of members of the *zhensovet* in the textile factory, apart from a passing down of information. The focus of the work of the *zhensovety* is on local needs and difficulties. There is, however, some contact with *zhensovety* in other factories. Visits of members of one *zhensovet* to another take place, partly to learn what others are doing: members also learn more about general activities in other factories and offices at conferences encouraged by the Soviet Women's Committee. The 'newness' in their organisations is obvious as members seek ideas about how best to proceed, not always certain about how much they should be doing.

When asked how *glasnost'* affected the work of the *zhensovet*, the women in the textile factory laughed nervously and one commented:

> There are difficulties with *glasnost'*. You must understand how it is. We have to experience it and it is new for us. We have to learn. It is complicated for us because it is hard to criticise others, especially those in positions of authority. We are not used to doing it in large meetings and at first we were afraid. And of course it is hard to take criticism; it hurts. *Glasnost'* entails talking to people and listening to their problems. We have to concentrate on what people say.

Such frank remarks about *glasnost'* were not forthcoming in interviews with the other two *zhensovety*. In the boot and shoe factory, the one *zhensovet* member whom I was allowed to interview said she did not know how to respond to the question of how *glasnost'* affected her work since there were no serious problems in the factory and there was a very strong trade union which looked after workers' interests. Women could already place weekly food orders through the factory to save time queuing. An entire building was under construction to cater to women's daily needs, including shopping. Workers would also soon enjoy the luxury of a sauna in the factory grounds. She was also unclear how the activities of the *zhensovet* tied in with *perestroika* and remarked 'it is hard to say how we are involved with *perestroika*'. Unlike the fixed monthly meetings of the *zhensovet* in the textile factory, here it seemed that there was no routine time for meetings. Similarly, there was no time set aside for women workers to come to talk to the *zhensovet*, as had been arranged in the textile factory. Neither had a questionnaire been sent out to women asking what changes they would like to see.

From walking round, however, one could see that working conditions were indeed excellent. There was new Italian machinery, space, light, little noise and no obvious dust levels. The medical wing was expanding, efforts were being made to house workers and the factory had its own House of Culture.[16] Many of the tasks taken on with enthusiasm by the *zhensovet* in the old textile factory had already been tackled in the modernised boot and shoe factory by the trade union. Thus there was not as great a need for the *zhensovet*. The overlap in the brief of the *zhensovet* and trade union limited the role of the former due to the effectiveness of the latter. Though the *zhensovet* had not asked women what their needs were, a channel for complaints already existed in the form of a suggestion box posted in the corridor by the trade union office which allowed workers to express their views – anonymously if they so wished. Issues could also be raised through the factory newspaper.

The role of *glasnost'* in the work of the third *zhensovet* was similarly not seriously considered. A member of the university's women's council said no more than that the implications of *glasnost'* and *perestroika* for the work of the *zhensovet* was 'a big question'. The activities of the *zhensovet*, however, illustrated new approaches to problems. These included lectures on sex, health, the problems of coping with difficult children, psychological counselling and legal advice. These topics were not openly discussed in the past, but were ignored, dismissed, or superficially treated. In this *zhensovet*, they are recognised as important in women's lives. The *zhensovet* has its own room in the university and any woman connected with the institution from cleaners and cooks to students and teachers can go there to discuss problems. If a woman feels in need of psychological counselling, then the *zhensovet* will arrange it.

The general goals of the university *zhensovet* were similar to those of the women's council in the textile factory. It hoped to arrange for more facilities to make the purchase of food easier and to attend to problems of family life and health. Gearing itself to the goal of strengthening the family, it organised a 'Family Day' in the Spring of 1987: a member of the *zhensovet* recounted that 'we showed films. There were exhibitions of children's paintings. There were computer games for the children. Over 1,000 people came and it was a great success, so we decided to have one every year.' Other women's councils have organised similar 'family holidays' under the slogan 'Strong family – strong power' (*Krest'ianka*, no. 6, 1987, p. 4).

The university *zhensovet* is also in the process of forming 'information groups' whose members work on particular topics. For example, a newly formed 'statistics group' collects data on women within the university. The general impression created by this *zhensovet* is that its members are well-organised and resourceful and in little need of guidance. The *zhensovet* holds a regular monthly meeting and a larger Plenum twice a year. It also works under the party committee.

The work of the *zhensovety* therefore varies according to institutional setting. This is in accord with their brief, which emphasises the need to address local problems. These vary according to workplace, district and republic, despite inevitable similarities such as overcoming problems of food purchase.

Problems faced by the zhensovety

A common criticism of the 1920s and 1960s was that party committees failed, in practice, to develop a positive attitude towards women's organisations. Writing just one year after the *zhensovety* were revived by Gorbachev, Mel'nik made the same charge. Citing the experience of Moldavia, where by January 1987 there were 2,000 *zhensovety* involving 22,000 women, Mel'nik argued that the *zhensovety* did not always receive the necessary encouragement and attention from those in authority. He observed that leaders in the enterprises, party and trade unions often failed to respond appropriately to requests put to them by *zhensovety*. For instance, when the republic level *zhensovet* in Moldavia approached a party committee in the field of civil aviation to invite its members to become involved in the setting up of a new *zhensovet* in their workplace, they declined to take part. They did not even turn up at the election of its members (Mel'nik, 1987, p. 63).[17] Pukhova also mentioned in her speech to the 19th All-Union Conference of the CPSU that male indifference to women's organisations persists. She regretted that 'Far from everywhere do party organisations take this new social movement seriously or extend support to the *zhensovety*' (*Izvestiia*, 2 July 1988, p. 10).

Yet, the members of the *zhensovety* themselves often have a hazy idea about what they should be doing and frequently hesitate to take the initiative without being told what to do. Using the example of women's councils in Moldavia, Mel'nik charged that they are not sufficiently active. He claimed that 'the women's councils still struggle half-heartedly' to create an appropriate atmosphere for making demands and for criticising past inadequacies; they overlook problems and are unwilling to tackle them. Pukhova echoed this criticism: 'the influence of the *zhensovety* on specific social questions is inadequate. Not all of them understand their role nor realise what their place is in society under the new conditions' (*Izvestiia*, 2 July 1988, p. 10). Critics feel that the opportunities available to the *zhensovety* under Gorbachev are not being confidently explored. 'Old ways' of waiting to be told what to do by the party and fears of speaking out against officials probably hold the women back. Deeply embedded in Soviet political culture is a resistance to initiative, independence of thought, and spontaneity.

Soviet women today, however, do not have to fear involvement in women's organisations as some may have done in the 1920s when delegates' meetings and women's clubs came under ideological attack. The theoretical strain suffered by early Soviet Marxism between the existence of women's institutions and an ideology based on divisions of class rather than gender, is no longer so apparent. This is due to the different functions of the women's institutions of the 1920s and 1980s and to the very different social and political contexts. The *zhensovety* are not now perceived as threatening to Soviet society in any fundamental way, as the *Zhenotdel* was in the 1920s. Although the *Zhenotdel* had the status of a party department, rather than a social organisation, policies on women were unpopular and controversial both inside and outside the party. They upset a highly traditional social fabric in which women were subordinate to men, and in Muslim areas tightly controlled by them. In the 1920s the existing family unit was under attack. By contrast, the family unit is hardly being undermined by the efforts of the *zhensovety* to make shopping easier. Instead, both men and women benefit. Moreover, by offering women easier access to food purchases, the *zhensovety* actually reinforce the traditional notion that shopping is 'woman's work', about which men are unlikely to complain. Furthermore, even if contemporary women's organisations are concerned with women's issues, these tend now to be seen as in the interest of all citizens since how women lead their lives affects economic productivity, population size, the rearing of children and domestic life. It is in a context of awareness of these broader issues that the *zhensovety* operate, rather than one in which the 'backwardness' of women calls for the promotion of women's liberation, as in the 1920s.

In the past many also feared that the *Zhenotdel* would deviate from party priorities and promote bourgeois feminism in a fragile socialist state that required class unity, not unnecessary gender divisions. Although some administrators are slow to take the *zhensovety* seriously today, this is far removed from the deep suspicion of women's issues in the 1920s for reasons of ideological dogmatism, fear, prejudice and male chauvinism. In the 1980s, the *zhensovety* are seen as rather weak social organisations, subservient to goals decided elsewhere. In the 1920s there was anxiety that women's organisations would not be so subservient. The volatility of the early years of Bolshevik power and the recent origin of the state's institutions generated instability rather than predictability. There were uncertainties about the end result of work among women, even though the *Zhenotdel* came under party authority. By contrast, the 1980s are relatively stable and the *zhensovety* are not viewed as dangerous power bases for a feminist alternative. Instead, they appear to be tame 'helpers' of the CPSU.

Indeed, the *zhensovety* have yet to champion radical proposals. Although Gorbachev has commented on the importance of promoting women, and despite the attention that Tereshkova and Pukhova have drawn to the poor promotion record of women, the *zhensovety* have not yet declared in favour of the preferential hiring of women over men or affirmative action programmes. The *zhensovety* have not challenged men's leadership roles. In the 1920s, however, the *Zhenotdel* was calling upon women to assume political tasks and was attempting to give women a much higher profile in the party, soviets, trade unions and administration. Mobilising women politically was more threatening to prevailing images of male and female roles, than the concentration of the *zhensovety* on shopping and social problems.

Although the *zhensovety* are relatively weak political organisations, revived to carry out party policy, as specialised institutions for women, they nevertheless provide an institutional base from which to exert pressure on topics which concern women. If their members use them to their advantage, new opportunities for women could result. Similarly, if conferences of women become a regular event (in the 1920s they were convened at the local level several times a year), they could become more than a channel for the CPSU to get its messages across to women, and enable women to influence the political agenda. Alexandra Biriukova has remarked that the solutions to many problems affecting women 'depend upon women themselves. They must, and should, be more active.' In her view, the *zhensovety* offer the appropriate channels for this action (Biriukova, 1987, p. 4). She may not have very radical action in mind, but feels that the *zhensovety* could produce results if only women take advantage of them.

Conclusion

Although a thaw in politics and society took place in the immediate post-Stalin years, it was not defined in terms of a systematic restructuring of all aspects of society. Some very lively debates raged under Brezhnev, but they were targeted at selected problems. By contrast, Gorbachev's ambition is to transform Soviet economics, politics and society. This ambition is more broadly conceived at the level of theory than those of his predecessors and is potentially more far-reaching in practice. Although Gorbachev's policies are resisted by sections of the Soviet population and encounter obstacles in the rigidities of the Soviet system, change is evident in policy discussions and ideological debate. Many Soviet citizens cynically complain that *perestroika* has brought no positive results, that self-financing in the factories is not working, that consumer goods are not improving in quality, that queues are not shortening and that nothing has changed in practice, but the way in which problems are discussed has radically altered. The wind of change is blowing, affecting the woman question, as well as all aspects of discussions on the economy, politics, history and culture.

Although in the 1970s debates about female roles led to an airing of many views, the range of topics under scrutiny is broader today and the space for disagreement wider. Although there are limits to *glasnost'* which set the parameters of debate, and still restrict what, and how much, is said about prostitution, contraception, sexuality, and a predominantly male leadership, topics which lack firm answers can nevertheless be approached in a range of ways. Although the woman question still awaits the fresh theoretical overhaul called for at the All-Union Conference of Women, numerous aspects of this question are already being considered, and at least the call has been made. Although ideological old-faithfuls, such as the importance of strengthening the family, are likely to go unchallenged, appropriate ways of running it under socialism, and various ways of running it (including single parenthood) are being discussed. Although non-topics still exist, such as the extent of discrimination against women under socialism, many recent articles address aspects of this question without systematically analysing it, and rare calls have been made for an end to patriarchy. Despite the fact that the percentage of women on the Central Committee remains very low (a reflection of their absence from top administrative jobs in the party and state hierarchy) if women wish to pursue further the issue of promotion, they have the legitimacy of Gorbachev's statements to protect them. Although the *zhensovety* are not radical institutions designed to mobilise women into 'high politics', or to redefine political agendas in a feminist direction, women could attempt to harness them for issues beyond arranging shopping orders, once this basic service has been provided.

The future course of the *zhenskii vopros* is not clear, but it is more open-ended than it has been for the past 50 years of Soviet history. How much Soviet ideology on women will be allowed to evolve and how extensive debate will be is uncertain. Authoritarian regimes can abruptly curtail discussion and impose rigid lines. It is also uncertain the extent to which *perestroika* will alter the daily lives of women at home, in the workplace and in politics and whether *glasnost'* will prompt a thorough redefinition of popular expectations of gender roles. Neither black pessimism nor unbounded optimism is warranted by developments since 1985.

Notes

1. The incidence of AIDS in the USSR has prompted more articles on contraception and prostitution, since prostitutes are seen as dangerous carriers and condoms a means to prevent transmission. One reader wrote in to the newspaper *Komsomol'skaia Pravda* complaining that although condoms were the only readily available means of protecting oneself against AIDS, they were generally unavailable in cities. He called for the sale of condoms in shops and for condom slot machines on the streets (*Komsomol'skaia Pravda*, 28 October 1987, p. 3). Interestingly, the dearth of contraceptives was not a matter for public debate when pregnancy was the only consequence. Now a more dramatic disease could be prevented through their use, they have become an issue which concerns men. A general debate about the relevance of contraceptives to women's liberation has not yet blossomed.

2. Gorbachev, however, was not the first to coin these terms. *Glasnost'* was used in the nineteenth century in calls for more openness at a time of autocracy and censorship. *Perestroika* has been used in different periods of Soviet history. In the 1930s frequent references were made to a 'restructuring' of economy and society; under Khrushchev there were remarks about the 'restructuring' of education.

3. *Khozraschet* is hard to implement in the Soviet economy because it was introduced without the necessary price reforms upon which its success is predicated. Price reforms are scheduled for 1990–1991, but these are highly controversial. Critics feel that socialism will be compromised by the inevitable price increases and many citizens are anxious that the cost of living will exceed wages.

4. I. Kon has recently suggested that since single-parent families are widespread they should be analysed as one form of family life. He challenged those who referred pejoratively to single-parent families as incomplete units which were missing something by pointing out that they could be just as happy as any other family.

   Kon singled out for particular attention the implications of the 'culture of divorce' for the subsequent life of mother and child. Rebutting the many articles which suggest that divorce ruins lives and gives rise to problem children, Kon claimed that this need not be so if parents proceeded in a civilised manner. He argued that children merely begin a 'new stage' of family life when one parent leaves. This transition could be eased if parents behaved in a supportive rather than destructive manner. Kon concluded that 'The culture of divorce is the most reliable indicator of the general cultural level of the individual.' Kon regretted that the ideal marriage was rare and the ideal divorce even rarer (Kon, 1987, p. 14). Nevertheless, he highlighted the complexities of divorce and suggested that stereotypes of life in single-parent families obscured their variety.

5. Attempts to study the complexities of modern family life have benefitted immensely from *glasnost'*. There have been numerous calls for more sophisticated research. Agarkov, for instance, has argued for better appreciation of the complexities of 'crisis situations in the family', including the relevance of psychological problems and sexual difficulties (Agarkov, 1987). Solodnikov has called for more detailed analysis into the nature of marital relations before divorce, the circumstances that provoke the decision to separate and the pressures on couples from members of their social circles (Solodnikov, 1986, p. 76).

   Past patterns of thinking are also challenged in numerous round-table discussions that have been taking place on Soviet television, in journals, at conferences and in universities. The weekly popular journal *Nedelia*, for instance, printed a round-table discussion in December 1987 on 'What sort of family we need'. Various views were expressed including the opinion that it was outmoded to award medals to mothers of large families to reward reproductive labour. A woman also deserved the title of 'heroine' if she reared two well-behaved children, pursued a career and helped a paralysed father. Another participant pointed out that a common question was how many children were needed to meet demographic goals, but now it was time to ask how many children working women needed, and what children themselves thought. A third stressed the importance of the quality of childrearing rather than the quantity. Admittedly, some of the points made in the round-table were made in debates of the 1960s and 1970s as well. *Glasnost'* is keeping these alive, prompting deeper reflection and adding new topics (*Nedelia*, no. 47, 23–29 November 1987, pp. 17–18).

6. Kozlov, for instance, has argued that strengthening the family is 'one of the conditions of the acceleration of the socio-economic development of the country' and a 'component part of the *perestroika* of the whole system of social relations' (Kozlov, 1987, p. 122). He believes that the family is in need of *perestroika* precisely because of its instability and points out that more than 60 per cent of young families admit to 'persistent arguments, conflicts and longstanding disagreements' (Kozlov, 1987, p. 115). Thus, the current task of the CPSU, and one element of *perestroika*, is to ask why this is the case and to work out what can be done to alter the situation.

7. The topic of domestic labour has been the focus of several sociological enquiries. Bozhkov and Golofast are advocates of comparative analysis of the domestic division of labour across Soviet republics. Their work on Russia, Latvia and Tadzhikistan has led them to conclude that 'male' and 'female' domestic roles vary according to a range of factors. Their findings give backing to the thesis that there are no necessarily fixed 'male' or 'female' chores in the home. They show that several variables account for domestic behaviour patterns, and thereby indicate the complexities of domestic interaction that Soviet writings of the past frequently overlooked. They argue that the nature of the domestic division of labour reflects the socio-economic position of husband and wife as well as their ideological and cultural characteristics (Bozhkov and Golofast, 1986).

M. Dzhunus"aev has linked the nature of the domestic division of labour more directly to equality of the sexes. Looking at 'egalitarian families' in Chimkentskii *oblast* in Kazakhstan, Dzhunus"aev found that 62.4 per cent of men and 81.2 per cent of women felt that chores should be equally divided. Dzhunus"aev argued that men who were less in favour of 'equality in daily life' (*raventsvo v bytu*) harboured stereotypes of 'male' and 'female' activities. Moreover, these stereotypes were anachronistic in 'the changing historical conditions of modern family life' (Dzhunus"aev, 1985, p. 107). Inequalities between men and women in domestic life persisted because husbands failed to meet the 'norms and ideals of socialist relations towards women' (Dzhunus"aev, 1985, p. 109). This echoes Fourier's position, adopted also by Marx, that the level of humanity can be gauged by the nature of man's relation to woman.

8. The most conservative position of all, as argued by economist Vladislav Kulikov at a conference on *perestroika* in Sweden, holds that more women should stay at home since the economy will soon not need them. This is based on the assumption that *perestroika* will result in economic efficiency, streamlining and an end to labour shortages (*Dagens Nyheter*, 11 January 1988). I am grateful to Riitta Pittman for this reference.

   A less extreme version of this is presented by G. Sergeeva, who argues in those republics where the participation rate of women in the economy is high, the conditions exist for tackling demographic problems: 'We recommend that in these republics the level of female participation in the economy should lower a little. This would more fully answer the harmonious combination of woman's professional function and motherhood' (Sergeeva, 1987, p. 125).

9. The Soviet Women's Committee was set up after the Second World War and grew out of the Soviet Women's Anti-Fascist Committee which was established in 1941. The Committee has its headquarters in Moscow and is made up of representatives from all Soviet republics. Its main official field of activity is 'developing co-operation with women's organisations abroad in order to promote peace, friendship and mutual understanding' (Soviet Women's Committee, 1983, p. 2). It meets in plenary session once a year. The daily activities are directed by a Presidium. From 1968 to 1987 Valentina Tereshkova, a pilot and astronaut and Hero of the Soviet Union, chaired the Committee. Zoia Pukhova, a woman with extensive experience of the textile industry, then took over the chair. Pukhova was born in 1936 and worked as a weaver in a textile factory from 1952 to 1973, when she became director of the Ivanovskii weaving factory (*Izvestiia*, 3 February 1987, p. 1).

10. Also in her speech to the 19th All-Union Party Conference Pukhova reported that night-shifts for women were banned by law except in exceptional circumstances which made them necessary. For 50 years this had been ignored (*Izvestiia*, 2 July 1988, p. 10).

11. Delegates to the All-Union Conference of Women made similar criticisms of poor working conditions. They lamented filthy surroundings, high dust and gas levels, tasteless canteen food and poor quality work clothes. They also noted that laws protecting female labour are sometimes ignored. For example, women who have recently given birth are not supposed to be allocated night-shifts until their newborn are over 1-year-old. It was pointed out that this legal protection 'has for a long time lost all meaning' (*Izvestiia*, 2 February 1987).

12. When asked in the Soviet press if discrimination against women existed in the USSR the sociologist Maia Pankratova recently replied, 'we have no conscious discrimination'. However, for 'historical and present-day reasons – our country lacks a sufficient number of energetic, talented and clever women from whom we could select the very best to be our leaders' (*Moscow News*, July 1988, p. 11).

Given that the education level of Soviet women exceeds that of men, this statement lacks credibility. Pankratova also claimed that opinion polls indicate that male chauvinism is not thought to exist in the USSR. By November 1988, Soviet women were voicing arguments which challenged Pankratova's views (Kuznetsova, 1988; Voronina, 1988). I am grateful to Jim Riordan for drawing Kuznetsova's article to my attention.

13. The lives of Muslim women have recently been given extensive coverage in the Soviet press. 'Vestiges of the past' were discussed in the 1960s and 1970s too, but today more attention is paid to the extent of traditional customs and to male violence against women resulting from them. One newspaper article reported that in one district of Turkmenia 95 per cent of marriages proceed only after the bride-price has been paid. Arranged marriages are widespread. If daughters object to their parents' choice they have to run away from home in order to marry whom they wish. This can provoke two sorts of reaction from parents. The first is to disown the daughter and the second to murder her. Death is felt to be a just punishment since not only did the daughter shamefully disobey her father, but she also robbed him of the bride-price (*Pravda*, 29 April 1986, p. 6; *Trud*, 29 April 1987, p. 2). Wives are also required by custom to return to their parents' house to live if their husbands have not paid the agreed bride-price in full by a particular date (*Trud*, 29 April 1987, p. 2). The strain of the clash of Muslim traditions and Soviet values on young women sometimes results in suicide by fire. This tragic practice has been known to exist for some time, but has not been discussed in the Soviet press. With the help of *glasnost'* it is now mentioned (*Le Monde*, 11 August 1987).

The general emphasis in these articles is that the restrictions faced by Muslim women are oppressive and stunt personal development. The recommendation is that women should fight for their rights. In order to illustrate the benefit of this, one article focused on the example of a woman driven into the countryside against her will by a man who wanted to marry her. The general pattern is for abducted women to be shamed into marrying their abductors, whether or not they want to, in order to avoid disgrace in the eyes of neighbours. This woman, however, refused to do so under threat of shame, subsequently endured the condemnation of the locals and with her parent's approval took her abductor to court, where he was punished (*Pravda*, 29 April 1986, p. 6).

Tamara Dragadze at the School for African and Oriental Studies of the University of London has made the point that many criticisms found in the Soviet press of 'vestiges of the past' in Muslim areas are particulary 'Russian' and exhibit a shallow understanding of the customs which they criticise which are often highly valued by Muslim women.

14. Since infant mortality rates have been released numerous articles have discussed their significance. The picture is a bleak one. In the Chenen-Ingush Autonomous republic more than 40 babies for every 1,000 births die in the first year of life (*Nedelia*, no. 7, 16–22 February 1987, pp. 16–17). Here one gynaecologist is responsible on average for 700 pregnant women, instead of the specified 150. In parts of Soviet Central Asia 55 babies out of every 1,000 born die (*Current Digest to the Soviet Press*, vol. 39, no. 6, March 11 1987, p. 21). Such high infant mortality rates are put down to negligence and a lack of sanitation. Often basic equipment is not available such as scales for weighing children, beds and hot water bottles. Indeed, there is a shortage of over 29,000 paediatric beds in one republic. Moreover, some maternity homes lack running hot water and a supply of oxygen. The clear message of critical journalism is that child deaths could frequently be avoided by better care and improved facilities.

15. The following discussion will therefore be limited, drawing on a slim range of

sources and relying heavily on interviews conducted in Moscow in December 1987 with members of three *zhensovety*.

16. Houses of Culture are generally separate buildings on the site of a factory which provide entertainment for the workers; films are shown, plays put on and dances organised.

17. Despite what he sees as the incredibly broad brief facing the *zhensovety* to take initiative in 'all spheres of production and political life and in government and social administration', Mel'nik believes that their activities 'have become more specific and purposeful', thereby facilitating 'constant attention' to their problems from party organs (Mel'nik, 1987, p. 63). While such scrutiny may be of some use to those *zhensovety* lacking in ideas, it is questionable how much 'constant attention' from the party women with initiative would find desirable.

7 Conclusion

Can anything be said with confidence about changes in the use of ideology in relation to the woman question? The arguments made by Engels, Lenin, Kollontai and Armand about the need to end domestic drudgery, to mobilise women into the labour force, to encourage political participation and to introduce legal equality and social services as the enabling conditions of equality of the sexes remain at the core of Soviet ideology. Since 1917 ideological writings on women's liberation under socialism have consistently included the themes of productive work, participation in politics, protection of equal rights in law and provision of maternity leave, kindergartens, public dining rooms and laundries; but some of them have been emphasised more than others in particular periods of Soviet history and their ideological salience has therefore varied. For example, improved social services edged on to the agenda under Khrushchev when it appeared that the low level of women's political activity was due to factors other than underdeveloped political consciousness. In due course, under Brezhnev, this became a much more visible issue when lack of provision was clearly affecting economic performance and the birth rate and also when improved services became more feasible than in earlier years. In the 1970s, economic problems and economic possibilities shaped the way in which the issue of kindergarten provision was raised.

Another example is provided by the argument that one aspect of women's liberation is participation in politics. Women's political roles were more topical in the 1920s and 1950s, for different reasons, than in the 1930s and 1970s. In the 1920s, ideology exhorted women to support the revolution, participate in delegates' meetings, join the party and vote for the soviets. Political roles were in the limelight since the Bolsheviks aimed to expand and consolidate their rule. The party also supported a drive to raise women's political consciousness on the grounds that women were more politically backward than men and *Zhenotdel* leaders were especially committed to involving women in political activity as part of their liberation. Political survival was a pressure behind the ideological salience of political roles in the 1920s; de-Stalinisation of the political system and a reinvigoration of the party and soviets under Khrushchev prompted a renewed focus on women's political roles. The theme of women and politics was less prominent under Stalin and Brezhnev since, in the 1930s, enforced rapid industrialisation and in the 1970s economic and demographic problems, took precedence.

The ideological claim that women's participation in the work-force is integral to socialism and to women's liberation has similarly been stressed more in some periods than others, and given a different interpretation. In the 1930s and 1940s, particularly heavy emphasis was given to women's roles as industrial workers and collective farmers. The image of women as 'a great army of labour' was promoted when industrialisation was paramount and participation in the war effort crucial. The development of the economy and defence needs were reliant upon female labour. The importance of economic roles for women was not ignored in the years before Stalin's central planning, but the socio-economic and political context of the 1920s affected when, how and by whom this importance was stressed. The theme of the importance of work in the labour force for women's liberation remained a central one in *Kommunistka*, the journal of the *Zhenotdel*. It was advocated with less enthusiasm in other journals and with less commitment by many men on party committees than it would be a decade later. Traditional cultural settings also shaped the attitudes of party men to factory work for women; often, Artiukhina lamented, new female factory workers were treated with derision and amusement. The situation in the labour market also affected attitudes. From 1921 to 1928 the New Economic Policy resulted in growing unemployment among women, which persisted into 1929. After 1928 there was stronger official commitment from the party for a widespread mobilisation of women into work because jobs were created by an expanding economy. The opportunities for the employment of women in the 1920s and 1930s differed, affecting how seriously work for women was viewed by trade unionists and party members. Bold images of women industrial workers and farmers were much less widespread in the 1920s, as the covers of women's magazines such as *Delegatka, Rabotnitsa* and *Krest'ianka* illustrated.

But the treatment of the woman question under Stalin cannot be explained merely by the requirements of industrialisation. The adoption of a crude socialist realism in literature, art and propaganda produced images of smiling female tractor drivers at a time when the rural population was being coerced into collectivisation. The aim to portray life under socialism as it should be, or would be, rather than as it actually was, gave rise to pictures of confident and capable women joyfully participating in the labour force. Alongside these unreal images a 'Thank you Stalin' literature blossomed in which women gushingly praised their leader and the Soviet state for delivering equality in law and in production at a time when these rights were often neither honoured nor promoted. These images and thanks to Stalin were not necessary to industrialisation *per se*, but to the personal and political elements of Stalinist rule and how it approached industrialisation. The official adoption of socialist realism and the personality cult of a highly authoritarian leader influenced the presentation of female roles and helped to create a large gap between the rhetoric of official ideology and the reality of the problems of everyday life.

The Stalin years provide an apt illustration of how the original spirit of recommendations may be modified later. By the 1930s, the theme that participation in the labour force was essential to women's liberation was replaced in many writings by the assertion that the construction of socialism required women to take jobs. The normative goal of women's liberation was thus subordinate to the practical means of building an economy to suit the distant end of socialism. Nevertheless, whilst images of confident working women catered to economic growth, they also created positive role models.

The 1930s also show how the representation of female roles in ideology is sometimes characterised by apparent contradictions. For example, during industrialisation under Stalin, the stakhanovite movement stressed images of strong women industrial workers who rose above gender stereotypes and took traditional 'men's jobs' at which they excelled by exceeding output quotas. At the same time, contradictory pictures were produced of supportive housewives who devoted themselves to looking after their stakhanovite husbands and who thereby indirectly contributed to economic growth. The juxtaposition of these discordant images poses a problem of ideological inconsistency only if we assume that the liberation of women and changes in gender roles are the fundamental objectives. Since both images were based on the economic priority of creating a heavy industry in metals, mining and energy, not women's liberation, the inconsistency was not present in the minds of Soviet propagandists of the 1930s. A problem remained for those who felt that the earlier ideas of Armand and Kollontai were betrayed, but they were not strong enough to make their voice heard. The formal objective of women's liberation was never jettisoned but the Soviet state often gave low priority to it, subordinating it to the means of achieving socialism in the form of industrialisation and economic development; this subordination often led to its displacement.

Women's economic and political roles have been persistent themes in the history of the USSR, although they have been treated in different ways at different times. Some arguments incorporated into Marxist writings about female roles have been much less durable. For example, Kollontai insisted in the 1920s that the meaning of revolution for changing relations between the sexes should be an important subject for reflection under socialism. Political and cultural pressures have always restricted debate about this wide-ranging topic. Elements of Kollontai's arguments have, however, been taken up after the passage of many years. Kollontai's remarks on the significance of 'passion' resurfaced in 1976 in *Komsomol'skaia Pravda*. A sociologist argued that marriages needed to be strengthened and that passion between husband and wife would help to ensure lasting union. Although Kollontai was cited as the inspiration for the suggestion, an isolated reference to the letter of her work entirely overlooked its spirit (*Komsomol'skaia Pravda*, 14 April 1976, p. 4). In the 1980s, the closest writers have come to Kollontai's link between revolution and sexuality is to suggest that sexual problems and psychological difficulties must be considered when examining marital breakdown. This is a very pale reflection of Kollontai's project to extend Marxist theory to incorporate the relationship between changing interpersonal relations and political change. The CPSU in its 'leading and guiding' role has never permitted the ideological space for this.

The examination of the topic of domestic labour has also been uneven, although it has occupied a more central ideological position than Kollontai's thoughts on sexuality. After 1917, reactions against conservative values and the fervour of revolution prompted some

Marxists to advocate a restructuring of the home. The views of Armand, Kollontai and Trotsky, however, were not warmly embraced by the party or the people; meagre economic resources meant that the infrastructure for supporting changes in domestic roles – such as a supply of kindergartens, and restaurants – was inadequate. Armand's argument that the success of socialism depends upon women's liberation and upon changes in the home has never really been accepted by the CPSU. The argument had shortlived popularity and was never seriously incorporated into Soviet ideology. Traditional gender relations and popular conceptions of woman's place in the home have never been rigorously challenged by the party. In the 1970s and 1980s, the topic resurfaced out of a concern to ease the double burden, to reduce the probability of divorce and to increase the birth rate; it was not with the intent of promoting female self-determination nor securing the success of socialism. On the issues of domestic labour and male–female relations, politics has served to perpetuate traditional gender relations rather than to refashion them. Women's congresses and conferences, however, raised the issue of domestic labour in the 1920s, 1960s and, most recently, in 1987; but only in the late 1980s is it beginning to receive mention in important party gatherings as, for example, by Zoia Pukhova in her capacity as Chair of the Soviet Women's Committee. Recent writings are also returning to the topic with greater analytic rigour, even advocating 'egalitarian families' and an end to patriarchy.

The policies of the CPSU affect which female roles are emphasised in different periods of history and also whether women's organisations have a role to play in promoting them. The CPSU has countenanced women-only groups in the 1980s without the accompanying fears of 'bourgeois feminism' that it voiced in the 1920s. When Gorbachev suggested at the 27th party Congress that the *zhensovety* should be revived, he was apparently untroubled by the thought that they would lead to feminist separatism and divide the working class. Sixty years earlier party congresses drew attention to the potential dangers of the *Zhenotdel*, of which separatism was one. For cultural reasons too, feminism was seen as a greater threat by party members in the 1920s since it challenged the ways in which traditional families and villages were run. The very different contexts partly account for the different ways in which women-only organisations are viewed, but the deliberate political purposes of male leaders of the 1920s and the 1980s also play a vital role.

Political pressures influence the nature and limits of debate about women's roles but they are not the only factors. In the climate of freer discussion after Khrushchev came to power, more open examination of the difficulties faced by women might have been expected. But many issues did not come openly onto the agenda; restrained references gently moved women's issues forward. The stress on de-Stalinisation under Khrushchev which caused women's political roles to be considered, and the continued 'solved' status of the woman question, restricted discourse and prevented more open discussions. Livelier debate took place under the rather more staid, stable and increasingly stagnant leadership of the Brezhnev years. In the 1970s, low birth rates and falling economic productivity were regarded as pressing problems and required examination of different aspects of the woman question. Ideological developments of the late 1960s and 1970s, fuelled by reactions to unrealistic claims made by Stalin and rash predictions voiced by Khrushchev, legitimised analyses of female roles. The recognition of non-antagonistic contradictions under developed socialism allowed the conflicting pressures of the female 'double burden' to be discussed in some detail. Thus interaction between social context, economic problems, political factors and ideological developments affected debate about female roles.

The introduction, in the late 1960s, of the concepts 'developed socialism' and 'non-antagonistic contradictions' and, in the mid-1980s, *perestroika* and *glasnost'*, allowed increasing scrutiny of basic problems for women. Ideologically-permitted space for discussion about women's lives greatly increased. The core tenets of Soviet ideology remained intact, but the approved party line was no longer rigid, as under Stalin and to a lesser extent under Khrushchev, and debates on aspects of the woman question followed. In periods when ideological lines are not taut nor clearly defined and when there is more open debate, specialists approach female roles from different angles, often taking different aspects of women's lives as their starting points. The resulting image of women's lives projected by debate is then much more complex, and solutions to problems are more controversial and open-ended. This was the case under Brezhnev and continues to be so under Gorbachev. The multifaceted implications of the woman question become clearer when ideology is not locked in a strait-jacket; so does the link between the recommendations of specialists and policy-making. However, the precise nature of the link between recommendations and policy outcomes is hard to establish since decision-makers are influenced by numerous factors. Nevertheless, in periods characterised by non-antagonistic contradictions and *glasnost'*, we can more easily identify different arguments about female roles, specify their relevance to several policy areas, and assess the extent to which political, economic, cultural and demographic pressures affect how women's liberation under socialism is interpreted.

The content of Soviet ideology can also set limits to policy options and justifications of policy. Marxism does not, for instance, allow women to be declared inferior to men, even if this notion is embedded in popular culture. The official adoption of unequal pay according to sex for like work would also be ideologically unsound. Explicit arguments that women should be denied equal opportunities to education, work and political office, would be difficult to make in a Marxist state. In practice, policies may not always be implemented and laws administered exactly in the way defined by the party. Equal opportunities in hiring and promotion may be flouted and preference given to men. For cultural reasons, men may be seen as the main breadwinner. Out of concern for production and efficiency, women may be viewed as a more unstable component of the labour force due to maternity. The legal provision for part-time work may not be seriously taken up by management, despite requests from the female work-force, because the priorities of plan fulfilment override the introduction of flexible working hours. Policy implementation, however, although sometimes guided by ideology, is not determined in detail by it. The flouting of ideology and official policy in practice is a different matter from the use of ideology in political statements and discussions about policy.

The examples cited demonstrate that a complex of factors affects the use of ideology and its recommendations concerning women at work, at home and in politics. Ideology can inspire policy. Its normative prescriptions about equality and women's liberation triggered early legislation on political rights and equal pay and lifted restrictions on marriage and divorce. Its recommendations about the need for kindergartens and creches prompted commitment from the party to develop widespread childcare facilities. But commitment does not necessarily lead to provision. When material resources are lacking or when other policies are of higher salience, such as political survival, de-Stalinisation, economic growth or population expansion, then less attention is likely to be paid to the importance of kindergartens to women's liberation. Moreover, how kindergartens are approached, if they are approached, is likely to be in terms of their relevance to other issues, such as economic productivity.

Elements of ideology can also be ignored altogether. The extremely low proportion of rural women in the party and on the soviets was not a topic of widespread concern in the 1930s, despite the lipservice to equal rights and 'factual equality'. New ideas can be incorporated into ideology, but soon be shed from it. The notion that success of socialism depends upon women's liberation quickly lost its place after the demise of the *Zhenotdel* and the advent of forced industrialisation and collectivisation. It had enjoyed popularity among a relatively small group of women revolutionaries and was not incorporated into the mainstream of official ideology.

These different uses of ideology all challenge the claim made in the West in the 1960s that ideology was no more than an *ex post facto* justification of policy. However, there are striking examples of arguments about female roles being concocted *ex post facto* to justify policy decisions. In 1936 when abortion was declared illegal, the reason given for the volte-face in policy was that socialism, unlike capitalism, provided conditions which protected families, making abortion superfluous. Arguments about emancipation typical of the 1920s were ignored in rationalisations for the 1936 banning of abortion. The same applied in 1955 when abortion was legalised again. The practical problem that women were resorting to illegal abortions, despite the health risks, underpinned the change in law. The *ad hoc* justification was that abortion could be legalised because of improvement in women's 'cultural level' and their awareness of the importance of their maternal function. While ideology may serve as an *ex post facto* justification of policy, it can also combine this function in some policy areas with an initiating role in other areas. When lines on why abortion is legal or illegal are pragmatically switched, arguments about maternity leave, kindergarten provision and a supply of restaurants as prerequisites for women's liberation remained unchanged. It is not helpful to view ideology entirely as a rationalisation of policy.

This book has tried to show that the elements of ideology which are emphasised at any given time are affected by an interaction of economic, political, cultural and doctrinal pressures; the use of ideology also carries implications for policy on women and for debate about female roles. The declaration that the woman question has been solved means that no special policies for promoting equality of the sexes are needed since equality either already exists or will automatically come about. Investigations need not, therefore, be carried out into the problems that women face in the economy, politics and home, since either they confront none or they have difficulties which will disappear when other problems are solved. Conversely, declaring the woman question unsolved carries with it a requirement to investigate female roles and to analyse the position of women in society in order to make informed policy recommendations. How extensive this investigation and analysis becomes depends upon how the solution to the woman question is conceived. Propositions about the nature of equality affect which questions about female roles are asked, what sort of data are gathered and the kinds of policy proposals that are introduced.

These concepts and propositions not only set the boundaries of enquiry, but also give direction to the theoretical debate. In this sense, ideology may shape the range of issues that come onto the agenda and set limits to acceptable conclusions. Developed socialism, with its non-antagonistic contradictions, exposed problem areas long excluded from debate and gave a new breadth to debate. Despite the linkage in the early 1980s of the woman question to the population problem, broad scope for discussion remained because of the continued use of the concept of 'non-antagonistic contradiction'; this ensured that a return to the ideological strait-jacket of the Stalin years with its numerous 'solved' problems could not take place. The boundaries of debate expanded even further with the advent of *glasnost'*. The greater the ideological space for debate, the more likely that women's lives will be more soberly assessed and the difficulties that they face analysed. More realistic appraisals of female roles, however, with inputs from economists, sociologists and demographers generate a range of conclusions, some of which might seem at variance with the spirit of Marxism. Under Gorbachev some economists are advocating a 'restructuring' of female labour, directing it more into the home; this jars with many of the arguments voiced at the 1987 All-Union Conference of Women.

The use of ideology, then, has changed since 1917, depending upon policy priorities, the nature of political leadership and conceptual developments. Despite core consistencies, the aspects of ideology on women which are emphasised shift, as does the degree of debate about them. The use of ideology and emphases on themes within it are, therefore, likely to change again. Women's role in the labour force may be increasingly downplayed if unemployment becomes part of Soviet experience. Images of woman as mother and nurturer might then be promoted and portrayals of women as stakhanovite labourers could be relegated to the dustbins of history. Alternatively, the two images could remain because some women may be encouraged to concentrate on reproduction and others invited to make contributions to an economy in need of women as a skilled labour resource. The 'long and thorny path' to women's liberation under socialism is somewhat open-ended as the Soviet state moves into the 1990s.

Selected Bibliography

Soviet sources

(excluding titles listed under Soviet dissertation abstracts, Soviet dissertations, and Soviet statistics)

Abilova, G. A. (1970) *Zhenshchiny Azerbaidzhana – aktivnye stroiteli kommunizma* (Baky, Izdatel'stvo Elm).

Agarkov, S. T. (1987) 'Disgarmonichnyi brak', *Sotsiologicheskie issledovaniia*, no. 4, pp. 81–5.

Agranova, S. (1936) 'Itogi zhenskikh s''ezdov i zadachi komsomola', *Revoliutsiia i Natsional'nosti*, no. 3 (March), pp. 43–6.

Akopian, G. (1939) *Zhenshchiny strany sotsializma* (Moscow, Gosudarstvennoe izdatel'stvo politicheskoi literatury).

Aleksandrov, N. F. and Bruskina, B. G. (1961) *Politiko-massovaia rabota sredi zhenshchin* (Checheno-Ingushskoe knizhnoe izdatel'stvo).

Alieva, S. M. (1962) 'Rabota partorganizatsii Azerbaidzhana po podgotovke zhenskikh kadrov v gody pervoi piatiletki', *Voprosy Istorii Kompartii Azerbaidzhana*, no. 26, pp. 75–105.

Alkhazova, A. (1964) *Dela zhensoveta* (Makhachkala, Dagestanskoe knizhnoe izdatel'stvo).

Aminova, R. (1977) *The October Revolution and Women's Liberation in Uzbekistan* (Moscow, Nauka).

Aralovets, N. (1947) *Zhenshchina-velikaia sila Sovetskogo obshchestva* (Moscow, Moskovskii rabochii).

Armand, I. F. (1975) *Stat'i, rechi, pis'ma* (Moscow, Politizdat).

Artiukhina, A. (1928a) 'Bol'she samokritiki', *Kommunistka*, no. 4 (April), pp. 29–35.

Artiukhina, A. (1928b) 'Likvidatsionnyi zud nyzhno uniat',' *Kommunistka*, no. 6 (June), pp. 3–8.

Artiukhina, A. (1930a) *Delegatka na bor'bu za kadry* (Moscow–Leningrad, Gosudarstvennoe izdatel'stvo).

Artiukhina, A. (1930b) 'Zhenrabotu vesti vcei partiei v tselom', *Kommunistka*, no. 1–3 (January), pp. 6–10.

Artiukhina, A. (1936) 'Velikaia zabota zhenshchine-materi', *Rabotnitsa*, no. 16 (July), pp. 3–4.

Ashirov, N. (1978) *Musul'manskaia propoved'* (Moscow, Politizdat).

Astapovich, Z. A. (1971) *Velikii oktiabr' i raskreposhchenie zhenshchin Srednei Azii i Kazakhstana*, 1917–1936 (Moscow, Mysl').

Babintsev, I. and Turetskii, V. (1936) 'O raskreposhchenii zhenshchin v Azerbaidzhane', *Revoliutsiia i Natsional'nosti*, no. 3 (March), pp. 51–5.

Bairamsakhatov, N. (1979) *Novyi byt i islam* (Moscow, Politizdat).

Baltianskii, M. (1971) 'Bereg Sem'i', *Rabochaia Gazeta*, 13 August.

Baranskaia, N. (1969) 'Nedelia kak nedelia', *Novyi Mir*, 11 (November), pp. 23–55.

Belkin, M. S. (1936) 'K voprosu o vrede abortov', *Rabotnitsa i Krest'ianka*, no. 14, p. 22.

Bil'shai, V. (1959) *Reshenie zhenskogo voprosa v SSSR* (Moscow, Izdatel'stvo politicheskoi literatury).

Biriukova, Aleksandra (1987) 'Oktiabrem zavoevano', *Sovetskaia Zhenshchina*, no. 10, pp. 2–4.

Bozhkov, O. B. and Golofast, V. B. (1986) 'Razdelenie truda v gorodskoi sem'e', *Sotsiologicheskie issledovaniia*, no. 4, pp. 68–75.

Brazhnikova, E. F. (1961) *Zhenskie sovety na altae* (Barnaul, Altaiskoe knizhnoe izdatel'stvo).

Chatskii, L. Dr (1926) 'Abort ili preduprezhdenie beremennosti?' *Rabotnitsa i Domashniaia Khoziaika*, no. 2, 28 July, p. 3.

Chirkov, P. M. (1978) *Reshenie zhenskogo voprosa v SSSR: 1917–1937* (Moscow, Mysl').

Demysheva, Z. (1960) 'Eto ne o sovetskikh zhenshchin', *Partiinaia zhizn'*, no. 8 (April), pp. 72–3.

Dirzhinskaite, L. (1975) 'Sovetskaia zhenshchina – aktivnyi stroitel' kommunizma', *Partiinaia zhizn'*, no. 20 (October), pp. 23–8.

Dmitrieva, G. (1975) Mezhdunarodnaia Zashchita Prav Zhenshchiny (Kiev, Vishcha shkola).

Drozdetskaia, N. (1961) 'Politicheskaia rabota sredi zhenshchin' *Partiinaia zhizn'*, no. 14 (July), pp. 23–8.

Dugarzhapova, Ts. (1965) 'Zhenskie sovety', *Partiinaia zhizn'*, no. 17 (September), pp. 53–5.

Dzhabarly, Dzhafar (1979) 'Sevil', in *Dzhafar Dzhabarly: P'esy* (Baku, Iazychy), pp. 12–70.

Dzhunus"aev, M. D. (1985) 'Raspredelenie domashnego truda v Kazakhskoi sem'e', *Sotsiologicheskie issledovaniia*, no. 1, pp. 106–9.

El'darova, R. A. (1963) *Zhenshchiny gor: politicheskaia rabota sredi zhenshchin Dagestana* (Moscow, Sovetskaia Rossiia).

Emel'ianova, E. D. (1971) *Revoliutsiia, partiia, zhenshchina* (Smolensk, gosudarstvennyi pedogogicheskii institut).

Frolov, V. (1934) *Zhenshchiny v kolkhozakh – bol'shaia sila* (Severnoe kraevoe otdelenie, Partizdat).

Frumkina, M. (1921) 'O rabote sredi evreiskikh rabotnits', *Kommunistka*, no. 10–11 (March–April), pp. 34–5.

Furtseva, E. (1960) 'Zhenshchiny i stroitel'stvo kommunizma', *Pravda*, 8 March, p. 2.

Gasanova, A. I. (1963) *Raskpreposhchenie zhenshchiny–gorianki v Dages-*

tane: 1920–1940 (Makhachkala, Dagestanskii filial Akademii Nauk SSSR).

Gasanova, A. I. (1969) *Podgotovka zhenskikh kadrov v Dagestane i ikh rol' v khoziaistvennom i kul'turnom razvitii respubliki: 1945–1965* (Makhachkala, Institut istorii, iazyka i literatury).

Glavpolitrosvet klubnyi otdel (1926) *Klubnyi kruzhki i massovaia rabota* (Moscow, izdatel'stvo doloi negramotnost').

Golubeva, V. (1926) 'K diskussii po voprosam brachnogo i semeinogo prava', *Kommunistka*, no. 1 (January), pp. 50–3.

Golubeva, V. (1980) 'The other side of the medal', in *Woman and Russia: First Feminist Samizdat*, trans. Women in Eastern Europe Group (London, Sheba) pp. 51–6.

Gorbachev, M. (1987) *Perestroika i novoe myshlenie dlia nashei strany i dlia vsevo mira* (Moscow, Politizdat).

Gorbachev, M. (1988) 'On progress in implementing the decisions of the 27th CPSU Congress and the tasks of promoting perestroika', *19th All-Union Conference of the CPSU: documents and materials* (Moscow, Novosti), pp. 5–93.

Gruzdeva, E. B. (1979b) 'Uchastie zhenshchin v obshchestvennom proizvodstve kak forma realizatsii ikh ravnopraviia v sotsialisticheskom obshchestve', in E. Klopov (ed.) *Vo imia cheloveka truda* (Moscow, Profizdat).

Gruzdeva, E. B. and Chertikhina, E. S. (1983) *Trud i byt Sovetskikh zhenshchin* (Moscow, Politizdat).

Guliev, Zh. B. (1972) *Pod znamenem Leninskoi natsional'noi politiki* (Baku, Azerbaidzhanskoe gosudarstvennoe izdatel'stvo).

Gurova, N. M. and Krivenko, N. A. (1960) *Zhenshchiny Donetskoi magistrali* (Stalino-Donbass, Knizhnoe izdatel'stvo).

Iankova, Z. A. (1975) 'Razvitie lichnosti zhenshchiny v Sovetskom obshchestve', *Sotsiologicheskie issledovaniia*, no. 4, pp. 42–51.

Iankova, Z. A. (1978) *Sovetskaia zhenshchina* (Moscow: Izdatel'stvo politicheskoi literatury).

Iankova, Z. A. (1979) 'Kul'turno-psikhologicheskie problemy ukreplenie sem'i', *Sotsiologicheskie issledovaniia*, no. 2, pp. 36–45.

Institut Marksizma-Leninizma pri TsK KPSS (1983–1987) vols 1–14 *Kommunisticheskaia partiia Sovetskogo Soiuza v rezoliutsiiakh i resheniiakh s"ezdov, konferentsii i plenumov TsK* (Moscow, Politizdat).

Kaganovich, L. (1930) 'Reorganizatsiia partapparata i ocherednye zadachi partraboty', *Kommunistka*, no. 1–3 (January), pp. 3–5.

Kalygina, A. (1926) 'Delegatskie sobraniia krest'ianok', *Kommunistka*, no. 7 (July), pp. 27–35.

Karaseva, L. (1946) *Slavnye docheri nashei rodiny* (Moscow, Gospolitizdat).

Kazakov, A. (1931) *Organizatsiia zhenskogo truda v kolkhozakh* (Moscow/Samara, Gosudarstvennoe izdatel'stvo srednevolzhskoe kraevoe otdelenie).

Kazantseva, E. (1958) 'Chto daet differentsirovannaia rabota s liudmi', *Partiinaia zhizn'* no. 13, pp. 44–7.

Khodakov, N. M. (1981) *Molodym suprugam*, 3rd edn (Moscow, Meditsina).

Khorvat, F. (1982) *Liubov', Materinstvo, Buduschchee* (Moscow, Progress publishers).

Khrushchev, N. S. (1956) 'Otchetnyi doklad TsK KPSS', *XX s"ezd kommunisticheskoi partii sovetskogo soiuza, stenograficheskii otchet,* vol. 1 (Moscow, Gosudarstvennoe izdatel'stvo politicheskoi literatury), pp. 9–120.

Khrushchev, N. S. (1959) 'O kontrol'nykh tsifrakh razvitiia narodnogo khoziaistva SSSR na 1959–1965 goda: doklad', *Vneocherednoi XXI s"ezd kommunisticheskoi partii sovetskogo soiuza, stenograficheskii otchet,* vol. 1 (Moscow, Gosudarstvennoe izdatel'stvo politicheskoi literatury), pp. 12–120.

Khrushchev, N. S. (1962) 'Otchet TsK KPSS XXII s"ezdy KPSS', *XXII s"ezd kommunisticheskoi partii sovetskogo soiuza, stenograficheskii otchet,* vol. 1 (Moscow, Gosudarstvennoe izdatel'stvo politicheskoi literatury), pp. 15–132.

Kollontai, Alexandra (1984) *Selected Articles and Speeches* (Moscow, Progress publishers).

Kon, I. (1987) 'Roditeli i deti', *Nedelia,* no. 50 (14–20 December), p. 14.

Kondakova, N. I. (1981) *Opyt KPSS v Reshenie Zhenskogo Voprosa* (Moscow, Mysl').

Konstantinov, F. V. (1974) *The Fundamentals of Marxist-Leninist Philosophy* (Moscow, Progress publishers).

Kosolapov, R. I., Pechenev, V. S. and Markov, V. S. (1983) *Developed Socialism: Theory and Practice* (Moscow, Progress publishers).

Kotelenets, A. I. (1977) *Zhenshchiny strany sovetov* (Moscow, Politizdat).

Kotliar, A. E. and Turchaninova, S. Ia. (1975) *Zaniatost' zhenshchin v proizvodstve* (Moscow, Statistika).

Kozlov, V. (1987) 'Liniia na ukreplenie sem'i', in P. Ia. Slezko (ed.) *Perestroika: problemy, poiski, nakhodki* (Moscow, Politizdat).

KPSS v Rezoliutsiiakh i Resheniiakh S"ezdov, Konferentsii i Plenumov TsK, (1970–1982) 8th edn, 14 vols (Moscow, Politizdat).

(1934), *Krest'ianka v zapadnoi oblasti* (Moscow-Smolensk, Krest'ianskaia gazeta).

Kriakvin, T. (1960) 'Nasha rabota sredi zhenshchin', *Partiinaia zhizn',* no. 15 (August), pp. 51–4.

Kuznetsova, K. S. (1979) *Velikii Oktiabr' i raskreposhchenie zhenshchin Severnogo Kavkaza i Zakavkaz'ia: 1917–1936* (Moscow, Mysl').

Kuznetsova, L. (1988) 'What every woman wants?', *Soviet Weekly,* 26 November, p. 15.

Liubimova, S. (1926a) *Dnevnik zhenotdelki* (Tashkent, Sredazkniga).

Liubimova, S. (1926b) *Za novyi byt* (Tashkent, Sredazkniga).

Liubimova, S. (1958) *V pervye gody* (Moscow, Gosudarstvennoe izdatel'stvo politicheskoi literatury).

Mamedov, S. G. (1973) *Stranitsy zhizni* (Baku, Ishyg).

Materialy XXII s"ezda KPSS (1961) (Moscow, Gospolitizdat).

Materialy XXIII s"ezda KPSS (1966) (Moscow, Politizdat).

Materialy XXIV s"ezda KPSS (1972) (Moscow, Politizdat).

Materialy XXV s"ezda KPSS (1976) (Moscow, Politizdat).

Materialy XXVI s"ezda KPSS (1981) (Moscow, Politizdat).

Materialy XXVII s"ezda KPSS (1986) (Moscow, Politizdat).

Materialy XVII s"ezda professional'nykh soiuzov SSSR (1982) (Moscow, Profizdat).

Matveev, G. K. (1978) *Sovetskoe Semeinoe Pravo* (Moscow, Iuridicheskaia Literatura).

Melikhova, E. V. (1976) *V te surovye gody* (Leningrad, Leninizdat).

Mel'nik, A. (1987) 'Zhensovety – vazhnaia forma razvitiia, trudovoi i obshchestvennoi aktivnosti zhenshchin' *Partiinaia zhizn'*, no. 2 (January), pp. 59–63.

Miatieva, A. (1973) *Dela i dumy zhenshchin* (Ashkhabad, Izdatel'stvo 'Turkmenistan').

Mikhailiuk, V. B. (1981) *Legendy i Pravda o Zhenskom Trude: za fasadom burzhuaznykh teorii* (Moscow, Izdatel'stvo politicheskoi literatury).

Mironova, Z. V. (1957) *Pravda*, 9 March, p. 1.

Mishova, A. D. (1960) 'Krupitsy opyta', in *Nash sovremennitsy* (Syktyvkar, Komi knizhnoe izdatel'stvo), pp. 82–9.

Mitskevich, A. V. (1959) 'Rasshirenie roli obshchestvennykh organisatsii v period razvernutogo stroitel'stva kommunizma', *Sovetskoe Gosudarstvo i Pravo*, vol. 9, pp. 24–33.

Mochalov, B. (1980) *Requirements of Developed Socialist Society* (Moscow, Progress publishers).

Mollaeva, M. (1978) 'Rastet sotsial'naia aktivnost' Sovetskikh zhenshchin', *Partiinaia zhizn'*, no. 5 (March), pp. 57–62.

Murav'eva, N. (1965) 'Nekotorye voprosy raboty sredi zhenshchin', *Partiinaia zhizn'*, no. 3 (February), pp. 8–15.

Murmantseva, V. S. (1979) *Sovetskie zhenshchiny v velikoi otechestvennoi voine* (Moscow, Mysl').

Musaeva, T. A. (1964) *Bor'ba za razvitie narodnogo obrazovaniia v Azerbaidzhane v gody pervoi piatiletki* (Baku, izdatel'stvo akademii nauk Azerbaidzhanskoi SSSR).

Nadezhdina, V. A. (1985) *Rukovodstvo delegatskimi sobraniiami – odna iz form raboty partii po resheniiu zhenskogo voprosa* (Leningrad, Vestnik LGU, seriia istoriia, iazyk, literatura).

(1960) *Nash Sovremennitsy* (Syktyvkar, Komi knizhnoe izdatel'stvo).

Nashi besedy (1962) 'Vzaimnoe uvazhenie v sem'e, zabota o vospitanii detei', *Partiinaia zhizn'*, no. 10 (May), pp. 59–65.

Nechaev-Ianotson, S. (1936) 'Dvenadtsat' detei', *Rabotnitsa*, no. 18 (June), pp. 10–11.

Neliubin, A. (1983) *Massovo-politicheskaia rabota po mestu zhitel'stva* (Moscow, Moskovskii rabochii).

Nemirova, N. (1962) 'Zhensovet deistvuet', *Partiinaia zhizn'*, no. 17 (September), pp. 49–50.

Nikul'kova, A. (1932) *Massovaia rabota sredi kolkhoznits* (Novosibirsk, Partizdat).

Novikova, E. E., Sidorova, T. N. and Turchaninova, S. Ia. (1984) *Sovetskie zhenshchiny i profsoiuzy* (Moscow, Profizdat).

Nukhrat, A. (1935) 'Zhenshchina na II s"ezde kolkhoznikov', *Revoliutsiia i Natsional'nosti*, no. 3 (March), pp. 23–32.

Otdel Rabotnits i Krest'ianok (1927) *Zhenskie kluby na vostoke* (Moscow, izdatel'stvo okhrana materinstva i mladenchestva).

Otradinkskii, Dr (1926) 'Bor'ba c abortami', *Delegatka*, no. 10, May, pp. 15–16.

Ov-ezov, B. (1965) 'Vydvizhenie i vospitanie zhenskikh kadrov', *Partiinaia zhizn'*, no. 1 (January), pp. 8–13.

Pankratova, M. G. and Iankova, Z. A. (1978) 'Sovetskaia zhenshchina: (sotsial'nyi portret)', *Sotsiologicheskie issledovaniia*, no. 1 (January–March), pp. 19–28.

Peredovaia (1956) 'Voprosy priema v partiiu', *Partiinaia zhizn'*, no. 8 (April), pp. 3–8.

Peredovaia (1960) 'Zhenshchina – aktivnyi stroitel' kommunizma', *Partiinaia zhizn'*, no. 5 (March), pp. 3–7.

Perevedentsev, V. I. (1975) 'Sem'ia: vchera, segodnia, zavtra', *Nash sovremmenik*, no. 6 (June), p. 120.

Perevedentsev, V. I. (1977) 'Edinstvenny v sem'e', *Literaturnaia Gazeta*, 16 March, p. 12.

Perevedentsev, V. I. (1979) *Demograficheskie problemy SSSR* (Moscow, Znanie).

Perevedentsev, V. I. (1982) 'Vosproizvodstvo naseleniia i sem'ia' *Sotsiologicheskie issledovaniia*, no. 2, pp. 80–8.

Pod''iachikh, Petr (1966) 'Narodnonaselenie i progress' *Literaturnaia Gazeta*, 22 February, p. 4.

Podliashuk, Pavel (1973) *Tovarishch Inessa* (Moscow, Politizdat).

Polianskaia, E. (1933) *Zhenshchina v sovete i v kolkhoze* (Leningrad, Lensoveta).

(1932), *Primernyi plan raboty delegatskogo sobraniia kolkhoznits za 1932 god* (Mozhaisk, 'za kolkhoz').

(1932), *Programma dlia zhendelegatskikh sobranii (posobiia dlia rukovoditelei)* (Rostov on Don, Partizdat).

Radzhabov, R. A. (1975) *Obshchestvennye organizatsii Azerbaidzhana i ikh rol' v privlechenii mass k upravleniiu Sovetskim gosudarstvom, 1920–1932* (Baku, Azerbaidzhanskoe gosudarstvennoe izdatel'stvo).

Rakhimova, I. (1967) 'Zhenshchina – aktivnyi stroitel' kommunizma', *Partiinaia zhizn'*, no. 10 (May), pp. 57–62.

Rakitina, Z. (1929) 'Delegatskie sobraniia v rekonstruktivnyi period', *Kommunistka*, no. 21 (November), pp. 38–42.

Resolutions of the 19th All-Union Conference of The CPSU (1988), *19th All-Union Conference of the CPSU: Documents and Materials* (Moscow, Novosti), pp. 118–60.

Riabushkin, T. (ed.) (1978) *Demograficheskie problemy sem'i* (Moscow, Nauka).

Riabushkin, T. (1983) 'The demographic policy of developed socialist society', in *Demographic Processes* (Moscow, Social Sciences Today), pp. 43–56.

Riabushkin, T. and Galetskaia, R. (1983) 'Introduction', in *Demographic Processes* (Moscow, Social Sciences Today), pp. 5–9.

Rizel', F. (1932) 'Zhenshchina-natsionalka v bor'be za khlopkouborochnuiu', *Revoliutsiia i Natsional'nosti*, no. 9 (September), pp. 30–6.

Rogov, L. (1936) 'Na gosudarstvennoi i obshchestvennoi rabote', *Vlast' Sovetov*, no. 11 (June), pp. 17–18.

Rogovin, V. E. (1987) 'Usilenie zaboty o sem'e, o polozhenii zhenshchiny-materi', in Mikul'skii, K. I., Rogovin, V. E. and Shatalin, S. S., *Sotsial'naia Politika KPSS* (Moscow, Politizdat), pp. 220–30.

Rzhanitsina (1983) *Female Labour under Socialism: The Socio-economic Aspects* (Moscow, Progress publishers).

Saltykov, S. (1960) 'Chem zanimat'sia zhenskim sovetam?', *Partiinaia zhizn'*, no. 17 (September), pp. 50–3.

Samoilova, K. (1920) 'Voprosi organisatsii: organisatsionnye zadachi', *Kommunistka*, no. 6 (November), pp. 26-8.

Samoilova, K. (1921) *Organizatsionnye zadachi otdelov pabotnits* (Tula, Izdanie Tul'skogo gubkoma).

Semsashko, N. (1926) 'Pochemu ne zapretiat delat' aborty', *Rabotnitsa*, no. 19 (October), p. 17.

Sergeeva, G. P. (1987) *Professional'naia zaniatost' zhenshchin: problemy i perspektivy* (Moscow, Ekonomika).

Shishkan, N. M. (1976) *Trud zhenshchin v slovüakh razvitogo sotsializma* (Kishinev, Izdatel'stvo shtiintsa).

Shitarev, G. (1961) 'O novykh formakh partiinoi raboty', *Partiinaia zhizn'*, no. 11 (June), pp. 9–16.

Shitkina, M. (1926) 'Delegatki – prakticheskie stroiteli', *Rabotnitsa i Krest'ianka*, vol. 17–18 (September), pp. 1–2.

Shuvalov, E. L. (1978) *Praktikum po geografii naseleniia* (Moscow, Prosveshchenie).

Smidovich, S. (1926) 'O novom kodekse zakonov o brake i sem'e', *Kommunistka*, no. 1 (January), pp. 45–50.

Smirnova, D. (1963) 'Sovetskaia zhenshchina', *Partiinaia zhizn'*, no. 5 (March), pp. 8–13.

Sokolova, O. (1926a) 'K postroeniiu i rabote delegatskikh sobranii rabotnits', *Kommunistka*, no. 7 (July), pp. 19–35.

Sokolova, O. (1926b) *Tseli i zadachi delegatskogo sobraniia* (Moscow–Leningrad, gosudarstevennoe izdatel'stvo).

Solodnikov, V. V. (1986) 'Predrazvodnaia situatsiia v molodoi sem"e', *Sotsiologicheskie issledovaniia*, no. 4 (October–December), pp. 76–80.

Sonin, M. Ia. (1978) 'Ravnye prava, neravnye nagruzki', *Ekonomika i organizatsiia promychlennogo proizvodstva* (Novosibirsk) (May–June), pp. 5–18.

Soveshchanie zhenshchin-delegatok XIV Vserossiiskogo i 5 Vsesoiuznogo S"ezdov Sovetov (1929) May (Moscow, Izdanie TsIk Soiuza SSR).

Soviet Women's Committee (1983) *Soviet Women's Committee* (Moscow, Soviet Women's Committee).

Sozaeva, A. O. (1973) *Sotsialisticheskaia kul'tura, ateizm i zhenshchina* (Nal'chuk, El'brus).

Stishova, L. I. (ed.) (1986) *V budniakh velikikh stroek; zhenshchiny-kommunistki, geroini pervykh piatiletok* (Moscow, Politizdat).

Stoiakina, A. S. (1962) *Zhenskie sovety* (Moscow, Izdatel'stvo Sovetskogo Rossiia).

Sultanova, A. I. (1957) 'Rol' zhenshchin Azerbaidzhana v razvitii ekonomiki

i kul'tury respubliki', Doklad zam, predsedatelia Soveta Ministrov Azerbaidzhanskoi SSR, tov. Sultanovoi, A. I. (Baku).

Sultanova, A. I. (1964) *Schastlivye zhenshchiny Sovetskogo Azerbaidzhana*
(Baku, Azerbaidzhanskoe gosudarstvennoe izdatel'stvo).

Tatarinova, N. I. (1979) *Primenenie truda zhenshchin v narodnom
khoziaistve SSSR* (Moscow, Izdatel'stvo politicheskoi literatury).

Telen', L. (1988) 'Kakaia zhe ona, zhenskaia dolia?', *Sotsialisticheskaia
industriia*, no. 18 (22 January), pp. 2–3.

Tettenborn, Z. (1936) 'Materinstvo v sovetskoi strane', *Vlast' Sovetov*,
(June), pp. 7–8.

Tomskii, I. E. (1969) *Zhenshchiny Iakutii* (Iakutsk, Iakutskoe knizhnoe
izdatel'stvo).

Tsetkin, K. (1926) *Kavkaz v ogne* (Moscow-Leningrad, Moskovskii
rabochii).

Tupitsin, V. (1987) 'Sposobstvovat' ukrepleniiu sem'i, iskoreniat' p'ianstvo,'
Partiinaia zhizn', no. 1 (January), pp. 66–99.

Unanian, K. (1960) 'Vovlekat' domokhoziaek v obshchestvennuiu zhizn'',
Partiinaia zhizn', no. 8 (April), pp. 49–51.

Uritskii, S. (1934) *Krest'ianka v zapadnoi oblasti*, (June), p. i.

Vagabov, M. B. (1975) *Kalym – vrednyi perezhitok* (Makhachkala, Dagestanskoe knizhnoe izdatel'stvo).

Valentei, D. (ed.) (1983a) *Demograficheskaia politika v SSSR* (Moscow
Finansy i statistika).

Valentei, D. (1983b) 'Control of demographic processes', in *Demographic
Processes* (Moscow, Social Sciences Today), pp. 10–27.

Vesnik, E. E. (1936) *Nash opyt* (Sotsekizdat Ukrainy).

Vishnevskii, A. G. (1977) *Brachnost', rozhdaemost', smertnost' v Rossii i v
SSSR* (Moscow, Statistika).

Volkova, Z. A. (1984) *Komissiia profkoma po voprosam truda i byta
zhenshchin, okhrany materinstva i detstva* (Moscow, Profizdat).

Volkova, Z. A., Mel'nikova, E. A. and Novikova, E. E. (1979) *Komissiia po
rabote sredi zhenshchin pri FZMK* (Moscow, Profizdat).

Voronina, Ol'ga (1988) 'Muzhchiny sozdali mir dlia sebia', *Sovetskaia
zhenshchina*, no. 11, pp. 14–15.

Zagorskii, N. and Pirozerskaia, A. (1929) *Krasnye ugolki v bor'be za novyi
byt* (Moscow–Leningrad, gosudarstvennoe izdatel'stvo).

Zakhovaeva, K. (1961) 'Bol'she vnimaniia rabote sredi zhenshchin',
Partiinaia zhizn', no. 6 (March), pp. 16–21.

Zdorovets, G. (ed.) (1961) *Khoziaika strany gor: materialy raboty 8-go
s"ezda zhenshchin Dagestana* (Makhachkala, Dagestanskoe knizhnoe
izdatel'stvo).

(1936) *Zhenshchina – bol'shaia sila, pervoe kraevoe soveshchanie zhen
stakhanovtsev severnogo kraia, 15–17 aprelia 1936 goda, stenograficheskii otchet* (Sevkraigiz, ogiz).

(1931), *Zhenshchina v bor'be za khlopok* (Moscow–Tashkent, Ob'edinenie
gosudarstvennykh izdatel'stvo, Sredneaziatskie otdelenie).

Zhvinklenie, A. (1987) 'Semeinaia integratsiia kak ob"ekt issledovaniia',
Sotsiologicheskie issledovaniia, no. 1, pp. 70–3.

Soviet dissertation abstracts

Abdurazhimov, M. A. (1971) *Preodolenie perezhitkov proshlogo i stanovlenie novoi morali v semeinom bytu v period stroitel'stva kommunizma*, candidate degree dissertation abstract, Makhachkala.

Abdydaev, S. A. (1972) *Nektorye osobennosti konservatsii religioznykh predrassudkov sredi zhenshchin*, candidate degree dissertation abstract, Frundze.

Agaev, M.–B. Kh. (1972) *Razvitie brachno-semeinykh otnoshenii v usloviiakh stroitel'stva kommunizma*, candidate degree dissertation abstract, Makhachkala.

Akhmedov, A. P. (1965) *Dal'neishee razvitie i ukreplenie semeinykh otnoshenii v period stroitel'stva kommunizma*, candidate degree dissertation abstract, Baku.

Alibekova, G. Kh. (1972) *Sotsial'nye prichiny sokhraneniia ostatkov fakticheskogo neravenstva zhenshchin v bytu pri sotsializme i puti ikh preodoleniia*, candidate degree dissertation abstract.

Azhibaeva, A. D. (1966) *Vozrastanie roli zhenshchin v obshchestvennom proizvodstve – zakonomernost' epokhi sotsializma*, candidate degree dissertation abstract, Alma Ata.

Brova, S. V. (1968) *Sotsial'nye problemy zhenskogo truda v promyshlennosti*, candidate degree dissertation abstract, Sverdlovsk.

Eremina, Z. I. (1972) *Problemy ispol'zovaniia zhenskogo truda v narodnom khoziaistve SSSR v sovremennykh usloviiakh*, candidate degree dissertation abstract, Saratov.

Gasanov, N. N. (1970) *Razvitie semeino-brachnykh otnoshenii u narodov Dagestana v period stroitel'stva kommunizma*, candidate degree dissertation abstract, Moscow.

Gavrilkina, M. P. (1974) *Obshchee i osobennoe v reshenii zhenskogo voprosa v SSSR*, candidate degree dissertation abstract, Moscow.

Gruzdeva, E. B. (1979a) *Vozrastanie roli zhenshchin-rabotnits v obshchestvennom proizvodstve i sovershenstvovanie ikh byta v usloviiakh razvitogo sotsializma*, candidate degree dissertation abstract, Moscow.

Gulieva, M. A. (1978) *Razvitie massovogo ateizma sredi zhenshchin Azerbaidzhana v usloviiakh sotsializma*, candidate degree dissertation abstract, Baku.

Iman-Zade, S. (1954) *Osvobozhdenie Azerbaidzhanki – odno iz vazhneishikh zavoevanii Velikoi Oktiabr'skoi sotsialisticheskoi revoliutsii, 1917–1939*, candidate degree dissertation abstract, Baku.

Iuk, Z. M. (1968) *Voprosy ratsional'nogo ispol'zovaniia zhenskogo truda v Belorusskoi SSR*, candidate degree dissertation abstract. Minsk.

Kalashnikov, A. P. (1977) *Sotsial'naia aktivnost' zhenshchin-proizvodstvennits v usloviiakh razvitogo sotsializma*, candidate degree dissertation abstract, Rostov.

Kiselev, V. I. (1972) *Osnovnye tendentsii sotsial'nykh preobrazovanii brachnykh otnoshenii pri sotsializme*, candidate degree dissertation abstract, Saratov.

Kozachenko, V. I. (1969) *Sotsial'no-ekonomicheskie problemy ispol'zovaniia zhenskogo truda v kolkhozakh*, candidate degree dissertation abstract, Kishinev.

Kuznetsov, V. K. (1970) *Sotsial'no-gigienicheskoe issledovanie prichin aborta*, candidate degree dissertation abstract, Moscow.

Lukashuk, Iu. M. (1976) *Sotsial'no-ekonomicheskie problemy ispol'zovaniia zhenskogo truda*, candidate degree dissertation abstract, Moscow.

Lysakova, A. S. (1966) *Likvidatsiia ostatkov neravenstva zhenshchiny v bytu v protsesse kommunisticheskogo stroitel'stva v SSSR*, candidate degree dissertation abstract, Moscow.

Main, N. E. (1974) *Sotsial'noe ravenstvo i obshchestvenno-politicheskaia aktivnost' zhenshchin v usloviiakh razvitogo sotsializma*, candidate degree dissertation abstract, Kazan'.

Nagiev, N. Kh. (1971) *Kommunizm i sotsial'noe ravenstvo polov*, candidate degree dissertation abstract, Baku.

Panova, N. V. (1970) *Zhenskii trud v sotsialisticheskom proizvodstve*, candidate degree dissertation abstract, Vil'nius.

Samokhina, Z. V. (1972) *Puti preodoleniia ostatkov neravenstva zhenshchin i muzhchin v usloviiakh razvitogo sotsialisticheskogo obshchestva*, candidate degree dissertation abstract, Moscow.

Sattarov, M. M. (1965) *Bor'ba formirovanie i utverzhdenie nauchno-ateisticheskogo mirovozzreniia u Azerbaidzhanskogo naroda v period sotsialisticheskogo i kommunisticheskogo stroitel'stva*, doctoral degree dissertation abstract, Baku.

Shishkan, N. M. (1969) *Sotsial'no-ekonomicheskie problemy povysheniia effektivnosti obshchestvennogo truda zhenshchin*, candidate degree dissertation abstract, Kishinev.

Zagrebel'nyi, B. P. (1977) *Formirovanie otnoshenii sotsial'nogo ravenstva zhenshchin i muzhchin-kolkhoznikov v usloviiakh razvitogo sotsializma*, candidate degree dissertation abstract, Kiev.

Zulalova, Z. A. (1975) *Formy proiavleniia religioznosti sredi zhenshchin i voprosy nauchno-ateisticheskogo vospitaniia*, candidate degree dissertation abstract, Baku.

Soviet dissertations

Gasanbekova, M. D. (1979) *Deiatel'nost' Dagestanskoi organizatsii KPSS po dal'neishemy povysheniiu-politicheskoi i proizvodstvennoi aktivnosti zhenshchin v usloviiakh razvitogo sotsializma, 1966–1975*, candidate dissertation, Baku.

Muradov, Sh. M. (1971) *Sotsial'no-ekonomicheskie problemy ispol'zovaniia zhenshkikh trudovykh resursov v Azerbaidzhanskoi SSR*, doctoral dissertation, Baku.

Sozaeva, A. O. (1971) *Sotsial'isticheskaia kul'tura i ee rol' v osvobozhdenii zhenshchin iz-pod vliianiia islama*, candidate dissertation, Moscow.

Soviet newspapers, journals and magazines

Bakinskii Rabochii
Current Digest to the Soviet Press
Delegatka, 1923–1931
Izvestiia
Kommunistka, 1920–1930
Krest'ianka
Moscow News
Nedelia
Patiinaia zhizn'
Pravda
Sotsiologicheskie issledovaniia, 1978–1988
Sovetskaia zhenshchina
Rabotnitsa, 1923–1988
Rabotnitsa i Domashniaia Khoziaika, 1926
Rabotnitsa i Krest'ianka, 1922–1941
Vestnik Statistiki

Soviet statistics

TsSu SSSR (1972) *Narodnoe khoziaistvo SSSR 1922–1972, iubileinyi statisticheskii ezhegodnik* (Moscow, Statistika).
TsSu SSSR (1975a) *Zhenshchiny v SSSR* (Moscow, Statistika).
TsSu SSSR (1975b) *Naselenie SSSR* (Moscow, Statistika).
TsSu SSSR (1978) *Narodnoe khoziaistvo SSSR v 1977g* (Moscow, Statistika).
TsSu SSSR (1979) *O predvaritel'nykh itogakh vsesoiuznoi perepisi naseleniia 1979 goda* (Moscow, Statistika).
TsSu SSSR (1984) *Zhenshchiny v SSSR 1984: statisticheskie materialy* (Moscow, Finansy i statistika).
TsSu SSSR (1985) *Zhenshchiny v SSSR 1985: statisticheskie materialy* (Moscow, Finansy i statistika).
TsSu SSSR (1987) *Zhenshchiny v SSSR 1987: statisticheskie materialy* (Moscow, Finansy i statistika).

Non-Soviet sources

Agonito, Rosemary (1977) *History of Ideas on Woman: A Source Book* (New York, Capricorn).
Apter, David E. (1964) *Ideology and Discontent* (New York, Free Press).
Arendt, Hannah (1958) *The Origins of Totalitarianism* (Cleveland, Meridian Books).
Aristotle (1862) *The History of Animals*, trans. Richard Cresswell (London, Henry G. Bohn).

Aristotle (1943) *Generation of Animals*, trans. A. L. Peck (London, Heinemann).

Aristotle (1973) *Politics*, trans. Ernest Barker (Oxford, Oxford University Press).

Aron, Raymond (1968) 'The end of the ideological age?', in Chaim I. Waxman (ed.) *The End of Ideology Debate* (New York, Funk and Wagnalls), pp. 27–48.

Atkinson, Dorothy (1978) 'Society and the sexes in the Russian past', in Dorothy Atkinson, Alexander Dallin and Gail Warshofsky Lapidus (eds) *Women in Russia* (Hassocks, Sussex, Harvester), pp. 3–38.

Atkinson, Dorothy, Dallin, Alexander and Lapidus, Gail Warshofsky (eds) (1978) *Women in Russia* (Hassocks, Sussex, Harvester).

Attwood, Lynne (1985) 'The new Soviet man and woman – Soviet views on psychological sex differences', in Barbara Holland (ed.) *Soviet Sisterhood* (Fourth Estate, London), pp. 54–77.

Attwood, Lynne (1988) *The New Soviet Man and Woman – Sex Role Socialisation in the Soviet Union*, PhD thesis, University of Birmingham.

Barnes, Samuel H. (1966) 'Ideology and the organization of conflict: on the relationship between political thought and behaviour', *Journal of Politics*. vol. 28, no. 3 (August), pp. 513–30.

Bebel, August (1971) *Woman under Socialism* (New York, Schocken Books).

Beck, Carl, Fleron, Frederic J., Lodge, Milton *et al* (1973) *Comparative Communist Political Leadership* (New York, David McKay).

Bell, Daniel (1965) 'Ideology and Soviet politics', *Slavic Review*, vol. 24, no. 4 (December), pp. 591–603.

Berlin, Isaiah (1979) *Russian Thinkers*, Henry Hardy and Aileen Kelly (eds) (Harmondsworth, Middlesex, Penguin).

Berliner, Joseph S. (1964) 'Marxism and the Soviet economy', *Problems of Communism*, no. 13 (September–October), pp. 1–11.

Bialer, Seweryn (1980) *Stalin's Successors: Leadership, Stability, and Change in the Soviet Union* (Cambridge, Cambridge University Press).

Bill, James A. and Hardgrave, Robert L. Jr (1973) *Comparative Politics: The Quest for Theory* (Columbia, Ohio, Charles E. Merrill Publishing Company).

Bobroff, Anne (1974) 'The Bolsheviks and working women, 1905–1920', *Soviet Studies*, vol. 26, no. 4 (October), pp. 540–67.

Breslauer, George W. (1980) 'Khrushchev reconsidered', in Stephen F. Cohen, Alexander Rabinowitch and Robert Sharlet (eds) *The Soviet Union Since Stalin* (Bloomington, Indiana, Indiana University Press), pp. 50–70.

Bridger, Susan (1987) *Women in the Soviet Countryside: Women's Roles in Rural Development in the Soviet Union* (Cambridge, Cambridge Univesity Press).

Browder, Robert Paul and Kerensky, Alexander F. (1961) *The Russian Provisional Government: Documents*, 3 vols (Stanford, California, Stanford Univesity Press)

Browning, Genia K. (1985a) *A Consideration of the Relationship Between the Status of Women in the USSR and their Position in the Political Leadership, with Special Reference to the Role of Soviet Women's Groups in Raising Women's Political Consciousness*, PhD thesis, Polytechnic of the South Bank.

Browning, Genia K. (1985b) 'Soviet politics – where are the women?', in Barbara Holland (ed.) *Soviet Sisterhood* (London, Fourth Estate), pp. 207–36.

Browning, Genia K. (1987) *Women and Politics in the USSR* (Wheatsheaf, London; St Martin's, New York).

Buckley, Mary (1981a) *Ideology and Soviet Women*, PhD dissertation, Vanderbilt University.

Buckley, Mary (1981b) 'Women in the Soviet Union', *Feminist Review* 8 (Summer), pp. 79–106.

Buckley, Mary (1985) 'Soviet interpretations of the woman question' in Barbara Holland (ed.) *Soviet Sisterhood* (London, Fourth Estate), pp. 24–53.

Buckley, Mary (ed.). (1986a) *Soviet Social Scientists Talking: an Official Debate about Women* (London, Macmillan).

Buckley, Mary (1986b) 'Soviet religious feminism as a form of dissent', *Topic*, Journal of Washington and Jefferson College, vol. 40 (Fall), pp. 5–12.

Buckley, Mary (1988a), 'Soviet ideology and female roles' in Stephen White and Alex Pravda (eds) *Ideology and Soviet Politics* (London, Macmillan), pp. 159–79.

Buckley, Mary (1988b) 'Female workers by hand and male workers by brain: the occupational composition of the 1985 Azerbaidzhan Supreme Soviet', *Soviet Union*, vol. 14. No. 2, pp. 229–37.

Chambre, Henri (1955) *Le Marxisme en Union Sovietique* (Paris, Seuil).

Chambre, Henri (1967) 'Soviet ideology', *Soviet Studies*, vol. 18, no. 3 (January), pp. 314–27.

Chernyshevskii, N. G. (1961) *What is to be Done?* (New York, Vintage Books).

Christenson, Reo M., Engel, Alan S., Jacobs, Dan, Rejai, Mostafa and Walzer, Herbert (1975) *Ideologies and Modern Politics* (London, Nelson).

Clements, Barbara Evans (1979) *Bolshevik Feminist* (Bloomington, Indiana, Indiana University Press).

Clements, Barbara Evans (1985) 'Baba and Bolshevik: Russian women and revolutionary change', *Soviet Union*, vol. 12, part 2, pp. 161–84.

Cohen, Stephen F. (1977) 'Bolshevism and Stalinism', in Robert C. Tucker (ed.) *Stalinism: Essays in Historical Interpretation* (New York, W. W. Norton and Company Inc.), pp. 3–29.

Cohen, Stephen F. (1980) *Bukharin and the Bolshevik Revolution* (Oxford, Oxford University Press).

Comey, David Dinsmore (1962) 'Marxist-Leninist ideology and Soviet policy', *Studies in Soviet Thought*, vol. 2, no. 4 (December), pp. 301–20.

Converse, Philip E. (1964) 'The nature of belief systems in mass publics', in David E. Apter (ed.) *Ideology and Discontent* (New York, Free Press), pp. 206–61.

Daniels, Robert V. (1966) 'The ideological vector', *Soviet Studies*, vol. 18, no. 1 (July), pp. 71–3.

De George, Richard T. (1968) *The New Marxism* (New York, Pegasus).

Desfosses, Helen (1976) 'Demography, ideology and politics in the USSR', *Soviet Studies*, vol. 28, no. 2 (April), pp. 244–56.

Deutscher, Isaac (1968) *Stalin* (Harmondsworth, Middlesex, Penguin).

Dobb, Maurice (1978) *Soviet Economic Development Since 1917* (London, Routledge and Kegan Paul).

Dodge, Norton (1966) *Women in the Soviet Economy* (Baltimore, Johns Hopkins University Press).

Donaldson, Robert H. (1972) 'The 1971 Soviet Central Committee: An assessment of the new elite', *World Politics*, vol. 24, no. 3 (April), pp. 382–409.

Donaldson, Robert H. and Waller, Derek J. (1970) *Stasis and Change in Revolutionary Elites: A Comparative Analysis of the 1956 Party Central Committees in China and the USSR* (Beverley Hills, Sage).

Dostoevsky, Fyodor (1988) *The Brothers Karamazov* (Harmondsworth, Middlesex, Penguin).

Edmondson, Linda (1984) *Feminism in Russia, 1900–1917* (London, Heinemann).

Ellenstein, Jean (1976) *The Stalin Phenomenon* (London, Lawrence and Wishart).

Engels, Friedrich (1968) 'The origin of the family, private property and the state', in *Karl Marx and Friedrich Engels: Selected Works* (London, Lawrence and Wishart), pp. 455–593.

Evans, Alfred B. Jr (1977) 'Developed socialism in Soviet ideology', *Soviet Studies*, vol. 29, no. 3 (July), pp. 409–28.

Fainsod, Merle (1958) *Smolensk Under Soviet Rule* (Cambridge, Massachusetts, Harvard University Press).

Fainsod, Merle (1963) *How Russia is Ruled* (Cambridge, Massachusetts, Harvard University Press).

Farnsworth, Beatrice Brodsky (1978) 'Bolshevik alternatives and the Soviet family: the 1926 Marriage Law debate', in Dorothy Atkinson, Alexander Dallin and Gail Warshofsky Lapidus (eds) *Women in Russia* (Hassocks, Sussex, Harvester), pp. 139–65.

Farnsworth, Beatrice Brodsky (1980) *Socialism, Feminism and Bolshevik Revolution* (Stanford, California, Stanford University Press).

Farrell, R. Barry (ed.) (1970) *Political Leadership in Eastern Europe and the Soviet Union* (Chicago, Aldine Publishing Company).

Feshbach, Murray and Rapawy, Stephen (1973) 'Labor constraints in the Five-Year Plan', *Soviet Economic Prospects for the Seventies*, US Congress, Joint Economic Committee, Compendium of Papers, 93rd Congress, 1st session (Washington, DC, Government Printing Office, 27 June), pp. 485–563.

Feshbach, Murray and Rapawy, Stephen (1976) 'Soviet population and manpower trends and policies', *Soviet Economy in a New Perspective*, US Congress, Joint Economic Committee, Compendium of Papers, 94th Congress, 2nd session (Washington, DC, Government Printing Office, 14 October), pp. 113–54.

Finer, S. E. (ed.) (1979) *Five Constitutions* (Harmondsworth, Middlesex, Penguin).

Fleron, Frederic (1970) 'Representation of career types in Soviet political leadership', in R. Barry Farrell (ed.) *Political Leadership in Eastern Europe and the Soviet Union* (Chicago, Aldine Publishing Company), pp. 108–39.

Fleron, Frederic (1973) 'System attributes and career attributes: the Soviet leadership system, 1952 to 1965', in Carl Beck, Frederic J. Fleron, Milton Lodge *et al.* (eds) *Comparative Communist Political Leadership* (New York, David McKay Company, Inc.), pp. 43–85.

Florinsky, Michael T. (1971) *The End of the Russian Empire* (New York, Collier).

Fourier, Charles (1971) *The Utopian Vision of Charles Fourier: Selected Texts on Work, Love, and Passionate Attraction*, translated and edited by Jonathan Beecher and Richard Vienvenu (Boston, Beacon Press).

Friedgut, Theodore H. (1979) *Political Participation in the USSR* (Princeton, New Jersey, Princeton University Press).

Friedrich, Carl and Brzezinski, Zbigniew (1965) *Totalitarian Dictatorship and Autocracy*, 2nd edn (New York, Praeger).

Geertz, Clifford (1964) 'Ideology as a cultural system', in David E. Apter (ed.) *Ideology and Discontent* (New York, Free Press), pp. 47–76.

Geertz, Clifford (1973) *The Interpretation of Cultures: Selected Essays* (New York, Basic Books).

Glickman, Rose (1978) 'The Russian factory woman, 1880–1914', in Dorothy Atkinson, Alexander Dallin and Gail Warshofsky Lapidus (eds) *Women in Russia* (Hassocks, Sussex, Harvester), pp. 63–83.

Goldman, Marshall I. (1983) *USSR in Crisis: The Failure of an Economic System* (New York, W. W. Norton and Company).

Hahn, Jeffrey W. (1977) 'The role of Soviet sociologists in the making of foreign policy', in Richard Remnek (ed.) *Social Scientists and Policy Making in the USSR* (New York, Praeger), pp. 34–58.

Harasymiw, Bohdan (1969) 'Nomenklatura: the Soviet Communist Party's leadership recruitment system', *Canadian Journal of Political Science*, vol. 2, pp. 493–512.

Harris, Nigel (1967) 'The Owl of Minerva', *Soviet Studies*, vol. 18, no. 3 (January), pp. 328–39.

Hayden, Carol Eubanks (1976) 'The Zhenotdel and the Bolshevik Party', *Russian History*, vol. 3, no. 2, pp. 150–73.

Hayden, Carol Eubanks (1979) *Feminism and Bolshevism: The Zhenotdel and the Politics of Women's Emancipation in Russia, 1917–1930*, PhD dissertation, University of California at Berkeley.

Heitlinger, Alena (1979) *Women and State Socialism: Sex Inequality in the Soviet Union and Czechoslovakia* (London, Macmillan).

Heldt, Barbara (1987) *Terrible Perfection: Women and Russian Literature* (Bloomington, Indiana, Indiana University Press).

Hempel, Carl (1952) *Fundamentals of Concept Formation in Empirical Science*, International Encyclopedia of Unified Science, vol. II, no. 7.

Hill, Ronald J. (1985) *Soviet Union: Politics, Economy and Society* (London, Frances Pinter).

Holland, Barbara (ed.) (1985) *Soviet Sisterhood* (London, Fourth Estate; Bloomington, Indiana University Press).

Holt, Alix (1977) *Alexandra Kollontai: Selected Writings* (New York, W. W. Norton and Company).

Holt, Alix (1980) 'Marxism and women's oppression: Bolshevik theory and practice in the 1920s', in Toya Yedlin (ed.) *Women in Eastern Europe and the Soviet Union* (New York, Praeger), pp. 87–114.

Holt, Alix (1985) 'The first Soviet feminists', in Barbara Holland (ed.), *Soviet Sisterhood* (London, Fourth Estate; Bloomington, Indiana University Press), pp. 237–65.

Hough, Jerry F. (1976) 'Party "saturation" in the Soviet Union' in Paul Cocks, Robert V. Daniels and Nancy Whittier Heer, *The Dynamics of Soviet Politics* (Cambridge, Massachusetts, Harvard University Press).

Hough, Jerry and Fainsod, Merle (1982) *How the Soviet Union is Governed* (Cambridge, Massachusetts, Harvard University Press).

Jancar, Barbara Wolfe (1978) *Women under Communism* (Baltimore, Johns Hopkins University Press).

Jansson, Jan Magnus (1959) 'The role of political ideologies in politics', *International Relations*, vol. 1 (April), pp. 529–42.

Johnson, Chalmers (ed.) (1970) *Change in Communist Systems* (Stanford, California, Stanford University Press).

Joravsky, David (1966) 'Soviet ideology', *Soviet Studies*, vol. 18, no. 1, pp. 2–19.

Juviler, Peter H. (1978) 'Women and sex in Soviet law', in Dorothy Atkinson, Alexander Dallin and Gail Warshofsky Lapidus (eds) *Women in Russia* (Hassocks, Sussex, Harvester), pp. 243–65.

Kautsky, John H. (1968) *Communism and the Politics of Development* (New York, John Wiley and Sons).

Keep. John (1968) 'October in the provinces', in Richard Pipes (ed.) *Revolutionary Russia* (Cambridge, Massachusetts, Harvard University Press), pp. 180–216.

Lane, David (1985) *State and Politics in the USSR* (Oxford, Basil Blackwell).

LaPalombara, Joseph (1968) 'Decline of ideology: a dissent and an interpretation', in Chaim I. Waxman (ed.) *The End of Ideology Debate* (New York, Funk and Wagnalls), pp. 315–41.

Lapidus, Gail Warshofsky (1978) *Women in Soviet Society: Equality, Development and Social Change* (Berkeley, University of California Press).

Leedy, Frederick A. (1973) 'Demographic trends in the USSR', *Soviet Economic Prospects for the Seventies*, US Congress, Joint Economic Committee, Compendium of papers, 93rd Congress, 1st session (Washington, DC, Government Printing Office, 27 June), pp. 428–563.

Lenin, V. I. (1970) *Selected Works*, 3 vols (Moscow, Progress publishers).

Lenin, V. I. (1977) *On the Emancipation of Women* (Moscow, Progress publishers).

Lewin, Moshe (1968) *Russian Peasants and Soviet Power* (London, Allen and Unwin).

Lewin, Moshe (1985) *Soviet Society in the Making* (London, Methuen).

Lichtheim, George (1967) *The Concept of Ideology and Other Essays* (New York, Vintage).

Lichtheim, George (1970) *A Short History of Socialism* (London, Weidenfeld and Nicolson).

Lipset, Seymour Martin (1968) 'The end of ideology?', in Chaim I. Waxman (ed.) *The End of Ideology Debate* (New York, Funk and Wagnalls), pp. 69–86.

Lodge, Milton C. (1969) *Soviet Elite Attitudes Since Stalin* (Columbus, Charles E. Merrill).

Lowenthal, Richard (1970) 'Development vs. utopia in communist policy', in Chalmers Johnson (ed.) *Change in Communist Systems* (Stanford, California, Stanford University Press), pp. 33–116.

McAuley, Mary (1977) *Politics and the Soviet Union* (Harmondsworth, Middlesex, Penguin).

McCauley, Martin (1983) *Stalin and Stalinism* (Harlow, Essex, Longman).

McCauley, Martin (ed.) (1987) *Khrushchev and Khrushchevism* (London, Macmillan).

Mandel, William M. (1975) *Soviet Women* (Garden City, New York, Anchor Books).

Marx, Karl (1968) 'Critique of the Gotha Programme', in *Marx and Engels: Selected Works* (London, Lawrence and Wishart), pp. 315–35.

Marx, Karl (1975a) 'Economic and Philosophic Manuscripts of 1844' in *Karl Marx and Friedrich Engels: Collected Works* (London, Lawrence and Wishart), vol. 3, pp. 229–346.

Marx, Karl (1975b), Letter to Vera Zasulich, London, March 8, 1881 in *Marx and Engels: Selected Correspondence* (Moscow, Progress publishers), pp. 319–20.

Marx, Karl and Engels, Friedrich (1969) *The German Ideology* (New York, International Publishers).

Massell, Gregory J. (1974) *The Surrogate Proletariat: Moslem Women and Revolutionary Strategies in Soviet Central Asia, 1919–1929* (Princeton, New Jersey, Princeton University Press).

Mawdsley, Evan (1987) *The Russian Civil War* (London, Allen and Unwin).

Medvedev, Roy (1982) *Khrushchev* (Oxford, Basil Blackwell).

Meyer, Alfred G. (1966) 'The functions of ideology in the soviet political system', *Soviet Studies*, vol. 17, no. 3 (January), pp. 273–85.

Meyer, Alfred G. (1970) 'Theories of convergence', in Chalmers Johnson (ed.) *Change in Communist Systems* (Stanford, California, Stanford University Press), pp. 313–41.

Meyer, Alfred G. (1978) 'Marxism and the women's movement', in Dorothy Atkinson, Alexander Dallin and Gail Warshofsky Lapidus (eds) *Women in Russia* (Hassocks, Sussex, Harvester), pp. 85–112.

Mickiewicz, Ellen (1977) 'Regional variation in female recruitment and advancement in the communist party of the Soviet Union', *Slavic Review*, vol. 36, no. 3 (September). pp. 441–54.

Mill, John Stuart and Taylor, Harriet (1870) *The Subjection of Women* (New York, Appleton and Co.).

Millar, James R. (ed.) (1971) *The Soviet Rural Community* (Urbana, University of Illinois Press).

Minar, David W. (1961) 'Ideology and political behaviour' *Midwest Journal of Political Science*, vol. 5 (November), pp. 317–31.

Moore, Barrington, Jr (1950) *Soviet Politics – The Dilemma of Power* (Cambridge, Massachusetts, Harvard University Press).

Moses, Joel C. (1978a) 'Women in political roles', in Dorothy Atkinson, Alexander Dallin and Gail Warshofsky Lapidus (eds) *Women in Russia* (Hassocks, Sussex, Harvester), pp. 333–53.

Moses, Joel C. (1978b) *The Politics of Female Labor in the Soviet Union*, Western Societies Program Occasional Paper, No. 10 (Ithaca, New York, Cornell University).

Nietzsche, Friedrich (1977) 'Woman as dangerous plaything', in Rosemary Agonito, *History of Ideas on Woman: A Source Book* (New York, Capricorn), pp. 267–9.

Nove, Alec (1972) *An Economic History of the USSR* (Harmondsworth, Middlesex, Penguin).

Orwell, George (1951) *Nineteen Eighty-Four* (London, Secker and Warburg).

Pipes, Richard (1974a) *Russia Under the Old Regime* (Harmondsworth, Middlesex, Penguin).

Pipes, Richard (1974b) *The Formation of the Soviet Union* (New York, Atheneum).

Polan, A. J. (1984) *Lenin and the End of Politics* (London, Methuen).

Porter, Cathy (1978) *Alexandra Kollontai* (London, Virago).

Pravda, Alex (1988) 'Ideology and the policy process', in Stephen White and Alex Pravda (eds) *Ideology and Soviet Politics* (London, Macmillan), pp. 225–52.

Putnam, Robert D. (1971) 'Studying elite political culture: the case of "ideology"', *American Political Science Review*, vol. 65, no. 3 (September), pp. 651–81.

Putnam, Robert D. (1973) *The Beliefs of Politicians: Ideology, Conflict and Democracy in Britain and Italy* (New Haven, Connecticut, Yale University Press).

Rabinowitch, Alexander (1978) *The Bolsheviks Come to Power* (New York, W. W. Norton).

Rorlich, Azade-Ayse (1986) 'The "Ali Bairamov" Club, the journal Sharg Gadini and the socialization of Azeri women: 1920–30', *Central Asian Survey*, vol. 5, no. 3–4, pp. 221–39.

Rosenberg, William G. (1985) 'Russian labor and Bolshevik power', *Slavic Review*, vol. 44, no. 2 (September), pp. 213–38.

Rosenhan, Mollie Schwartz (1978) 'Images of male and female in children's readers', in Dorothy Atkinson, Alexander Dallin and Gail Warshofsky Lapidus (eds) *Women in Russia* (Hassocks, Sussex, Harvester), pp. 293–305.

Rywkin, Michael (1982) *Moscow's Muslim Challenge: Soviet Central Asia* (London, C. Hurst and Company).

Sacks, Michael Paul (1976) *Women's Work in Soviet Russia: Continuity in the Midst of Change* (New York, Praeger).

Sartori, Giovanni (1969) 'Politics, ideology and belief systems,' *American Political Science Review*, vol. 63, no. 2 (June), pp. 398–411.

Sartori, Giovanni (1970) 'Concept misformation in comparative politics', *American Political Science Review*, vol. 64, no. 4 (December), pp. 1033–53.

Schlapentokh, Vladimir (1987) *The Politics of Sociology in the Soviet Union* (Boulder and London, Westview Press).

Schlesinger, Rudolf (1949) *Changing Attitudes in Soviet Russia: The Family in the USSR* (London, Routledge).

Schopenhauer, Arthur (1891) *Studies in Pessimism*, trans. T. Bailey Saunders (London, Swan Sonnenschein and Co.).

Schurman, Franz (1968) *Ideology and Organisation in Communist China* (Berkeley, University of California Press).

Scott, Hilda (1974) *Does Socialism Liberate Women?* (Boston, Beacon Press).

Shaw, William H. (1978) *Marx's Theory of History* (Stanford, California, Stanford University Press).

Shils, Edward (1955) 'The end of ideology?', *Encounter*, vol. 25, pp. 52–8.

Shils, Edward (1958) 'Ideology and civility: on the politics of the intellectual', *Sewanee Review*, vol. 66 (Summer), pp. 450–80.

Skilling, H. Gordon and Griffiths, Franklyn (eds) (1971) *Interest Groups and Soviet Politics* (Princeton, Princeton University Press).

Smith, Gordon B. (1988) *Soviet Politics: Continuity and Contradiction* (London, Macmillan).

Smith, Steve A. (1983) *Red Petrograd: Revolution in the Factories* (Cambridge, Cambridge University Press).

Soloman, Susan Gross (ed.) (1983) *Pluralism in the Soviet Union* (London, Macmillan).

Sternheimer, Stephen (1983) 'Communications and power in Soviet urban politics', in Everett Jacobs (ed.) *Soviet Local Politics and Government* (London, George Allen and Unwin), pp. 131–56.

Stites, Richard (1975) 'Kollontai, Inessa and Krupskaia: a review of recent literature', *Canadian–American Slavic Studies*, vol. 9 (Spring), pp. 84–92.

Stites, Richard (1978) *The Women's Liberation Movement in Russia* (Princeton, Princeton University Press).

Swafford, Michael (1978) 'Sex differences in Soviet earnings', *American Sociological Review*, vol. 43, no. 5 (October), pp. 657–73.

The Woman Question (1975) *Selections from the Writings of Karl Marx, Friedrich Engels, V. I. Lenin, Joseph Stalin* (New York, International Publishers).

Tinbergen, Jan (1961) 'Do communist and free economies show a converging pattern?', *Soviet Studies*, vol. 12, no. 4 (April), pp. 333–41.

Tolstoy, L. (1988) *Anna Karenina* (Harmondsworth, Middlesex, Penguin).

Trotsky, Leon (1970) *Women and the Family* (New York, Pathfinder Press, Inc.).

Trotsky, Leon (1972) *The Revolution Betrayed* (New York, Pathfinder Press, Inc.).

Tucker, Robert C. (ed.) (1977) *Stalinism: Essays in Historical Interpretation* (New York, W. W. Norton and Company, Inc.).

Turgenev, Ivan (1982) *First Love* (Harmondsworth, Middlesex, Penguin).

Venturi, Franco (1960) *Roots of Revolution* (Chicago, University of Chicago Press).

Voinovich, Vladimir (1978) *The Life and Extraordinary Adventures of Private Ivan Chonkin* (Harmondsworth, Middlesex, Penguin).

Vucinich, Wayne S. (ed.) (1968) *The Peasant in Nineteenth-Century Russia* (Stanford, California, Stanford University Press).

Waters, Elizabeth (1989) 'In the shadow of the Comintern: the communist women's movement, 1920–1943', in Sonia Kruks, Rayna Rapp and Marilyn Young (eds) *Promissory Notes: Women in the Transition to Socialism* (New York, Monthly Review Press), pp. 29–56.

Waxman, Chaim I. (ed.) (1968) *The End of Ideology Debate* (New York, Funk and Wagnalls).

Weinberg, Ann (1974) *The Development of Sociology in the Soviet Union* (London, Routledge and Kegan Paul).

Welsh, William A. (1973) 'Introduction: the comparative study of political leadership in communist systems', in Carl Beck, Frederic J. Fleron and Milton Lodge *et al.* (eds) *Comparative Communist Political Leadership* (New York, David McKay).

White, Stephen (1979) *Political Culture and Soviet Politics* (London, Macmillan).

White, Stephen (1988) 'Ideology and Soviet politics', in Stephen White and Alex Pravda (eds) *Ideology and Soviet Politics* (London, Macmillan), pp. 1–20.

White, Stephen and Pravda, Alex (eds) (1988) *Ideology and Soviet Politics* (London, Macmillan).

Winter, Ella (1933) *Red Virtue: Human Relationships in the New Russia* (New York, Harcourt Brace and Company).

Wittgenstein, Ludwig (1968) *Philosophical Investigations*, trans. G. E. M. Anscombe (New York, Macmillan).

Wolchik, Sharon L. and Meyer, Aldred G. (eds) (1985) *Women, State and Party in Eastern Europe* (Durham, Duke University Press).

Wollstonecraft, Mary (1978) *Vindication of the Rights of Women*, Miriam Brody Kramnick (ed.) (Harmondsworth, Middlesex, Penguin).

Women in Eastern Europe Group (trans.) (1980) *Women and Russia: First Feminist Samizdat* (London, Sheba).

Index